Your Children
Need Music

Marvin Greenberg is professor of Education in the Curriculum Research and Development Group at the University of Hawaii, and is nationally known for his writings and practical experience in music education for young children.

A SPECTRUM BOOK

Prentice-Hall, Inc., Englewood Cliffs, N.J. 07632

Marvin Greenberg

A GUIDE FOR PARENTS
AND TEACHERS OF YOUNG CHILDREN

Your Children
Need Music

Library of Congress Cataloging in Publication Data

Greenberg, Marvin.
  Your children need music.

  (A Spectrum Book)
  Bibliography: p.
  Discography: p.
  Includes index.
  1. Music—Instruction and study—Juvenile. I. Title.
MT740.G73   372.8'7   78-31110
ISBN 0-13-977116-6
ISBN 0-13-977108-5 pbk.

Drawings of coconut shells, rhythm sticks, sand blocks, tone block, wood block, guira, and claves are from Music Handbook for the Elementary School *by Marvin Greenberg and Beatrix MacGregor (West Nyack, N.Y.: Parker Publishing Co., Inc., 1972), and are reprinted with permission.*

A SPECTRUM BOOK

Printed in the United States of America

10 9 8 7 6 5 4 3 2 1

Editorial/production supervision and interior design by Maria Carella
Cover design by Michael Freeland; cover illustration by Mona Mark
Manufacturing Buyer: Cathie Lenard

Prentice-Hall International, Inc., *London*
Prentice-Hall of Australia Pty., Limited, *Sydney*
Prentice-Hall of Canada, Ltd., *Toronto*
Prentice-Hall of India Private, Limited, *New Delhi*
Prentice-Hall of Japan, Inc., *Tokyo*
Prentice-Hall of Southeast Asia Pte., Ltd., *Singapore*
Whitehall Books, Limited, *Wellington, New Zealand*

Music is the universal language of mankind. . . .

HENRY WADSWORTH LONGFELLOW

*There is no truer truth obtainable
By Man than comes of music.*

ROBERT BROWNING

*Education in music is most sovereign,
because more than anything else,
rhythm and harmony find their way
into the secret places of the soul.*

PLATO

*Those that do teach young babes
Do it with gentle means and easy tasks.*

WILLIAM SHAKESPEARE

Contents

EDUCATING
THE YOUNG IN MUSIC

Preface

Music is a language—a means of communication. Rather than words or gestures, it uses tones and rhythm as its media of expression. And like verbal communication, music is a lot to learn for the young child. The infant, born into a new environment and hearing sounds that he does not understand, is probably overwhelmed by what he hears and has to learn. Yet, in the space of a few short years, the young child manages to understand and communicate both the languages of words and music. How the adult can help the young child to learn the tonal and rhythmic language of music is the subject of this book.

Music enjoys an important role in the lives of most young children. Babies are often rocked to sleep by soothing lullabies and tunes sung by their parents. Two-year-olds enjoy experimenting with sound patterns when given a tambourine or xylophone. And most preschool teachers have at least some musical experiences for their children. Music and young children fit as well with each other as the completed pieces of a preschool puzzle.

Most adults instinctively know that music is beneficial for the young child. Yet, few adults really understand the role of music in the education of the very young; and even fewer know how to educate the young through music. Limited resources are available that describe the educational process involved in music for young children. Books for parents and teachers of infants and preschoolers either ignore music education or have no more than a short section on how to use music with the very young. This book fills these gaps by providing all adults who work with children, from infancy to age five, with a basic awareness of the principles and practices of educating the young through music.

The book is organized into two sections. The first section provides background material on the nature of the child from birth to five years of age, how he learns, what we know about musical growth in the young child, and music as an art form to be experienced by the young. This section provides the basic framework for the musical activities to be used with young children. The second section provides specific "how-to-do-it" approaches for working with young children in music. This section contains hundreds of hints on organizing the environment, using materials, and working with children in music. Many of these suggestions appear in print for the first time. Each of the chapters has a selected reference list at the end that outlines additional recommended reading. A list of songs suitable for use with young children is found in the Appendix.

The information in this book is based upon the author's extensive research in the fields of music for young children and early childhood education. Much of the material is based on current and previous work on music curriculum projects for preschool children and broad experience in observing and working with infants and preschoolers. The appraoches suggested in the text have been carefully tested with young children from infancy through the preschool years. These approaches have wide applicability for a variety of young children in different educational settings, including the home, the infant-care center, the preschool, the day-care center, and the recreation facility.

As much as possible, the book emphasizes a practical approach based upon current theories of child development, psychology, and music education. Technical

language is kept to a minimum, since it is felt that the

reader could easily become discouraged if confronted with the language and vocabulary of child development and psychological theory and the specialized terminology and notation of music. Although the emphasis is on how to carry out musical activities, the reasons for performing these activities are also provided. Theory is provided as it relates directly to practice. The approach used in the book draws heavily upon the writings of childhood development experts, early childhood educators, and music educators concerned with the aesthetic and musical growth of children.

The book is unique in several ways. It translates child development and learning theory into a relevant approach to music education for the very young. It traces musical response from its origins in infancy, relying on research in the field and observations of young children. It starts at the beginning of the life cycle and presents a unified, sequential approach that is basic to later response in music. It outlines specific methods of educating the young in music during the first five years of life. It relates language acquisition to musical growth to an extent not previously done. This is also believed to be the first book of its type written by an educator with both training and extensive practical experience in music education *and* early childhood education that deals with music education for the child below age three.

The book is intended for all adults who have responsibility for the care of a young child or children up to five years of age. Parents, day-care workers, baby-sitters, preschool teachers and aides, educators of the handicapped, recreation workers, and child-care administrators will find many valuable suggestions on ways to use music with the very young. The book is also addressed to prospective child-care workers and parents—both of whom may someday work in early childhood education. Preservice and in-service music educators at all levels will find the text helpful in understanding the origin of human musical response and how this affects the musical education of people of all ages. Special educators and parents of the handicapped will find that most of the approaches suggested will work very well

with their children, since children, whether handicapped

or not, respond in basically the same ways to musical activities.

The book is appropriate for college-level courses in music or the arts for young children and can serve as a supplementary text for courses in music or early childhood curriculum and movement for young children. It can serve as a guide in workshops for parents and other adults interested in music for the very young. The text can also provide basic reference material for all preschool teachers and child-care workers seeking to improve what they do with children in music.

The author wishes to acknowledge the efforts of many people for helping him in various phases of writing this book. In particular, grateful appreciation is given to Hannah Lou Bennett, Principal of the University Preschool and Elementary School, Curriculum Research and Development Group, University of Hawaii, for her never-tiring encouragement and understanding in support of my work with young children; also to Elsie Quintal, Frances Fox, Carmen Sagadraca, and Carlos Gonzales of the Parent and Child Center, Honolulu, for allowing me to test out ideas on music for the very young; and to Karen Oshiro and the staff of Family Services Center, Honolulu, for their support when I first started working with preschoolers. I would also like to thank Ruth Pfieffer for the use of the song "Chua-Ay," which appears in the Appendix. Photographs were generously supplied by Betty McDowell and the Kindergarten and Children's Aid Association of Hawaii; Paulette Geiger, Myra Kaahumanu, Joan Malama, and Ampero Mateo of the Family Sevices Center; Elsie Quintal and Carlos Gonzales; Marian Rauch of the Kamehameha Schools, Honolulu; Marilyn Ferreira of the Waianae Coast Day Care Center, Waianae, Hawaii; Dr. Setsu Furuno and Katherine A. O'Reilly, School of Public Health, University of Hawaii; Linda Masui Asahina of the Keiki Music School, Honolulu; Jerry L. Miller of the Yamaha Music Center, Honolulu; Sally and Mike Gale, George Wellington, Elaine Hoomanawanui, Susanne Carvalho, and Sandra Shimabukuro, of Honolulu; M. Hohner, Inc. (Hicksville, New York), and American Music Conference, Ludwig Drum

PREFACE Company, and Scientific Music Industries (all of Chicago). Gratitude is also expressed to Brian Dees for his illustrations; to the many beautiful young children of Hawaii who served as my pupils as I taught them music; to Joe Murray of Prentice-Hall, Inc. for his support of the book; and to Maria Carella and Lynne Lumsden of Spectrum Books, Prentice-Hall, Inc., for their patience and guidance on the manuscript and production of this book.

Marvin Greenberg
HONOLULU, HAWAII

Introduction:
Music
and Education

Early Childhood Education: An Important Concern

The education of the young child between birth and age five is receiving increasing attention throughout our country. More and more parents want to find out: "What's best for my child?" Many researchers have become interested in how the infant develops and learns. Preschool programs are mushrooming. Thousands of adults are being trained for positions related to the care of young children. Early childhood courses are being added to many college programs. Many articles, curricula, and textbooks dealing with the education of the child below five have been published during the last few years. Several legislative bills on child care have caused heated debate at both state and national levels. Clearly, the education of the young is one of the "educational waves" of the present and future.

Why this increasing emphasis on early childhood education? Several reasons can be given:

1. Social and economic conditions, highlighted by the feminist movement, the increase in one-parent homes,

and the soaring inflation rate have caused many women
with young children to enter the job market. In order to
work, these women have had to secure day care for their
children by placing them in preschools, infant centers,
the homes of baby-sitters and relatives, and other child-
care facilities.

2. Workers in child-care fields, stimulated by the ideas
of contemporary psychologists and educators, have begun to concern themselves with the vital processes of
child growth and development from the prenatal period
through the preschool years. It is now believed that these
years are vital in shaping the social, emotional, physical,
and intellectual development of the growing human
organism.

3. There is increasing evidence that indicates that certain possibly critical emotional, intellectual, and language patterns associated with socioeconomic background are already present in the child by age five. Thus,
the federal government has poured millions of dollars
into government-sponsored Head Start schools and other
preschool programs for "disadvantaged" children in order
to help these children "catch up" with their more priv-
ileged peers.

4. The relatively poor job market in elementary education during the last few years has caused many young
adults who are interested in working with children to
seek training in early childhood education, a field where
there has been a steady growth of available positions.

5. Educators in special education are viewing planned
early educational experiences for the handicapped as
being an important way of alleviating their problems at
later levels of education. Early education for handicapped
children is now believed to be essential to their later
growth.

6. Publishers and magazine editors, sensing the interest
of educators and parents in early childhood education,
have begun to print countless books, articles, and other
materials for parents and teachers on the care and education of the young child. As a result, the general public
and the child-care profession appear to be more aware of
4 this important phase of education.

Music in Early Childhood Education: Why?

How does music education fit into the excitement that is gripping early childhood education? What can music offer to the growing child? Why is music a necessary part of every child's education?

"Music" and "the young child" are almost synonymous terms. They both invoke a sense of wonderment, enjoyment, laughter, movement, freedom, creativity, and expression. Music seems to be an essential, almost magical, element in the life of the young child. By nature he* seems to need music as part of his daily existence. He listens in rapt fascination as his mother sings and rocks him. He experiments with making vocal sounds long before he can talk. He enjoys tapping everything he can in order to make sounds. He chants a catchy rhyme or nonsense syllables as he plays in the yard. He looks forward to playing rhythm instruments in the preschool. He moves with enthusiasm to express the rhythmic feeling in a march or piece of rock music. The young child has many opportunities to engage in musical activities. He desires these activities, he partakes in them, he expresses himself through them, he learns from them, and he enjoys them.

Parents and child-care workers recognize the importance of music in the life of the young child. They use music with the child for a wide variety of reasons:

- to put him to sleep
- to calm him when he is angry
- to provide a pleasant background for eating or playing
- to help celebrate a birthday or holiday
- to develop pride in his ethnic heritage by using songs, dances, and recordings from his culture
- to teach him differences in sound

*Throughout this book, the infant or young child is referred to as "he"; the term here applies to both sexes. Similarly, the adult or teacher is referred to as "she," and this term also is applicable to both sexes.

- to help him develop understandings about music, e.g., slow–fast, high–low, loud–soft
- to help him release energy and tensions
- to teach him language patterns
- to make learning more fun
- to help him express his feelings through movement and dance
- to develop his gross and fine motor skills
- to develop social and group skills

It is evident that most adults view music as having great value in the education of the young, because it has the potential of doing so much for children.

What are some of the specific values of educating our young children in music? Music education can contribute significantly to a wide variety of goals. It can foster:

- *Creativity*, since musical experiences can stimulate exploration, experimentation, and the expression of new and different ideas;
- *Emotional response*, since musical experiences enhance the child's expression of feelings and sharpen awareness of the feelings of others;
- *Intellectual growth*, since musical experiences can stimulate the child to think, to solve problems, to develop understandings about sound, and to organize his perceptions in terms of relationships, comparisons, and concepts;
- *Language development*, since musical experiences can help the child acquire and use language in describing his musical experiences and can help him learn word and sound patterns through singing and listening;
- *Physical development*, since musical experiences, especially those involved in singing, playing instruments, and rhythmic movement, can help the child gain increasing control over his large and small muscles and can help him explore and experiment with the movement of his body;
- *Concepts of self*, since musical experiences can help the child know and appreciate himself as a person and foster cultural identity and pride.

Music-making through clapping rhythms is a joyful experience for young children. (Photo courtesy of Hannah Lou Bennett, University Preschool, University of Hawaii, and Will Kyselka, photographer)

Music, then, can contribute significantly to every child's social, emotional, intellectual, and physical development. Yet, music's main and most critical role in the education of young children is often neglected. This role is its contribution to the *aesthetic* growth of the human organism.

Music is an art form. It communicates ideas and feelings to us through its tones and rhythms. This communication develops in us a sense of richness, fulfillment, and beauty. The power of music to stir the deepest emotions in us is due to the *aesthetic dimension of music*. This dimension refers to the process of perceiving, feeling, organizing, and thinking about the musical experience. This process results in an expression that has meaning for the listener. The aesthetic dimension, so widely ignored in the general education of most of our children and youth, focuses on the way our senses and intellect react to the tonal and rhythmic beauty of music. This aesthetic reaction to what is beautiful in music is caused by the interplay between our emotional and intellectual responses when engaged in the musical experience. We listen to the music, we perceive its tones and rhythms, we respond emotionally to the music, we try to understand the tonal design of the music, and we gain aesthetic satisfaction. We listen, we perceive, we respond, we understand, we sense beauty and meaning, we enjoy. We want the child, at his own level, to be able to listen to the music, sense its emotional impact, perceive and think about its tones and rhythms, respond to its beauty, and develop an appreciation and need for musical experiences of all types. The aesthetic dimension of music education focuses on the tonal beauty of the music and its tonal effect upon the listener. Its concerns are:

• How does the music make us feel?
• What do we hear in the music?
• How can we express the music?
• Why do we react the way we do to the music?

Music and other art forms (dance, drama, the visual **8** arts, literature) are powerful means of educating our young. This power is derived from the aesthetic qualities of the arts. These qualities, when focused upon in the musical experience, can do much to educate both the intellect and the affect (feelings, emotions, attitudes, values). In the *intellectual area,* the musical experience can augment the child's potential to be creative, to develop concepts of music and the world of sound, to express himself verbally and nonverbally, and to solve problems. In the *affective area,* the musical experience can help develop the child's ability to express what he senses, feels, and thinks through sounds, instruments, his voice, and bodily movement. No one can doubt that the child, when participating in a meaningful musical experience, is engaged in a unifying and dynamic activity. Music, as well as the other art forms, has the capacity to unite the diverse elements of the child's experience to cause a significant, total response. This unity is caused by the emotional–intellectual interrelationships of the musical experience and how this interplay gives aesthetic meaning and fulfillment to that experience.

Unfortunately, adults often hinder rather than help the aesthetic development of young children. They often use music that does not represent the best examples from a particular style or culture. They may use a phonograph with poor sound quality or an instrument that is out of tune. They may sing poorly or use little expression when singing to children. They may inhibit the children's natural responses to create music or to move rhythmically to music. They may expose children to music selections (often contrived, trite children's songs) that are not representative of the world's musical heritage (see Chapter 3). Adults too often have had a significantly negative effect on the aesthetic education of children.

What can we do to foster creative and aesthetic growth through music? In our concern with developing the child's aesthetic sensitivity, we need to place emphasis on helping him sense and find beauty, wonder, and meaning through the musical experience. *Every child has an aesthetic potential that needs to be nurtured from birth.* In music, this potential involves a **9** capacity to create music, to sing, to move rhythmically, and to gain immense pleasure through listening to, performing, and creating music. Through musical experiences, we hope that the child will find beauty and understanding in the dancer's rhythmic movement, the violinist's performance, and a choral rendition of a church hymn. The long-range goal is to develop each child's aesthetic potential to the fullest. We need to help each child formulate his own taste and personal sense of what is or is not pleasing to him, based upon how he feels and what he understands about the musical experience. The task of educating the child through music involves developing his capacity to respond to the emotional values and cognitive significance of the musical experience. The goal is to help him:

- feel the emotional qualities in the music
- understand the tonal and rhythmic design of the music
- express the music and its impact on him
- enjoy the music
- attain aesthetic satisfaction through music

This book is dedicated to showing how this goal can be achieved through the first five years of life.

Selected Readings

The following books contain excellent introductions to the field of early childhood education:

Almy, Millie, *The Early Childhood Educator at Work*. New York: McGraw–Hill Book Co., 1975.

Hess, Robert, and Doreen Croft, *Teachers of Young Children*. Boston: Houghton Mifflin Co., 1972.

Hildebrand, Verna, *Introduction to Early Childhood Education*. New York: The Macmillan Co., 1976.

Hymes, James L., Jr., *Early Childhood Education: An Introduction to the Profession*. Washington, D.C.: National Association for the Education of Young Children, 1975.

 Teaching the Child Under Six (2nd ed.). Columbus, Ohio: Charles E. Merrill Publishing Co., 1974.

Landreth, Catherine, *Preschool Learning and Teaching*. New York: Harper and Row, 1972.

Leeper, Sarah H., Ruth J. Dales, Dora S. Skipper, and Ralph L. Witherspoon, *Good Schools for Young Children* (3rd ed.). New York: The Macmillan Co., 1974.

Morrison, George S., *Early Childhood Education Today.* Columbus, Ohio: Charles E. Merrill Publishing Co., 1976.

Read, Katherine H., *The Nursery School: A Human Relations Laboratory* (5th ed.) Philadelphia: W. B. Saunders, 1971.

Spodek, Bernard, *Teaching in the Early Years* (2nd ed.). Englewood Cliffs, N.J.: Prentice–Hall, Inc., 1978.

White, Burton, *The First Three Years of Life.* Englewood Cliffs, N. J.: Prentice–Hall, Inc., 1975.

The following texts are recommended for further reading on the aesthetic dimensions of music and the arts:

Aronoff, Frances W., *Music and Young Children.* New York: Holt, Rinehart and Winston, 1969. See Chapters 1 and 2.

The Arts, Education and Americans Panel, *Coming to Our Senses: The Significance of the Arts for American Education.* New York: McGraw–Hill Book Co., 1977.

Mursell, James L., *Education for Musical Growth.* Boston: Ginn and Co., 1948.

Reimer, Bennett, *A Philosophy of Music Education.* Englewood Cliffs, N.J.: Prentice–Hall, Inc., 1970.

Schwadron, Abraham A., *Aesthetic Dimensions for Music Education.* Washington, D.C.: Music Educators National Conference, 1967.

Smith, Ralph A., ed., *Aesthetic Concepts in Education.* Urbana, Ill.: University of Illinois Press, 1971.

The following texts are recommended as introductions to music education and the young child:

Andress, Barbara L., Hope M. Heimann, Carroll A. Rinehart, and E. Gene Talbert, *Music In Early Childhood.* Washington, D.C.: Music Educators National Conference, 1973.

Aronoff, Frances W., *Music and Young Children.* New York: Holt, Rinehart and Winston, 1969.

Association for Childhood Education International, *Music for Children's Living.* Washington, D.C.: The Association, 1955.

Jones, Elizabeth, *What is Music for Young Children?* Washington, D.C.: National Association for the Education of Young Children, 1969.

Nye, Vernice, *Music for Young Children,* Dubuque, Iowa: William C. Brown Co., 1975.

Pugmire, Mary Carolyn Weller, *Experiences in Music for Young Children.* Albany, New York: Delmar Publishers, 1977.

Sheehy, Emma D., *Children Discover Music and Dance.* New York: Teachers College Press, 1968.

Part One

FOUNDATIONS OF MUSICAL GROWTH

There are at least three factors that influence the ways we plan to develop musical responses in the child. These factors are **the child's growth and development, how the child responds to music, and the nature of music.**

We need to know how the child's growth and development affect the way he progresses from a fetus in his mother's womb into a five-year-old learner. We need to know how the young child responds to music in order to see how the child comes to understand and appreciate his world of music and the aesthetic nature of his experience. We need to know music — its materials, concepts and skills, and its ways of experience — so that we can do a better job of helping the child respond to his musical environment. Each of these three factors is discussed in the next few chapters and provides the essential foundations for educating the young child in music.

The years from birth to five are critcal in the young child's growth and development. (Photo courtesy of Kindergarten and Children's Aid Association of Hawaii)

1

The Young Child's Growth and Development

An effective music education program for the child from birth to age five depends to a large extent on the adult's understanding of the young child. The basis for success in working with children is to know how they develop as individuals and to relate this knowledge to ways of interacting with them. This chapter provides a brief summary of the developmental capabilities of children from birth to age five and will help us to understand how to develop their responses to music.

The Child from Birth to Five: An Overview

The first years of life witness a period of rapid physical, social, emotional, and intellectual growth. It is a time when the human organism matures from a totally dependent newborn baby into a child capable of running, jumping, playing with other children, thinking, speaking, writing, and responding musically. It is a time for learning how to learn, learning about his environment, and

19 for figuring out what things are, what the rules are, and

how things work. It is a time for learning about other
people, himself, his place in the world, what he can and
cannot do, how people feel about him, and how he feels
about himself.

The Infant

The newborn child appears to be completely helpless
when he enters our world. He sleeps most of the time,
is dependent on adults for most of his needs, and is
fragile and weak. His activities seem aimless and erratic.
Yet, the newborn already can perform several behaviors.
He can salivate, suck, defecate, urinate, vomit, sneeze,
yawn, kick, wave his arms and legs, shiver, tremble,
make some facial expressions, move his head, blink, cry,
grunt, and sigh. At birth, he is also able to respond to a
large array of sensory stimuli, including sound and
music.

The period from birth to one year is a time when
the infant learns some of the basic skills of living—how
to move, how to perceive the world through his five
senses (touch, sight, taste, smell, and hearing), how to
communicate through sound, how to react to objects
and events, and how to relate to other people. It is a time
when the child learns about emotional response and
love. It is a time when, more than ever, he needs the
physical care and emotional support given to him by an
adult.

The newborn child has a considerable capacity to
learn and adapt to what the environment demands or
provides. The child rapidly takes note of his immediate
environment, its objects, events, and people. Through
the use of his five senses, he gradually begins to get to
know the world. The newborn's sensory capacity extends
the infant's reach into his whole environment and accounts for most of what he learns during the first six
months of life.

One of the earliest responses of the infant to his
world is caused by sound.* The newborn child first

*A complete discussion on infants and sound/music appears on pp.
47–55. This section presents only an overview of the young child as
he responds to sound and music.

20

responds to the sensual stimulation of sounds. He then begins to discriminate sounds by responding to certain kinds (his mother's voice, the rattle, the squeaky rubber duck) more than others. Soon, he produces sounds that imitate those he hears in his environment. Hearing and reproducing sounds become very important parts of the life of the infant.

At about three months the visual and hearing senses become coordinated. At this stage, the child does not merely see what he sees or hear what he hears: rather, the infant learns to *listen* to what he sees and to *look* at what he hears. He begins to take note of various impressions that are not isolated phenomena but coordinated events. For example, he learns that a rattle can be sucked, looked at, grasped, and listened to as a source of sound. A composite of meanings and new interest arises as he interacts with his environment. He becomes aware of his perceptions and gives meaning to the information received by his senses. He sorts out the experiences and the different stimuli he finds in his world. He soon begins to use the accumulated information to learn more about his environment.

Between four and eight months of age the child refines his sensori-motor activities which have become established during the preceding months. But he now begins to take notice of the effects he can produce on his environment. He accidentally hits the rattle on the wood of the crib and notices the interesting patterns of sound he can make. He repeats this discovery and varies his actions to make other sounds. He learns to handle and use certain objects in the environment. He discovers that a spoon produces a sound when tapped against the floor, but not when held. He is experimental with objects, desiring to find out what the consequences are when he acts upon these objects. This is the beginning of the thinking process used in establishing cause-and-effect relationships.

The infant grows at an astonishing rate. Within a few months after birth, he shows an increase in his natural curiosity and response to his environment. He grows physically, sleeps less, develops some teeth, and learns how to smile. He begins to reach for and grasp objects. He becomes more mobile and may sit by himself at seven months and crawl at ten months. He moves around, pulls on things, and stands. By twelve months, he may be able to walk. His actions become more intentional and his activities more goal-directed. He not only grasps the drumstick, but he now intends to use it for a purpose. The child knows what the outcome will be when he hits the stick on the tambourine or the chair, and he directs his activity toward fulfilling this goal. He also learns that hitting the stick on the tambourine pleases his mother, but using it on glass or on his older brother makes his mother angry. He recognizes the connection between what he does and how things and other people react. During this time, the child also begins to develop the concept of *object permanence.* Basically, this means that the child knows an object is still present even though he cannot see it. Object permanence is the start of the child's ability to form images in his mind without having the concrete object or event in front of him. It is an essential aspect of the ability to think. By age one the child babbles and gurgles sounds that we call "baby talk." He begins to listen to and understand some of the words that people say. He may even say "ma-ma" and "bye-bye." Within the space of a short year, he has achieved a great deal in responding to, and learning about, his new environment.

The One-Year-Old

Between ages one and two, the infant exercises more and more control over his motor abilities. During this year, he will learn how to stand, walk, jump, climb stairs, hold a cup or pair of rhythm sticks, and make scribbling marks with a large pencil or crayon. As the child's mobility improves, he begins actively and enthusiastically to explore his surroundings. He is very curious about the bug crawling on the wall, the fire burning on the gas range, and the water swishing in the toilet bowl. He wonders about the sounds he hears from the radio, the steam rising from his cereal, and the water falling from the sky. Control over bodily functions enables many children to begin toilet training by age two.

Between ages one and two, the child begins to understand and use language. Visual discrimination improves, so that the child can now distinguish the form of a circle from that of a triangle or square. Emotions become more developed, and the child will show a variety of emotional tones such as anger, frustration, despair, jealousy, joy, loneliness, and love. At this age, he is still very dependent upon a familiar adult. He will develop self-help skills such as taking off his shoes and holding a spoon during feeding. During this period, the child continues to learn most and best through direct contact with objects and people. He must experience everything in order to learn about his world. He not only repeats what worked so far for him, but varies his approach to discover how he might change the results. He takes a drumstick and bangs a chair, another child, the floor, or a lamp. He uses the stick as an extension of his arm in order to get to a distant object. He is highly experimental and curious at this age as he tries to understand his ever-expanding and fascinating environment.

Musically, the one-year-old can now hold certain rhythm instruments with ease and use these to experiment with sound. He begins to play a steady pulse on these instruments, although still not synchronized with the music. He occasionally bursts out in dance as he hears music. He may begin to chant, using nonsense syllables, but is still unable to sing accurately. He remains enrapt with sound, especially as it occurs in the human voice. The second year of life, then, is a period of intense exploration, as the child— for the first time — has the mobility and intellectual capacity to move about and discover and respond to his environment.

The Two-Year-Old

Between ages two and three, the child continues to develop motor skills learned in the first two years of life as the basis for more refined motor development. He begins to run, jump from a chair, and walk up and down stairs. He can move his fingers independently. He gains bladder control.

The two-year-old, while continuing to rely mostly on sensori-motor experiences, now begins to use representations of objects or activities that are not tangibly before his eyes. He begins to form mental images about things and events in his world. If he has had prior experience in playing a drum, he may now imitate a drum being played, using a pillow or box. He may use a tone block as a make-believe drinking cup. Thus, at this stage, he begins to mentally represent things and actions which have been in his experience. He improves in his ability to think, problem-solve, put events in time sequence, reason, classify, and discriminate. He begins to learn the cause and effect of both his own actions and the actions of others. These processes take several years to develop. Although he still needs direct experiences in learning, he can also represent his experience through role playing, make-believe, and other play. A doll may now become his mommy, and a block his dog. A small table, chairs, and paper plates will become a means of representing how he feels and what he knows about his family's mealtime. The age of two is also a time for rapid growth in the child's ability to understand and use language for communication. His vocabulary increases from fifty to over one thousand words. He experiments with different kinds of language sounds, word order, and sentence patterns. He begins to learn some of the speech sounds of the language. He also starts to understand the relationships between different objects and events in the world.

The age of two is usually a time of negativism, when the "terrible two" first asserts his growing independence from his primary caretaker. He gives much more attention to his surroundings and to play materials than to other children. Cooperative play with other children is limited.

In music, the two-year-old begins to control his singing voice. He approximates the melody of a song. He chants and sings to himself at play. He also tries to clap or play instruments to the beat of music. He is freer in his movements to music. His creativity blossoms. He is

24

now capable of the muscular coordination needed to make up tunes, using his voice or a melody instrument such as the xylophone. The two-year-old, although frequently rebellious, is also a child reaching his peak of uninhibited curiosity and creativity.

The Three-Year-Old

The year from age three to four is a time in which fine-motor manipulative skills and gross motor skills become more developed. The child learns to run smoothly, walk stairs with alternating feet, pull strings through beads, play a triangle in a relatively controlled manner, put simple large puzzles together, and ride a tricycle.

The three-year-old's language abilities continue to improve. He asks questions to gain information. His vocabulary increases to well over one thousand words. He can learn prepositions such as *down, under,* and *in.* He can follow many simple directions. He begins mastery of the spoken grammar of his language. The three-year-old continues to learn by a variety of means, including repetition and self-motivated practice, imitation of adults and other children, and self-discovery. He starts to form clearer concepts of color, size, length, weight, time, and number. He can listen to short stories and play simple games such as "Simon Says" and "Red Light." He improves in his ability to recognize similarities and differences in objects. He begins to classify objects in his environment. He learns how to handle some emotions and find reasonable solutions to his negative feelings. He is also becoming more aware of the feelings of others. For the three-year-old, as well as for all young children, learning and play are inseparable. Play is the child's way of learning and expressing what he understands and feels about his world. It is the child's natural way of exploring, experimenting, and making inferences about the social and physical attributes of his world in order to formulate concepts and see relationships. The three-year-old actively seeks other children with whom to play, and his play lasts a longer time than previously. He is becoming more independent of adults. Sexual identity begins. His

25

self-concept becomes firmly set, and he develops most of the foundation for how he feels and thinks about himself.

Musically, the three-year-old can now sing some simple songs and phrases from songs. His ability to move with the beat of the music improves. He learns how to clap simple rhythmic patterns. He can follow the directions and motions of a simple singing game such as "Ring Around the Rosy" or "The Mulberry Bush." He continues to show a strong interest in creating his own music, using his voice or instruments. He begins to conceptualize musical elements such as loud–soft and fast–slow through bodily movement. The three-year-old, often delightful and self-assured in his relationship with adults, begins to show his individuality and capabilities as he gradually acquires some of life's skills and understandings.

The Four-Year-Old

By the time the child is almost five, he has acquired most of the basic characteristics and tools that will shape his life. He continues to make gains in motor control and coordination. He can now move his body in a variety of ways. He can climb ladders, walk backwards, and catch and throw a large ball. He can stand on one foot, hop, run smoothly, and walk a straight line heel to toe. He may start to learn how to skip and gallop. He will be able to handle scissors, pencils, crayons, and paste quite well. He may be able to write some letters of the alphabet, or even his name. He probably will be able to lace his shoes and lock a door.

At the age of four, language development is rapid. Vocabulary and sentence length are increasing, more sounds are articulated correctly, and new sentence forms are learned. Language is used more frequently to exchange ideas, find out information, and describe objects and events. This is a time for very active learning and rapid intellectual development. The child is a thinking human being, although he still has several more years to go before attaining the more abstract and complex thought processes characteristic of the older child and the adult. He still prefers working directly on or with objects and events, rather than thinking about them. He remains primarily activity-oriented and a "doer." He continues to rely heavily on his senses and on his motor ability in order to learn. He has a greater ability to remember things, and he often uses previous experience to conceptualize new learning. Attention span increases. Concepts such as time, weight, number, classification, and size continue to become refined. The child gains an increasing knowledge of the physical attributes of objects such as glass, water, metal, and paper. Socialization improves as the child is better able to get along with others and handle his own feelings in more socially acceptable ways.

In music, the four-year-old's expanding vocal range, rhythmic ability, and vocabulary allow him to sing more difficult songs. He is better able to synchronize his bodily movements to the rhythmic flow of the music. He now can handle most of the easy-to-play rhythm instruments with comparative ease. His past experiences in music enable him to create songs and tunes that are more varied and interesting. He moves with abandon and more musical expression as he interprets the music through his own body. By the age of five, the young child is ready to enter a new world—the environment of the kinder-garten—where new challenges await him.

Factors Influencing Growth and Development

As seen from the previous overview on child growth and development, there are many factors that determine what the child can do and learn, whether in a general way or in music. Some of these factors include: *endowment, maturation, stage of development, environment and experience,* and *individuality.*

Endowment refers to the inborn characteristics of **27** the child, as influenced by heredity and genetic factors.

These characteristics will partially determine the child's course of development and his interests, needs, and style of interacting with his environment. One child's rate of metabolism may make him more nervous or calmer than another child. One child's poor muscular coordination may cause him difficulty when he moves to music or plays instruments. Characteristics influenced by factors of endowment may be modified, at least to some extent, by the environment and through experience.

Maturation refers to the ability of the child, at certain stages of growth, to reach his potential capacities. His capacity to behave in a certain way has arrived. He is functionally ready to crawl, or to stand, or to walk, or to run. Maturation, shaped by genetic factors, is a progressive and dynamic unfolding process that takes place according to a predetermined schedule. The concept of maturation implies the fact that there are expected sequences for growth and a time for this unfolding. The child's abilities to grasp, turn his head, and reach for objects seem to occur at certain stages in the life of the child, in a set order, and they present themselves independent of what adults can do. Thus, it is not possible to teach a six-month-old baby to run, to sing, to play the piano, or to talk. Nor is it possible to teach a two-year-old to skip, play chords on the guitar, or write words. Both maturation and experience determine when these behaviors will occur in the human organism.

Stages of development is a phrase that refers to the various levels of growth at which the child shows definite characteristic behaviors true of most children. For example, most two-year-olds enter a stage of negativism in dealing with adults. And according to some writers, there are stages in social–emotional and intellectual development through which all humans proceed. The concept of stages notes that these characteristic behaviors indicate the need for certain experiences or events to occur at a particular level of development. It also implies that certain stages are critical in the child's development and that if these activities do not take place at that time, growth may be seriously hampered.

28   *Environment and experience* refer to the influences around the child that affect his development. These influences include factors in the physical environment—the foods, the climactic conditions, the sights, sounds, and smells—and the human environment—the type of interactions the child has with people around him. Environment and experience refer also to the context of the stimuli, i.e., the timing, intensity, variety, and emotional climate of the experience.

Individuality refers to the uniqueness of each child. This uniqueness is caused by variations in size, sex, physical health, reactions to sensory stimuli, level of activity, and experience. Differences in the child's genetic-heredity endowment, in combination with variations in what the child experiences, lead to highly individual ways of response. All children, though they do develop in generally similar ways, are unique individuals. Every child responds to the world in his own unique manner. No two children are alike.

A Sequence of Development

The young child seems to display an orderly sequence in the emergence of many new abilities. Much of what the young child does—e.g., learning to crawl, stand, and walk—is self-initiated and appears virtually independent of what the environment is like. On the other hand, some accomplishments depend to a great degree on the child's experience and environment, e.g., the ability to form sentences and understand directions or the ability to ride a tricycle. Nevertheless, the development of much of the child's physical, social, emotional, intellectual, language, musical, and other responses follows a definite schedule or timetable. The order of events seems to be fairly standard in all children. In Table 1 some aspects of this schedule are summarized. The age levels and sequence are not rigidly fixed and should not be taken literally, since the exact age that any child behaves in a **29** given fashion is subject to the influence of many genetic,

An Overview of Certain Aspects of Growth, Development, and Response in the Child Age 0 to 5

APPROX. AGE	MOTOR	SOCIAL– EMOTIONAL	INTELLECTUAL	LANGUAGE VERBAL AND MUSICAL
0 to 2 months	Uncontrolled isolated reflexes (sucking, grasping); frequent sleeping; lack of mobility; cannot turn body; large head; poor vision and focusing.	Infrequently smiles at human faces; begins to look at eyes of adults who hold him or talk to him; otherwise not social; few moods shown (anger, distress, satisfaction).	Reflex stage – experiences the initial rhythms of life, e.g., sucking, crying, breathing, feeding; isolated sensory intake.	Generally quiet due to sleepiness and grogginess; cries when distressed; makes occasional noises as howls, shrieks; little interest in listening to his own sounds; by 2 months cries more frequently; comforted by soft sounds, rocking, human voices; distressed by sudden loud or high-pitched sounds.
2 to 4 months	Awake more; rapid increase in weight, strength; supports head when lying on stomach; little control over head; hands open, with no grasp reflex; cannot turn over or reach for objects; follows slow-moving objects with eyes; interested in hands, fingers; begins to coordinate several behaviors (grasping, looking, sucking, hearing).	Frequent social smiles at all people; usually appears comfortable and happy; interested in the human face; still has limited number of emotional states; shows special interest in mother's face and voice; responds and laughs when tickled.	Begins to control and regulate initial rhythms of life and to coordinate various senses, e.g., hearing and looking at same object; learns only through senses; by 4 months marked increase in curiosity.	Less crying; makes more sounds than newly born, including squeals, shrieks of delight, gurgles; occasionally makes sounds when nodded to or spoken to; enjoys playing with his own sounds caused by his own saliva; continues to be comforted by soft sounds, rocking, human voices; responds more definitely to human voices, especially to mother's voice.
4 to 6 months	Vigorous large-muscle activity – – kicks, waves arms; can turn over; more control over head, and can self-support it; sits with pillows propped on three sides; uses hands to reach, and plays with objects placed in hands; coordinates hands and vision.	Develops strong relationship with caring adult(s); laughs, giggles, and continues frequent smiling; begins to use cry or sounds to get adult's attention; generally friendly to all adults.	Begins to incorporate environment into his sense of being and control; explores all objects within his reach, particularly those that can be grasped, chewed, swung, or batted.	Vowel-like coos; chuckles; eyes search for sound sources; continues liking sounds from human voices; begins to use more consonants in cooing, especially those formed by lips (m, b, p); becomes calm when music is played.

APPROX. AGE	MOTOR	SOCIAL – EMOTIONAL	INTELLECTUAL	LANGUAGE VERBAL AND MUSICAL	
6 to 9 months	Still unable to move about; readily turns over from back to stomach and vice versa; uses hands for support; likes to reach; grasps using thumbs and fingers; sits by himself; pulls himself to stand by about 8 months; begins to crawl; frequent "exercising" of arms, legs.	Very "sociable" with other people; frequent smiling continues; begins to show anxiety with strangers by 8 or 9 months; continues giggling and laughter; likes being played with; has more abrupt mood changes.	Continues exploration of environment; incorporates new objects and events into existing mental structure; begins to recognize that object is still there, even if out of view; will push aside obstacles to get at desired objects.	Babbles (makes one-syllable sounds) using vowels with some consonants; attempts to imitate "da," "ma" sounds made by adults; intonation patterns become distinct; utterances can signal emotions and emphasis; by 8 to 9 months begins to repeat sounds and sound patterns; may move arms to music; appears satisfied when music is played.	
9 months to 1 year	Continued mobility, but is very clumsy; crawls well; takes side steps, holding; begins to climb; by 1 year may walk when held by one hand.	More suspicious with strangers; quite moody; likes to watch actions of other people; very reliant upon familiar adults, especially the primary caretaker.	Refines the previous stage; interested in effect of motor actions on objects (cause-and-effect); begins to do things in definite time sequence; limited memory; frequent staring at objects.	Frequent sound play such as gurgling, bubble blowing; tries to imitate lots of sounds, often unsuccessfully; starts to respond to some words ("no!" and "here"); continues interest in sound and music.	
				VERBAL	MUSICAL
1 year to 1 year, 6 months	Stands momentarily alone; crawls faster; takes steps, first by holding adult's hand, then alone; climbs; walks clumsily; grasps and releases objects well; wants to touch and get into everything.	Begins to learn simple rules; very dependent upon familiar adults; often clings to or resists adult; very short attention span; understands what belongs to others but does not share; may be able to help with simple tasks; wary of strangers.	Very curious about his world; experimental with everything he can touch; begins to solve problems and learn cause-and-effect; time relationships (first ... then); continued frequent staring at objects, people.	Follows simple commands, and responds to "no"; repeats simple sound sequences more frequently and with greater accuracy; begins to say a few words: con-	Discriminates between many sounds; taps self-initiated beat and may move to music, but is not synchronized with it; babbles using different pitches and

An Overview of Growth . . . (cont.)

APPROX. AGE	MOTOR	SOCIAL – EMOTIONAL	INTELLECTUAL	LANGUAGE VERBAL AND MUSICAL	
				tinues sound play and babbling.	rhythmic patterns; enchanted by new, unusual sounds; may approximate pitches of simple patterns sung to him.
1 year, 6 months to 2 years	Stance and grasp developed; walks with stiff gait and is propulsive; sits on chair with fair aim; kicks and throws ball clumsily; begins to run; able to start toilet training; difficulty in building a three-cube tower; poor fine-motor coordination; better visual and hearing discrimination.	Plays alone, but likes being near adult; very dependent upon familiar adult; can help with simple tasks; very short attention span; does not share; may begin to resist adult; very shy with strangers.	Increased grasp of reality; can deal with some abstractions; remembers places he has been to; recognizes some pictures in books; names some foods, body parts; continues staring behavior; thinks through some actions before doing them.	Lots of sound play with several syllables and intricate intonation patterns; increases vocabulary to 20 to 200 words; points to objects upon direction; understands simple questions; forms two-word phrases ("see ball," "me cat"); little attempt to communicate information.	"Sings" and hums at play; gains some control of singing voice; continues to approximate pitches and rhythms; occasionally matches beat of music on rhythm instruments or through movement; likes to create tunes using voice or simple melody instrument; responds well to pattern repetition and rhymes; can learn finger plays.

APPROX. AGE	MOTOR	SOCIAL–EMOTIONAL	INTELLECTUAL	LANGUAGE VERBAL AND MUSICAL	
2 years to 2 years, 6 months	Runs, but falls frequently; walks up and down stairs (one foot forward only); controls bladder; well-developed handedness; improved fine-motor control.	Plays alone, but likes being near other children; frequent demands on adult's attention; often negative and rebellious; difficulty in sharing; may have tantrums; will separate from primary care-taker for short periods.	Recognizes objects, people in pictures; able to listen to simple stories and follow directions; begins to use objects to act out what is known (role play, make-believe); places shapes in correct puzzle form; notices what is missing in picture; forming concepts of body parts, number, size.	Vocabulary of between 50 and 400 words; uses two- and three-word phrases; begins to understand and use pronouns and prepositions; definite increase in using language to communicate.	Sings and hums at play; likes rhymes and repetition of tonal patterns (chants); frequently repeats sounds and patterns; enjoys nursery tunes; joins in on certain phrases of songs (still often not on pitch); freer and more frequent bodily response to music.
2 years, 6 months to 3 years	Jumps with two feet; begins to tiptoe; jumps from chair; better hand and finger coordination; moves fingers independently; builds tower of six cubes; learns to cut with scissors, but still has difficulty.	Emotionally still very dependent on adults; often is negative and rebellious; strong sense of "it is mine" (will snatch and grab toys); likes to watch other children play, but still prefers solitary play; frequent fights with other children; often rigid and persistent in behavior.	Enjoys looking at pictures; frequent role playing and make believe; has some sense of beginning, end, present, past, and future; forming concepts of weight, space, darkness, number, height, classification, length, thickness, etc.	Babbling stops; fast increase in vocabulary; uses three- and four-word utterances; tries to communicate; uses correct word order more often; applies some rules of grammar; understands most of what is said to him; is more intelligible in his speech; asks frequent questions.	Continues to sing tonal patterns that interest him; matches some pitches; sings spontaneously for family; interested in records and instruments; learns simple singing games; begins to synchronize music, playing rhythm instruments, and movement.

An Overview of Growth . . . (cont.)

APPROX. AGE	MOTOR	SOCIAL – EMOTIONAL	INTELLECTUAL	LANGUAGE VERBAL and MUSICAL	
3 years to 4 years	Runs smoothly with acceleration, deceleration; easily negotiates curves; walks stairs with alternating feet; jumps twelve inches; rides tricycle; stands on one foot; tiptoes; learns to manipulate scissors; pastes, strings beads, works with puzzles.	Gradually learns how to take turns; will separate from primary caretaker for extended periods; joins in play with other children; competitive; can share at times; helps put things away; likes to help and please adults; expresses extremes of affection or annoyance at adults.	More emphasis on thinking through problems before acting; notices relationships, details, discrepancies; remembers; puts himself in someone else's position, but still very egocentric; longer attention span; anticipates consequences; can dual-focus (does his "own thing" while noting what is around him); more complex cause-and-effect concepts; begins to classify.	Vocabulary of 1,000 plus words; uses sentences; more attention to correct grammatical structure, although errors abound; between 80 and 90% comprehensibility; articulates most sounds correctly but has difficulty with s, th, z, r, l, and others; more frequent use of adjectives, adverbs, prepositions; sentences become more complex.	More control of voice; better able to change pitch, dynamics, speed; can sing simple phrases and songs with increasing accuracy; moves more consistently to the music's beat; imitates simple rhythmic patterns; learns some singing games; forms concept of loud-soft, fast-slow; free in movement to music; likes to make up tunes with his voice.
4 years to 5 years	Jumps over rope; walks on a line; catches ball in arms; hops on one foot; climbs ladders, trees; walks backwards; handles scissors, paste, crayons, pencils, and other	More social with children and adults; usually plays fairly well with others; begins to choose friends; can learn simple social games; understands need for, and follows, rules;	Increasing memory and power to recall; better understanding of number, time; able to do easy and somewhat complex puzzles; sees likenesses and differences; states why	Names many objects, actions, colors; speaks in more complex sentences; frequent questioning;	Plays most rhythm instruments; echoes rhythmic patterns; moves and plays much better to

APPROX. AGE	MOTOR	SOCIAL – EMOTIONAL	INTELLECTUAL	LANGUAGE VERBAL AND MUSICAL	
	small objects; builds large block structures.	comforts those in distress; can do simple errands; more independent.	some events happen; begins to use analogies; longer attention span; classification concepts clearer.	makes only a few infantile substitutions in speech; uses at least 1,500 to 1,-800 words; understands many complex sentences; may be able to read simple words.	music's rhythmic flow; expanding concepts of high–low pitch, long–short tones, and differences in tone quality; sings songs of a wider vocal range and with better rhythmic and pitch accuracy; longer attention span in guided listening to records.

maturational, and environmental factors. There is a great danger in generalizing about what a child should be like at any age, since each child is unique and has his own rate of development. The specified ages for developmental levels should be taken only as approximations and rough guidelines.

Table 1 indicates that the development of certain skills in one area of development parallels the development of certain skills in other areas. The table shows that the "typical" child learns to respond in generally similar ways and along similar schedules. The child will normally proceed from one stage or level to another. Each stage seems to be dependent upon the preceding one. The table also indicates that the period of most rapid growth and change occurs during the first two years of life.

Two essential points related to music education for the young should be noted in connection with Table 1:

1. The table indicates that the origins of musical and verbal language stem from the same roots and that for the first year or more of life, language and musical growth involve the same processes and stages. *Both music and language have a common basis in the infant's earliest vocalizations* (see also pp. 55–61). At about one year of age, the child has needed background to learn both verbal language and the language of music. For the next several years of early childhood, there is a close relationship and mutual reinforcement between the way these two languages are learned.

2. Table 1 shows that a close relationship exists between musical growth and other developmental areas. For example, the ability to move to the beat, clap in time to it, or play it on an instrument rests in part on the child's ability to control his movements and synchronize them with the music. And the ability to sing songs depends in part on the child's language and intellectual abilities to pronounce and understand words and remember them in the proper sequence and on his motor ability to control his vocal cords in singing. Musical growth, then, is not an isolated phenomenon; rather, it goes hand in hand with other areas of development. *Musical growth is*

*directly affected by the child's overall motor,
social–emotional, intellectual, and language development.*

Summary

In educating the young child in music, we must be
concerned first and foremost with the individual child
as he develops from an almost totally dependent infant
to a relatively capable five-year-old. That age span is one
of rapid growth. The child learns to control and use his
large muscles and obtains better and more accurate fine-
motor control. The child develops a concept of self,
learns to express emotions, to get along with children
and adults, to follow rules, to express himself verbally
and musically, and to understand the world about him.
He relies heavily on his senses and his motor explora-
tions to understand his world. He learns cause and effect,
time and spatial relationships, and logical thinking. He
does these in a relatively sequential order, with many
behaviors dependent upon what he has experienced before. Language and musical acitivities relate to and
reinforce each other, especially at the earliest stages of
development. And most importantly, musical growth is
dependent to a great degree on the child's overall growth
patterns. Musical growth and education are not isolated
areas of concern; rather, they must be considered in the
context of the child's total development. A successful
program in music rests upon, and is related to, how the
child develops, and takes into account the needs, interests, and capacities of the growing young child.

Selected Readings

Ames, Louise B., and Frances L. Ilg, *Your Two Year Old* (149 pp.),
Your Three Year Old (167 pp.), and *Your Four Year Old* (152
pp.). New York: Delacorte Press, 1976.
*Practical guides that outline the charateristic patterns of each
age.*

Biehler, Robert F., *Child Development: An Introduction*. Boston: Houghton Mifflin Co., 1976.
A good introduction to the field.

Brazelton, T. Berry, *Infants and Mothers*. New York: Dell Publishers, 1969.
Describes the average, quiet, and active baby in each of the first twelve months of life.

Charles, C. M., *Teachers' Petit Piaget*. Belmont, Calif.: Fearon Publishers, 1974.
Hundreds of books and articles have sought to interpret the writings of Jean Piaget, noted psycholgist, for the layperson and educator. Charles' 60-page paperback does a commendable job and has a bibliography for further readings.

Erikson, Erik H., *Childhood and Society*. New York: W. W. Norton and Co., 1963.
A classic presentation of child-rearing practices and the growth of personality and character in young children.

Gesell, Arnold, Frances L. Ilg, and Louise B. Ames, *Infant and Child in the Culture of Today*, rev. ed. New York: Harper Publishers, 1974.
Emphasizes the developmental, maturational aspects of growth.

Garvey, Catherine, *Play*. Cambridge, Mass.: Harvard University Press, 1977.
Describes the key role of play in early childhood learning.

Gordon, Ira J., *Baby Learning Through Baby Play: A Parent's Guide for the First Two Years*. New York: St. Martin's Press, 1970.
A down-to-earth guide.

Holt, John, *How Children Learn*. New York: Pitman Publishers, 1967.
A very readable presentation of how to assist children in learning.

Infant Care, Department of Health, Education and Welfare Publication No. (OCD) 73-15, Children's Bureau Publication No. 8-1973. Washington, D. C.: U.S. Department of Health, Education, and Welfare, Superintendent of Documents, U.S. Government Printing Office, 1975.
An excellent, highly readable pamphlet on the growth and development of the infant.

Isaacs, Susan, *Intellectual Growth in Children*. London: Routledge and Kegan Paul, 1930.
Presentation of how young children learn, by the noted educator who so influenced the British Open Education movement.

Jersild, Arthur T., *Child Psychology* (7th ed.). Englewood Cliffs, N. J.: Prentice–Hall, Inc., 1975.
One of the most authoritative books on child growth and development.

Lugo, James O., and Gerald L. Hershey, *Human Development*. New York: The Macmillan Co., 1974.
An excellent source for various theories and models of how individuals develop.

The Young Child's Growth and Development

Sponseller, Doris, ed., *Play as a Learning Medium.* Washington, D. C.: National Association for the Education of Young Children, 1974.
An informative booklet on the central role of play in early childhood.

White, Burton L., *The First Three Years of Life.* Englewood Cliffs, N. J.: Prentice-Hall Inc., 1975.
Very readable book that stresses all aspects of the development of the young child.

Early childhood is a time for much musical experimentation and development. (Photo courtesy of Sally Gale)

2

The Young Child Learns Music

The young child has been shown to be an active learner during the entire period of early childhood. He is curious, inquisitive, enthusiastic, and eager to discover all he can about his world. In doing this, he learns through direct experience with objects, events, and people in his environment. This chapter discusses how the young child learns music in very much the same way as he learns everything else. The biological and environmental factors in musical response are discussed, and a detailed description of the child's developmental growth patterns in music is provided. Particular emphasis is placed on how the young child learns to respond to music and how he learns to sing. This chapter focuses, then, on the origins and development of musical response in the child from birth to age five.

Biological Factors

Music has been an essential part of human experience since the dawn of history. Even primitive people selected and organized sounds from nature to communicate their feelings and understandings of the world. Using music to communicate and express oneself is a natural consequence of being human. And this capacity to communicate through music crosses all cultural, geographical, and racial lines. *All* human beings have the capacity to communicate musically. And all human beings seem to have a strong need for the musical experience.

What are some musical behaviors that appear to be common to the human species and that exhibit themselves during the earliest years of life? If you watch a three-month-old infant from any culture or geographic area over an extended period, you might observe that if his hearing and overall physical growth are normal, he will:

- notice musical sounds by turning to the sound source and/or moving part of his body rhythmically;
- make and experiment with vocal sounds, using different pitches, dynamic levels, and durations;
- experiment with other sound sources (instruments?) available to him.

The infant is musically responsive, whether he lives in New York, New South Wales, or New Guinea.

The young child's capacity to respond to music is as much a part of his natural endowment as his learning to grasp objects or walk. Human babies are born into a species of animals that can behave and respond musically. In the human species, there is a strong biological tendency to react to musical sound. All babies, by nature, have a communicative capacity and competency in music.

The development of musical behavior and everything that transpires in the child's life rests on the biological, genetic foundations of the organism. As the child grows, changes will occur in his response to music and his environment. The impetus for this change is inherent within each child. With the proper encouragement and set of circumstances—i.e., with a supportive environment and education—this musical growth will unfold in an organized, sequential manner toward its more mature state.

44

We know very little about the biological aspects of musical responsiveness. One can guess that there are many biological mechanisms that affect musical responsiveness. Specific physical attributes in the young child's vocal mechanism might affect his singing abilities. The central nervous system and small-gross-motor functioning could affect the ability of the child to play instruments, move rhythmically to music, or hear fine discriminations in rhythm or pitch. Children differ in their hearing acuity in ways that may affect how they acquire certain complex musical skills. Certainly, being deaf makes it very difficult to respond to sound stimuli. This, in turn, markedly limits the deaf child's ability to respond to music. And there is some evidence, although meager, that heredity has an important role in determining musical talent.

Maturation plays a major role in the musical development of the young child (see also pp. 27–29, 55–65). For example, there appears to be a set sequence of vocal responses that the child must proceed through in order to learn to sing, and this probably cannot be quickened by giving the child additional practice. We know that the four-month-old child will coo and make sounds of definite pitch and duration, but no amount of additional exposure to singing or additional practice in singing will enable him to chant simple words on two alternating pitches. Similarly, the two-year-old may chant his own name, but no amount of additional practice will enable him to sing "The Farmer in the Dell" with accurate pitches, rhythms, and words. It seems that some aspects of musical development unfold in a relatively sequential manner, determined by maturational factors. The capacity and the impulse to communicate musically resemble the growth of life itself. The process is one of a gradual unfolding of one's potential to respond to and make music. Much of this growth may be attributed to heredity, maturation, and biological factors.

Given his own biological makeup, the child still needs opportunities to interact with his environment in order to progress at his own pace from one stage of musical development to the next (see discussion on stages of development in Chapter 1). Biological factors, although they play an important role in the musical development of the child, cannot be divorced from experience. Biological factors are a necessary but not sufficient condition for musical growth. Environment also plays a key role.

Environmental Factors

Although all children have certain inborn capacities to respond musically, the *environment* acts upon each child to change these capacities. This change is called "learning." The child's innate capacity to respond musically must be triggered by his environment. The child has the capacity to sing or to move rhythmically to music and will do so as an infant, but he will not progress unless there are models and opportunities from which he can learn. Research has indicated that more exposure to certain sensory experiences during infancy enables the human organism to respond more easily to these stimuli at later stages of development. Many studies have shown that early musical experiences can have significant impact on the child's musical growth. There is clear evidence that the control of musical experiences within the environment will shape the musical development of the child. Such early activities include vocalizing and singing, moving to music, listening to sound and music, and experimenting with environmental sounds and instruments. The first years of life, then, are *critical* for the general music and aesthetic education of all our children.

We now know that both the home and school environments affect the musical growth of young children. For example, a mother's frequency of singing with her young child can shape the child's overall musical responsiveness and singing abilities. *A musical home invariably accelerates the musical growth of the child.* Furthermore, several planned music programs emphasizing music perception and concept formation have shown that these programs generally facilitate musical development in comparison with music instruction that is unplanned, haphazard, or nonexistent. Clearly, environmental factors influence musical growth to a great extent.

We can conclusively state that the *innate genetic potential* of the child to respond to music, acting in conjunction with a *favorable musical environment*, accounts for musical ability and response. The young child's musical development and growth are products of an interplay between his biological tendencies and his environment. It is the *interaction* between heredity and environment that is the key to understanding how a child learns music. The parent, teacher, and other adults who work in music with the child from birth to five need to recognize that: (1) every child has the innate potential of responding and communicating musically at his own developmental level; and (2) a rich and varied musical environment must be provided for the child that will maximize his potential for musical response and growth. The child's natural capacity to respond to and enjoy music can be enhanced by continuous adult encouragement and support in a planned environment designed to foster musical growth. The time to begin this planned environment is at birth!

The Child Responds to Sound and Music

Let us now trace the origins of musical response in the child. When does it start? How does this response begin? How does it develop?

The growing child, from birth, is captivated by sound. He is curious about sound, what produces it, and how he can produce it. This curiosity forms the foundation for the young child's introduction to the world of music. His first responses to sound are the forerunners of musical growth and development.

The human capacity to respond to sound and music actually develops long before a child is born! One of the first recognizable signs of life in the unborn fetus is the **47** heartbeat—an automatic "musical" response. The beat of the heart begins during the third week following conception. This beat and other vibrations within the mother's womb surround the fetus until birth. As early as the third month of gestation, most fetuses will react to external sound stimuli by moving and changing their internal rates of breathing. By the sixth month, the fetus is equipped with practically all the machinery necessary for him to become a musically responsive human. His hearing apparatus, central nervous system, and vocal mechanisms have been formed, although these do need further maturation to be fully functional.

Prior to birth, the fetus is able to respond to vibrations that produce auditory sensation and to respond to touch and pressure stimulation. Numerous observers have noted that muscular contractions, kicking, and other movements are exhibited by the fetus when unusually loud and sudden noises are heard in the environment. For example, it is relatively common for mothers to report fetal activity when there is a loud, sudden noise, such as when the sides of a bathtub are struck by a metal rod as the mother bathes. During the late stages of pregnancy, some mothers have reported that a concert or recorded rock music often produces increased fetal activity. One study has shown that fetuses and infants both respond more to sounds of varying pitch than to sounds of varying loudness. A friend of the author reported that her fetus occasionally "danced" to recordings of Beethoven symphonies, especially those sections that were rhythmical, pulsating, and relatively loud. Unfortunately, researchers have not been able to determine whether these responses to sound before birth are the fetus's reactions to the physical vibrations that produce sound or whether the embryo actually "hears" the sound.

The newborn child can respond to sound and music almost immediately. He is quieted by one of the earliest and constant sounds he hears—his mother's heartbeat—as he sucks from her breast. Like the fetus, he will be jarred by loud and sudden sounds. He will attend to high-pitched sounds more readily than to other sounds. When the newborn child hears music, he will respond in one of several ways: He will become quiet after crying or being active; or he will become active or cry after being quiet; or he will make a verbal sound. Music will frequently quiet the child. Many infants will exhibit fleeting smiles when they hear soft human voices. Most will show the beginning of the ability to localize sound by responding differently to a sound coming from the right or left. Newborn infants will also show an adaptation to a steady recurring sound by decreasing their response to the continuing sound after several minutes. Many infants will move their entire bodies when hearing music, especially high-pitched voices or instruments. All of these responses occur before learning has had any effect or influence on their behavior.

The newborn's hearing, although not as acute as an adult's, enables him to receive various sounds from the environment. He can discriminate a wide range of sounds in his first months of life. As stated previously, he has a general sensitivity to loud, sharp sounds (as do most adults!). He also reacts uncomfortably to high-pitched sounds. Both loud and high-pitched sounds startle the infant, and sustained crying usually results. He reacts calmly to the lilting melody of a lullaby, especially when accompanied by an adult's rocking movements. He exhibits a more quieting and alerting behavior to soft, high-pitched instruments and female voices than to low-pitched instruments and male voices. Thus, at a very early age, the infant shows that he prefers the higher-pitched female voice. Even lively instrumental or vocal music, when played softly, will calm the infant. Researchers also note that the infant will stop his ongoing behavior and become quiet when stimulated by novel sounds. These sounds have two effects on the infant; they cause him to orient himself toward the source of the sound, and they inhibit his ongoing activity.

Musical sound is one of the principal means of soothing a child and showing warmth and affection. Parents all over the world use vocal means (speaking, chanting, singing) to show their love for the child. Many parents rhythmically rock their infants in their arms and laps as they sing, hum, or play a lullaby to calm them. **49** Infants seem to sense that the human voice is a means of expressing love, affection, and comfort. The sound of the female voice is especially effective for communicating this sense.

The infant does not seem to mind if the music he hears is "off-key." In fact, he probably cannot tell the difference! His main interest seems to be on the special qualities of the sound and on any movement he can observe as he hears the sound. His response is almost totally sensual and emotional. He apparently makes little connection between what he perceives at a particular moment and what he has heard before. As the infant attains more experience with music, his ear will become more attuned to musical qualities such as pitch, the beat and rhythm, and other musical elements.

How does the newborn baby view his first auditory experiences with music? No one is likely ever to find out. Probably it is a vague, undifferentiated, thoughtless perception. But right from the start of life, the newborn begins to organize his world of sound, and it becomes more orderly. There is increasing differentiation in his response to sound. The baby is able to recognize the voice of the mother who feeds him and the voice of the father who fondles him. He will awaken or quiet to his mother's voice at about age three to four months. The baby even learns to recognize differences in his parents' footsteps. He will respond to a tape recording of his own vocalizations by smiling, moving, and becoming slightly tense. After a few weeks the sounds that once were part of a confused medley become more recognizable, distinct, and meaningful to him.

Up to age two to three months, the baby is able to hear most sounds within adult hearing range. He may react with a bodily movement, an eye motion, or a cry, but he generally will not attempt to turn his head to the source of the sound. He does not yet connect his hearing response with his visual capacity. However, at about three months, the infant will begin to show some coordination between his hearing and his seeing. He will hear and then turn to the source of the sound, often with glee and surprise. By about the fifth month, the infant's eye—ear coordination improves to the point where he is

50

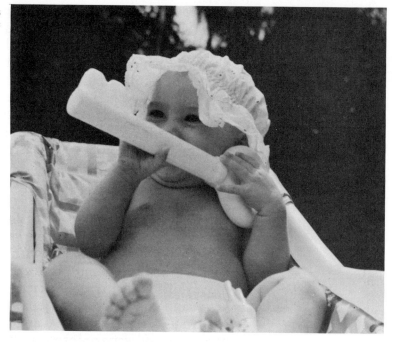

The infant experiments with the sound qualities of many objects in the environment. (Photo courtesy of Joseph and Katherine A. O'Reilly)

more accurate and reliable in turning his eyes and his body to the source of sound he hears.

The baby can recognize the visual and vocal features of the mother by the third month of life. The mother's smile, especially when accompanied by her voice, is an important means of eliciting the baby's smile response, which is strong at this age. By five months of age, the child recognizes the mother's voice, regardless of the words she uses, through its particular sound qualities. Research has shown that the five-month-old infant can identify the mother's voice from among many other voices, despite the physical absence of the mother. When hearing the mother's voice, the baby will often pay more attention to it than to any other sound and will frequently smile when he hears it.

Between ages four to six months, the infant begins to show a very strong interest in sound. He listens intently to any sounds and music in the immediate **51** environment and enjoys listening to and experimenting with sounds that he himself can produce, either vocally or by hitting or kicking objects in his vicinity. The sounds, which serve no practical purpose, are relished for their own emotional and aesthetic values. The child simply likes to listen to pleasant sounds and music. He will begin to respond to these sounds through movement and by making babbling or chuckling sounds with his voice. At this age, then, the child becomes acutely aware of sound as a source of pleasurable or discomforting stimulation.

Physical movements to music increase dramatically between the ages of four to eight months. The baby listens before he moves. His movements usually begin ten to twenty seconds after the start of the music. Rarely are the movements made with individual body parts such as the head, hands, or feet. Rather, the entire body moves. The most frequent types of movements are the sway and the bounce, either from a lying or a sitting position. The movements are rhythmic, regular, and repetitive and vary in intensity from small, smooth, and flowing movements to those that are large, jerky, and even violent in character. The movements, although steady and rhythmical in themselves, are never coordinated with the music's rhythmic flow. This synchronization develops at age two or later. Thus, it takes several years for the child to learn to move his body in conjunction with the music's rhythmic and dynamic elements.

At about six to seven months of age, the infant may seem to be responding to words he hears, but usually it is the sound and inflection of words, rather than their meanings, that interest him the most. However, by about the age of nine months, the infant will begin to respond selectively to a few simple words. Shortly afterwards, the first sounds that resemble words appear in the baby's vocalizations. For babies brought up in English-speaking homes, these words are almost always the same: "mama" and "da-da" (or some variation of "mother" and "father"), "bye-bye," and "ba-by."

Between ages six to nine months, the infant can use his eyes and hands in a coordinated fashion to grasp objects. He will grasp small objects and hit or bang them against any nearby object. He enjoys dropping objects, throwing them, and tapping them. He begins to focus on the consequences of hitting objects against different surfaces. He becomes fascinated with his own ability to make sound with objects and with the resulting sound produced. In effect, he seems to be experimenting with his newly acquired control of his own body as it acts on objects in his environment.

A major part of the nine-month- to two-year-old child's waking hours is spent looking at and listening to two or more adults or older children talk. Apparently, the child is enthralled by the sounds and intonations of spoken language, especially those sounds that he can understand. In addition, most children are now exposed to sound from the radio, television, and phonograph. Yet, few children under age three watch television or listen to the radio or phonograph for more than a few minutes at a time. Apparently, live sound sources are more relevant and interesting to very young children than sound sources from audio machines.

As the growing child becomes more mobile and develops some language ability, his musical responses also expand. By nine months, he may show displeasure at music he does not like. He appears to respond more to vocal than to instrumental selections (perhaps this is due to his increasing interest in speech sounds). Motor response to music becomes more frequent, and the length and intensity of his musical responses increase. As he learns to walk and talk during his second year of life, he begins to actively and enthusiastically explore his environment. He listens to some of the music and sounds on television or the radio. He enoys watching his older sister play the tonette or guitar. He is fascinated by the sounds of birds, cats, cars, planes, and clocks. He uses many objects in his environment—a dish, a spoon, a cup, a stick, a stone—to make a sound. He occasionally moves rhythmically (and clumsily!) to music he hears. He now moves his whole body from a standing, rather than a sitting, position. He begins to move individual body parts to the music. He likes to hear simple nursery rhymes and tunes and tries, often unsuccessfully, to join in. He enjoys having his primary caretaker sing to him. His world of music is constantly growing between the ages of one and two.

From ages two to three years, six months, the child continues his interest in sound and music. His ability to concentrate on and listen to the music increases. He may sit or lie down quietly and attend to the music for several minutes. He is enchanted by the sounds of words and the word repetition in books and rhymes. Listening to nursery songs is often a favorite activity. *Echolalia*—the constant repetition of words and sounds—is an enjoyable pastime. His physical movements to music become more varied and refined. He will begin to control his motor abilities so that he can bend his knees, sway, or clap to the music. He often enjoys moving to music with an adult, a sibling, or even a doll. He uses more space than previously when he moves to music. He has better control over playing rhythm instruments and slowly begins to synchronize his playing and bodily movements with the rhythm of the music. This synchronization provides evidence that he can focus on a musical element—rhythm—in his responses and can represent this element in his movements. He also begins to respond to the dynamics of a musical work. He will begin to learn simple singing games. He continues his high interest in hearing musical instruments and begins to listen more to music on television, radio, and the phonograph.

At about age three years, six months, and extending through age five and beyond, the young child's response to music undergoes a significant change. He begins to develop an awareness of tonal arrangement and order, which he internalizes and conceptualizes (see pp. 255–258). Music becomes more than just sound. It becomes a nonverbal means of expression and communication. It begins to fulfill the child's need for obtaining aesthetic satisfaction in life's experiences. It is at this age that music begins to be felt, thought about, and enjoyed for its aesthetic dimensions.

What can the four-year-old do in response to music? He can keep the beat of the music (although not always accurately), using his body or rhythm instrument to express this pulse; imitate rhythmic patterns that are clapped; identify certain sounds made by selected instruments; play many rhythm instruments, using them to accompany songs and instrumental pieces or to create his own tunes; he can move to the aesthetic qualities of recorded music. Significantly, at this age he can now talk about the musical experience and what he hears. Interestingly, repetitive spontaneous movements to music slacken at this age. The child appears to internalize the music rather than express it through physical movements. Specific movements of parts of the body are much more frequent than movements of the entire body. The child is able to coordinate his movements with the music to a longer extent than before. He enjoys singing games and dances. He shows interest in the meanings and story content of words of songs. His interest in play and imaginative activities makes him very responsive to creative bodily movement, especially when acting out a song's story or showing how objects or animals move. The child, upon reaching his fifth birthday, has learned a variety of new ways to respond to what he hears in music. In five short years, he has made tremendous strides in becoming a more musically responsive individual.

The Child Sings

All children, by nature, are vocal organisms. Even newborn babies are able to come forth with a variety of vocalizations, including the cry and soft, melodious cooing sounds, despite the fact that they have no obvious opportunities to "learn" how to make these sounds. Studies of the vocalizations of infants born to congenitally deaf parents also take note of the ability of the newly born to make sounds. Thus, it is apparent that early vocalizations are inherent or native to the newborn and can be developed through the child's ensuing interaction with his environment. There is evidence to support this notion, since children who sing well often come from families where singing is frequent. The infant's early vocalizations and his experiences in hearing

55

songs are the forerunners of singing and speaking abilities in the human species.

The young child learns how to vocalize and, gradually, to sing by progressing through five developmental stages (see also discussion on "stages of development," in Chapter 1). These stages closely parallel language development and include:

Stage 1. The First Vocalizations (ages birth to 3 months)

Stage 2. Vocal Experimentation and Sound Imitation (ages 3 months to 1 year, 6 months)

Stage 3. Approximation of Singing (ages 1 year, 6 months, to 3 years)

Stage 4. Singing Accuracy: Limited Range (ages 3 years to 4 years)

Stage 5. Singing Accuracy: Expanded Range (ages 4 years and up)

The age levels for the developmental stages are approximate, depending upon each child's innate musical capacities and his experiences. These levels are optimal; undoubtedly, many children, especially at Stages 3 to 5, will lag between three months to two years or more behind the age levels given. Without a supportive environment and musical education to encourage singing and aural discrimination, few five-year-old children will reach Stages 4 and 5—the ability to sing accurately.

Stage 1: The First Vocalizations

The first sounds made by the newborn child are reflexive and are caused by the normal developmental process. Many of these sounds will relate to the child's comfort level or his sucking behavior. They are usually made by accident and are a result of changes in tension in the muscles used for vocalization. The most frequent sounds are the cry and the coo.

The newborn child's first and most important means of communicating his needs and feelings is the cry. The sound is in every sense "musical," since it has tones of varying pitch and intensity levels, rhythmic impulse, and conveys meaning. The child enters into the world with an inborn capacity to cry—to make his own vocalizations in order to convey what he wants and how he feels. In fact, the baby's "birth cry" is his very first attempt at communication. This cry, although a primitive means of expression, serves as the prelude to speaking and singing in the human species.

The cry of the newborn is nasal, very monotonous, and is one breath long. It is quite unrhythmical, since it cannot be modified at this time by the baby's mouth opening and closing, as in speech. It is a "total" cry in that it can be seen in the infant's entire bodily movement. Soon, the cry gradually becomes more rhythmical as the baby begins to control his mouth muscles. By three months, the child's muscular and voice–breath coordination is developed to the point where the cry is more controlled and increasingly "musical."

All healthy babies cry with vigor and abandon. Yet each baby's cry becomes distinctive between one or two weeks after birth. Some cries are robust and loud; some are spiritless and soft. Some are sharp and short; some are smoother and more connected. Some are more melodious, i.e., their pitches are more varied; some are less musical. By the time a child is a few months old, he can communicate his various needs to his parents by using different types of cries. Similarly, the parents can often respond to the child's specific needs by listening carefully to the nature of his cry. The child soon learns that his cries are useful for getting someone's attention. He communicates his specific needs through specific cries. Interestingly enough, when a baby's cry is tape-recorded and replayed for the child, he will often lie motionless and stiffen, then relax, and finally move and vocalize while trying to reproduce what he has heard. Some studies have shown that the infant can distinguish his own cry at a very early age.

There is some evidence that there is a significant relationship between the frequency and type of crying behavior and the child's later ability to speak and do intellectual tasks. Perhaps those who cry with the greatest variation in pitch and intensity will learn to speak or sing better at a later age! In fact, the nature of the infant's cry may be the basis for his future musical development.

Within a month after birth, a child can make other sounds besides the cry. The most frequent sounds are the soft, melodic coos. These coos often use vowels, especially the open-mouthed *ah* and the narrow-opening *ih* (as in *big*). Other vowel sounds include "oo," "ee," and "uh." The aspirated "h" is the most frequently uttered consonant; this is probably linked to the infant's gasping for breath. The labial (lip) consonants *p*, *b*, and *m* are common. Although infants may be able to articulate as many as eight consonants, they will never use more than one in any individual vocalization. Other sounds the infant makes include the grunt, yawn, sigh, and sounds connected with sneezing, coughing, and belching. Vowel sounds predominate in all these vocalizations. During this early vocalization stage, the infant shows little interest in listening to his own sounds, except when they are replayed on a tape recorder.

To summarize, the basis of all singing, as well as spoken language, originates in the earliest vocal sounds made by the infant. These sounds—the coos, the sighs, and especially the cries—show a variety of pitches, tone qualities, rhythmic patterns, and levels of loudness and are in every sense musical. Within a few weeks after birth, the infant learns to control these sounds. Cries in particular become differentiated as the infant learns how to use certain cries for one type of request or emotion and another type of cry for another need or expression. By age three months, the infant has usually learned to control his earliest means of communication.

Stage 2: Vocal Experimentation and Sound Imitation

By the fourth month of life, the child begins to experiment with his vocalizations. Control over his vocal muscles and dexterity of the jaw, lips, and tongue increase. He can now prolong a cry, repeat a cry, and produce new sounds that somehow catch his attention. He begins to "babble" by repeating sounds in long strings or chains, as "ba-ba-ba-ba," and later makes sounds of two syllables, as "ba-ba." The infant often bathes himself in his own sounds, repeats them profusely, and varies them. He becomes more and more interested in listening to tape recordings of his own vocalizations. He produces different sounds when alone as compared with when his parents are present. Gradually, vocalization—which earlier served a basic need to the infant—becomes a source of sound play, pleasure, and aesthetic experience.

During the third and fourth months of life, the infant begins to be interested in listening to sounds that he can make with the saliva in his mouth. These sounds are called "gurgles." By five months of age, there is evidence of the infant's strong urge to experiment with his own sounds, especially when he has excess saliva in his mouth. He often delights in repeating the soft sounds he makes with his saliva.

The infant uses many utterances during this stage of vocal development. Squealing happy sounds occur between four to six months of age. The child will react to tickling and funny faces or sounds by squealing with glee. The babbling of various sounds becomes more frequent. At this stage, the baby makes many vocal inflections and intonations similar to those in adult speech. By age seven months, the baby shows that he is "tuning in" to the specific intonations and melody of adult speech by babbling sounds with these adult intonations. Listening to a typical five- to seven-month-old baby "speak" would reveal that he can squeal with delight, make guttural growls, make a series of sounds with rising and falling inflections, grunt in anger or pain, and coo. These utterances and babblings will often be in response to someone else's speech or singing. If there is someone in the room to respond to, the baby's speech will likely be more frequent.

Musical babbling, i.e., making speech sounds on various pitches, usually begins between six and nine months of age and parallels the infant's ability to move to music. These musical babbles follow the speech babbles that began at three or four months of age. Unlike

59

speech babbles, the musical babbles have definite pitch and do not have as many syllables as speech babbles. They usually lack definite rhythm and begin relatively high in pitch and then descend (as in a statement). Tones that repeat, or that move in very small intervals, or that slide down from the first tones are most frequent. The pitch range can vary from only a few tones to a distance of about eight scale tones, as from C to C or D to D. The pitches appear to center around middle C, or even below. These musical babbles are most frequently produced when an adult or older child sings to the infant.

Between six to nine months of age, the baby continues to experiment with his own vocalizations. Gurgling with his saliva is frequent, and he enjoys varying the sounds he makes, either by himself or with another person. The infant will attempt at times to repeat pitches of vocal sounds as an adult sings high and low pitches. At times, the infant's sound play will sound like adult sentences or a song. It will be accented, rhythmic, and tuneful.

Beginning about the seventh or eighth month of age, the infant's speech babbling becomes more refined. The child will begin to imitate vowel sounds, especially *ah* and *ih*. He will repeat these sounds after hearing an adult say them and will experiment with combining these sounds into different rhythmic patterns. Gradually he will add consonants—especially those formed by the lips (*b*, *p*, and *m*)—to these vowel sounds, resulting in sounds such as *pah, mah, bah, pih, bih,* and *mih*. He continues during this stage to experiment with babbling and gurgling and will increasingly repeat his own sounds. By age eleven months, the infant will begin to jabber by making babbling sounds, partial words, and distorted intonation patterns. It now appears that he is attempting to communicate. The melody and intonation patterns of the jabbers often sound like sentences and are frequently directed to the person talking to him. By age twelve to fifteen months, he may even appear to be singing songs through his jabbering. Between twelve and eighteen months, language learning becomes increasingly important, as the child begins to respond to words, repeat sound sequences, form words and two-word phrases, and vary his intonation patterns. And by one year, six months, the typical child is speaking. And now he is ready to sing!

Stage 3: Approximation of Singing

By eighteen months of age or later, most children have developed the ability to babble and understand some words, and they begin speaking. The musical babbles, which began between six and nine months of age, take on a new dimension. More and more "babbling songs" are heard, and they are more varied rhythmically and melodically than previously. These spontaneous babbles now contain definite rhythms, usually consisting of short tones followed by tones of longer duration, resembling

♫ ♩ ♫ ♩ ♩ or ♫ ♩ ♩ ♩.

Tones of three or four different durations are rare in these babbles. The "babbling songs" are often punctuated by rests, which depend more on the breath control of the child than on his musical purpose. The pitches of his songs become more definite, and more frequent and wider pitch intervals are used. Thus, by the age of two, most children can self-initiate "songs" through their musical babbles.

Soon the young child, at about age two or later, with experience and some adult guidance, will begin to learn songs he hears. First he notices and imitates the sound patterns of the words. Then he begins to imitate the rhythmic patterns of the words. At about age three, most children should be able to imitate the pitch as well as the words and rhythm. Nevertheless, there are some children who will not follow this sequence; rather, they will first learn the song's pitches, rather than its words and rhythms. In general, the sequence from learning words to rhythms to pitches persists through early childhood. During this stage the child will approximate the rhythms and the up-and-down pitch movements of a

61

tonal pattern and later, a complete song. He will raise and lower the pitches of the song, but will rarely if ever match all the tones. Some children during this stage will approximate the tonal pattern using a wide variety of tones in an extended range; most will confine themselves to tones with only slight variations in pitch level. However, by age three, most children will imitate simple songs that they have heard. Singing as we know it has been established in the young child.

The "approximation of singing" stage will last from about age one and a half to three and even beyond, depending upon the child's musical abilities and previous experience. Some children will remain at this stage for several years. Other children will move into the next developmental level—the singing accuracy stage—as early as age two and a half. Unfortunately, some children and adults never go beyond this stage of vocal development.

At the "approximation" stage, the child begins to incorporate singing into his daily activities. He will jabber tunefully to himself at play. He will attempt to sing or hum in imitation of his older sister, his mother, or a television performer. He will enjoy nursery rhymes and tunes and will try to join in on certain phrases. He will sing spontaneously to himself or for relatives, but usually will be inhibited in singing for other children. He enjoys such simple group music activities as "Ring Around the Rosy" or "The Farmer in the Dell." Singing begins to take on meaning in his day-to-day existence.

During this developmental stage, if the child is below age three, he will have difficulty pronouncing many of the words of a song. Indeed, most of the words may not have meaning for him. Thus, the use of selected phrases from songs—e.g., the "ding, ding, dong" pattern of "Are You Sleeping" or the "e-i-e-i-o" pattern from "Old MacDonald"—is indicated for the child below three who is at this singing stage. Of course, a four- or five-year-old child who is still in this "approximation" stage of singing will have much greater ability than the younger child to pronounce and understand the words of most **62** songs.

The "approximation" stage is critical to the development of the child's ability to sing and parallels the tremendous spurt occurring at the same time in language development. This stage is often neglected in the child's music education because of heavy emphasis on language learning during this period. One of the probable causes of poor singing responses of many children in preschool and elementary school is the inattention given to the young child's development in singing during the critical period from ages one and a half to three.

Stage 4: Singing Accuracy—Limited Range

After having many experiences in approximating the tones in a melodic pattern or a song, the child then will begin to sing the pitches and rhythms more accurately. This usually occurs with songs or patterns that have a limited tonal range with only a few different pitches. By about age three, most children, with experience and some previous training, will be able to sing tunes within the limited range of D to G above middle C:

A few children may sing in a range slightly higher than that. Most young children will find it physically impossible to sing lower than middle C or higher than third-space C above middle C. Generally, the first accurate pitches sung by young children will cluster around first-line E above middle C.

During this "singing accuracy" stage and usually occurring between ages three-and-a-half to four-and-a-half, many children will begin spontaneously to make up their own songs. Usually the words of these songs consist of nonsense syllables or words that immediately **63** come into the child's mind. The words are often repetitive. They may also be fragments from songs already familiar to him. The rhythms coincide with the word rhythms. The tunes may be original, but more frequently, they resemble or imitate tunes already familiar to the child. Usually both the rhythm and pitches are only partially accurate. Thus, it is not rare to find a four-year-old creating his own "original song" that strongly resembles one that everybody knows. For example, note the similarity in the melody and rhythm between an original song called "My New Dress" and the song "Skip to My Lou":

MY NEW DRESS
(from a tape of a four-year-old's original song)

See my new dress, See my new dress, See my new dress, It is ver-y nice.

Note: Actual tape rendition has many pitches that are only approximations of what are notated above. Original key on tape is D major.

Rhythmic accuracy in singing will improve during this approximation stage, but errors in rhythm still abound. The child can now sing faster and/or louder. Expressive singing, however, is negligible or absent, since the child is still too involved in learning how to match pitch and rhythms and how to articulate and remember the words to bother about the expressive aspects of singing.

Stage 5: Singing
Accuracy — Expanded Range

Beginning at about age four, with appropriate experience and training, the child will begin to expand his vocal range—upward to A, B, and C above middle C and downward to middle C or below.

Not until age five or later will the typical child be

64

able to reach the higher tones with much accuracy, due to an inability to control the physical mechanism needed to produce these tones. Nevertheless, the range does expand during the fourth year of life as the child gains increasing control of his singing apparatus. Rhythmic accuracy also improves, as does the articulation of words.

It is during this fifth singing stage that the child begins to express the musical aspects of the song and sing with attention to the song's dynamics and tempo. The child starts to use his voice more effectively to express the meaning and emotional content of the song and its words. He learns to add subtleties and nuances to his rendition of the song, which will enhance his ability to communicate how he feels about the particular musical experience. By the time the child reaches his fifth birthday, he should be well on his way toward using his voice as a primary means of expressing himself musically.

Summary

Human musical capacity is biological in nature and genetically transmitted, but is shaped to a large degree by environmental factors. These factors can encourage or inhibit musical response. Although all children respond in many ways to musical stimuli, it is only in supportive, varied, and planned environments that children will learn to respond in the more complex and meaningful ways that characterize the unique capacities of human beings in this area.

The young child responds to musical sound at birth and even earlier. He listens to all kinds of sounds in his immediate environment. He gradually differentiates between them. He makes sounds by hitting, dropping, and shaking objects. As he matures, he gains more skill in his musical responses as he moves to the music, plays instruments, creates musical patterns and tunes, and identifies different musical qualities and sounds. Vocally, the newborn child's repertoire of sounds is limited, but new sounds emerge very quickly. Some sounds (usually cries) are for hunger, some for pain, and some for discomfort. Some sounds (usually coos and gurgles) express his satisfaction. He listens intently to sounds made by others in his environment and to his own sounds. He hears new intonations and new patterns of sound. He imitates these. He varies them. He develops a new repertoire of vocalized sound. He reproduces the intonation and sound patterns of what he hears long before he can formulate sounds to convey meanings through words. He babbles musically. He begins to sing approximate pitch and rhythmic patterns of the songs and tunes he hears. He gains increasing competency in his ability to sing accurately. He learns to sing more complex tunes with wider pitch ranges and more difficult rhythms and words. By the age of five, his responses to music have increased tremendously, and his musical experience is well on its way toward helping him achieve aesthetic growth and musical enjoyment.

Selected Readings

Aronoff, Frances W., *Music and Young Children*. New York: Holt, Rinehart and Winston, 1969.
  Provides specific examples of how the preschooler responds at his own level of development.

Greenberg, Marvin, "Research in Music in Early Childhood Education: A Survey With Recommendations." *Bulletin No. 45*, Council for Research in Music Education (Winter 1976), 1–20.
  Summarizes most research findings on music in early childhood education; has a lengthy bibliography.

Hopper, Robert, and Rita C. Naremore, *Children's Speech: A Practical Introduction to Communication Development*. New York: Harper and Row, 1973.
  An introduction to speech development; has many implications for music education.

Lundin, Robert W., *An Objective Psychology of Music*. New York: The Ronald Press, 1967.

Contains a fine discussion of the origins of musical response. Deals with the heredity—environment issue, musical talent and heredity, racial differences in musical response, and the relationship between intelligence and musical growth.

Weir, Ruth, *Language in the Crib*. The Hague: Mouton, 1962.
A basic reference on infant "speech," with many implications for the origins of singing.

Participation in listening to and making music is the key to the child's
musical growth. (Photo courtesy of American Music Conference)

3

The
Musical
Experience

The first two chapters have discussed the developmental patterns of general and musical growth in the young child and some principles of learning. Understanding the child and how he responds to his environment are essential prerequisites to knowing what to do in music for the child. We now turn to another aspect that must be considered in planning a music program for the young child. We need to know about the nature of the subject matter being used in the educational process. Specifically, we concern ourselves with the subject matter of music and its:

- areas of experience
- materials
- concepts

Areas of Musical Experience

How does one educate the young child to achieve his aesthetic potential through music? What experiences are needed to help the child respond to music with feeling and with understanding? How can the adult help the child to achieve meaning and enjoyment through a variety of musical experiences?

Aesthetic growth is accomplished by having the young child participate directly in an aesthetic experience. In music, this means providing many musical experiences that involve the child in perceiving the music, feeling its impact, responding to it, understanding it, and enjoying it (see pp. 6–10). Although the first and most basic response to music for the young child is sensory (he will hear the sound stimuli), aesthetic growth means more than hearing the music. From the beginning of infancy, through a planned environment and education, we hope to capitalize on the child's interest in sound to focus his attention on the emotional–intellectual–aesthetic content of the music. To the extent that we are successful, we have helped the child to achieve aesthetic satisfaction and enjoyment.

There are three basic experiences in music that are needed for aesthetic growth. These experiences are:

- listening to music
- performing music
- creating music

The approach in each of these experiences emphasizes *doing*. The experiences are activity oriented, since the child from birth to five learns best through acting upon what he experiences. In music, this means primarily expressing the music's aesthetic qualities through the movement of the child's body or body parts as he listens to, performs, and creates music. By using the body, the child expresses what he perceives in the music, how he feels about the music, and what he understands in it. Anyone who has worked with the young child instantly recognizes bodily movement as being a basic response mode of the child to music. Examples of this type of response can be seen when:

- the one-year-old moves his head rhythmically to a

72   recording of "Skip to My Lou" or a Strauss waltz;

- the two-year-old swings his hands up and down when hearing a band at a parade;
- the preschooler moves his body for a singing game such as "The Mulberry Bush" or "The Hokey Pokey."

Listening to Music

Music is an aural art; i.e., all our feelings, understandings, and responses to music are derived from what we perceive through our ears. Every time we engage in a musical experience, we listen. *Every musical experience, then, is a listening experience.* Listening is the basis of all experience in music and is at the core of all efforts to educate the child musically. Listening to music is involved when:

- the infant stares intently at the sound source as his mother shakes the wrist bells or sings to him;
- the two-year-old tries to move rhythmically to the beat of rock music;
- the four-year-old chants a song about the seesaw as he plays in the yard.

Many children and adults *hear* music rather than *listen* to it. Hearing involves receiving the music's sound stimulus through the ear, but not responding aesthetically to the music. Listening involves hearing the music, paying attention to it, feeling its impact, and thinking about its tonal and rhythmic qualities. *Listening is an active process* whereby the listener reacts both emotionally and intellectually to the experience. As such, listening is a fundamental activity in all musical experiences for all children.

Performing Music

Another basic musical experience is performing music. Two principal ways in which the child can perform **73** music are through *singing* and *playing instruments*.

Singing involves using our own natural instrument—the voice—to make music. Playing instruments involves using a means other than our voices—e.g., a stick, a rattle, a pot, a guitar, a piano, a trumpet, or band or orchestra—to make musical sounds. A young child performs music when he:

- babbles interesting patterns of sounds with his voice;
- hits a stick rhythmically against a chair or fence;
- chants his name over and over again as he plays with blocks;
- plays the triangle to accompany "Twinkle, Twinkle Little Star."

Creating Music

All music that we listen to, at one time or another, was created (composed). Most of this music was composed for the voice, instruments, or a combination of the two. Some music, especially in contemporary times, has employed natural sounds found in the environment, sound using objects in the environment, and electronic and tape media. In creating music, the composer uses familiar musical elements to make new and interesting sound patterns that are pleasing to him or her. Examples of the creative response to music occur when:

- an infant experiments with making vocal sounds, using interesting sound and intonation patterns;
- a two-year-old takes a drum and tambourine and taps out interesting rhythmic patterns on each instrument and in combination;
- a four-year-old makes up a song about Big Billy Goat Gruff after hearing the story about the three billy goats and the troll.

As can be seen from these examples, young children and people of all ages from all walks of life can engage in the three basic activities of musical experience—listening, performing, and creating. Although

74

the sophistication of the activity varies with age and experience, the basic nature and impact of the activity can be quite similar. Thus, the young child and the musician—each at his or her own level—can have meaningful aesthetic responses as they listen to, perform, and compose music.

Music: The Material in Music Education

In listening to, performing, and creating music, what materials are most appropriate? Whether for the infant or the musician, the materials are sound and its sources. Since music is organized sound arranged in meaningful tonal and rhythmic relationships, sound must be the basic material and experience of music. These sounds include tones from traditional music resources, as the voice and instruments, as well as environmental and electronically produced sound. The music experience, then, is not a story about composers, or a discussion about the music's melody or loudness levels, or looking at pictures of instruments or composers. Rather, *the musical experience is direct experience with the materials of music themselves—the tonal and rhythmic aspects of sound—and all that the sounds attempt to communicate.* The basic materials of music, then, are the human voice, instruments, environmental sounds, and music from sound-producing equipment such as the phonograph, tape recorder, radio, television, records, and tapes.

Most of the areas of musical experience involve using a music *repertoire*, i.e., the various musical selections played for or performed by the person. Listening and performing activities, especially, utilize many songs and instrumental pieces. In working with the young child, many adults use a music repertoire that is very limited. Often, the only criteria used in the selection of music for the child is that "the child likes it." The music's inherent aesthetic value is often ignored. Usually, only a few Mother Goose tunes and singing games

75

are played or performed. The listening repertoire often consists of some marches, lullabies, stories about instruments, and musical selections for special occasions (birthdays, Christmas, Halloween). Instrumental selections are rarely played, except for rock music and "background" music to calm the child as he plays, eats, or sleeps. In most cases, the music repertoire for the young child is woefully inadequate—lacking in variety and in musical quality. We often tend to use the worst possible music in our attempts to foster aesthetic growth in young children!

One particularly questionable practice that many adults use in working with children is to expose them to "contrived children's music." This music, not a part of the world's musical heritage, may be a song to teach the days of the week, or counting skills, or names of the colors. Or it may be a song about traffic lights, or the fireman, or a trip to the market. Or it may be a recording of a vocalist singing about various family members or a storyteller narrating and singing "The Three Pigs" or "Cinderella." Most of the songs and recordings of this "contrived children's music" are designed to teach nonmusical learning. Although we know that this type of music sometimes accomplishes the intended, nonmusical purposes for which it has been designed, it is usually unmusical in its conception and is often poorly performed. At times, the voices of the singers are badly distorted a la Donald Duck records. One only has to visit a record shop's children's music section to become acquainted with the many poor-quality recordings available for young children. Singers and instrumentalists are often out of tune, and the words are often unintelligible. They do little more than superficially entertain the young. Unfortunately, many adults—including preschool teachers and parents—use this type of music as a substitute for better-quality music. Prolonged exposure to this trite "contrived children's music" will have a significantly negative influence on each child's aesthetic growth. "Contrived children's music" has no place in the music education of the young.

Many music educators, teachers, and parents—in working with the very young—have shown repeatedly that children will respond at their own levels to a much wider variety and quality of music than was previously supposed. In fact, some musics usually reserved for the college music student or professional musician—e.g., a movement from a Schubert symphony or Mozart string quartet, or progressive jazz, or primitive chants from Yemen, Hawaii, and New Guinea—have been more effective in obtaining musical responses in the very young than so-called children's music. The rhythmic response of most young children to a fourteenth-century French dance, a movement from a Bach concerto or cantata, a Yugoslavian folk tune, a Chinese rice-planting song, or a jazz arrangement by Duke Ellington is astonishing. To the young child whose aesthetic tastes have not yet been formed, the music is as meaningful as a Sousa march or rock music. And this music is certainly more significant and aesthetically satisfying than the music of an educationally contrived, marchlike song about tooth brushing, animals in the zoo, or the parts of the body.

Many parents and teachers of children of all ages, including the youngest infants, have demonstrated conclusively that all children can and should be given the opportunity to respond to the world of music as it exists in real life. If we are earnest in our desire to foster aesthetic and musical growth, we need to provide experiences with a much wider range of music than most young children hear. *The repertoire for any music education program for young children should be broad and reflect the vast heritage of music.* This world of music, reflected in the songs and recordings of many types of musical styles and cultures, should include a balance of:

- children's chants, play songs, and singing games
- nursery tunes and songs
- American folk music
- music of the child's ethnic background
- religious music
- patriotic music
- holiday and seasonal music
- rock music
- jazz

- popular, movie, and show music
- folk music from around the world
- classical music
- experimental music (electronic and tape)
- music for dancing and marching
- music of all historical periods

Three types of music that are often neglected in the musical education of the young child are classical music, folk music from around the world, and contemporary experimental music. We know that young children are very open to all types of music. It is amazing to see the musical responses of young children when a recording is played of a dramatic soprano singing an excerpt from an opera by Wagner or Verdi, or of a Renaissance French court dance, or a Bach church cantata. Similarly, the sounds from avant-garde electronic music often captivate the attention of an infant or preschooler. And who has not been surprised at seeing the child's spontaneous musical response to the drum beats of a tabla from India or the steel drums from Trinidad, or to the pounding of the hollow bamboo drums from Fiji or the playing of the xylophones to accompany the chants of West and Central Africa? *All* types of music should be experienced by the child from birth. He should hear the Japanese koto, the bamboo flutes from Iraq or Korea, the hardanger fiddle from Norway, the compositions of such contemporary composers as Boulez, Cage, Kay, Schuller, Stockhausen, and Webern; and the great vocal and instrumental masterpieces of the past—from the music of medieval times and the Renaissance to the masterworks by Bach, Mozart, Beethoven, Schubert, Brahms, Verdi, Debussy, Stravinsky, and others. The young child needs to hear music performed by the great concert artists such as Vladimir Horowitz or Beverly Sills, as well as by Ravi Shankar, Ornette Coleman, Louis Armstrong, Bob Dylan, and countless other performers. He needs to be exposed to music performed by such diverse groups as the Philadelphia Orchestra, the Viennese Boys' Choir, the Carpenters, a Hungarian folk choir, and the local high school band or orchestra. *We shape the musical responses and tastes of the young child by the music we play for him.* A child who only hears rock music and sings only nursery school songs is being deprived of mankind's vast musical heritage.

Almost any piece of music can be used in the musical education of the young child if it is presented in such a way as to elicit the child's response to it at his own level of maturity and musical understanding. The decision on which piece to use will depend on the prior experience of the child. Generally, the sequence will be from familiar to unfamiliar music and from simple, rhythmic music to more complex, subtle music. A further discussion on the materials to use for the young child is found on p. 104, and pp. 133–34, 174–78.

Concepts of Music

In participating in the basic experiences of listening to, performing, and creating music and in becoming acquainted with a wide variety of the world's representative music, the child will begin gradually to develop his own *concepts* about music. These concepts will emerge as a result of the child's many experiences with music and his growing ability to discriminate, see relationships, categorize, and generalize about them. The child's concepts of music, ever-changing and expanding, are broad understandings or ideas that the child constructs and restructures as a result of his experiences. They are the child's interpretation of what he hears and understands in the music, consistent with his own maturational level and prior experience. Concept development in music is indicative of how the child views and understands the world of musical sound.

Even the young child forms concepts about music. He normally will express his understanding through musical behavior. For example, he will smile only at the sound of his mother's voice. He will move more slowly as the music becomes slower. He will sing the correct **79** pitches of "Mary Had a Little Lamb." Using rhythm sticks, he will echo the beat or rhythmic pattern in the music. Through these behaviors, the young child shows his increasing conceptualization of what he knows about music.

At a very early age, the child will begin to form concepts about what he is experiencing in music. Concepts about tone, loudness, pitch, melody, rhythm, and other elements that comprise music will become refined as experiences expand. He will begin to sense that music is a series of organized sounds and silences that attempt to communicate musical meanings. He will differentiate between organized musical sounds and other sounds in the environment—a car or plane noise, a bird call, water splashing, the sound of the wind, and thunder. He will begin to learn that he can engage in many different types of musical experiences. He will recognize that music can communicate to him in ways different from all other modes of communication. He will develop particular attitudes and musical tastes about the music he hears. The child's concepts about music and its significance to his daily life will be constantly changing and expanding as he progresses through his life cycle.

Concepts of Tone

What are some of the musical concepts that begin to develop from birth to age five? Certainly, one of the child's earliest concepts is that of *tone*. The young child will begin to experience and later to conceptualize that:

1. A tone has *intensity* (its relative loudness and softness); some tones are louder (or softer) than others.

2. A tone has *duration* (its relative shortness and length); some tones are held longer than (or not as long as) others.

3. A tone has *pitch* (its relative highness and lowness); some tones are higher (or lower) than others.

4. A tone has *timbre* (its tonal quality, which, for example, helps us perceive differences between the sounds

of instruments and voices); each tone has a different quality than others.

Even a five-month-old infant reacts differently to tones of different intensity or pitch; and an eighteen-month-old child is normally able to make vocal sounds in imitation of various durations or point to rhythm instruments that have distinctive tone qualities after hearing several of their sounds. The young child, then, begins to build concepts about the basic ingredients of tone—intensity, duration, pitch, and timbre—at a very early age.

Concepts of Rhythm and Tempo

Another set of concepts the young child will develop as he listens to, performs, and creates music will relate to the musical element of *rhythm*—the flow or movement of tones through time. As the child obtains many new and varied experiences with music, he will form concepts about the *tempo* or speed of the music, the *beat* or steady pulse of the music, and the *rhythmic patterns*, or the long and short tones, of the music.

The young child will be able to form concepts about music's *tempo* or speed. Some of these understandings include:

1. Some pieces of music are relatively slow moving; some are relatively fast moving.

2. Many pieces keep the same tempo throughout; some pieces have a few or frequent changes of tempo.

3. Changes in a piece's tempo affect the speed of the music's beat or pulse; the faster the piece, the faster the beat or pulse.

4. Changes in a piece's tempo affect the music's mood. In general, the faster the tempo, the more irritated and/or frenzied is the mood; the slower the tempo, the **81** calmer and more restful is the mood.

Concepts of Beat

One important aspect of rhythm is *beat*—the steady pulse of the music. Awareness of beat is fundamental to understanding the rhythm of the music. It is the beat that is marched to, clapped to, or danced to as the child responds to a band in a parade, a folk song, or rock music. Some of the basic concepts the child will develop about beat include:

1. Most music has a regular, steadily recurring and continuous beat, or pulse, that pulsates with the rhythmic flow of the music.
2. Some pieces have slow-moving beats; some have fast-moving beats.
3. Some pieces have a strong feeling of beat—e.g., a march, most rock music; others have a weaker feeling of beat—e.g., a lullaby, most "mood" music.
4. The speed of the beat within a piece may change (see previous discussion on *tempo.*)
5. Some beats in a piece seem stronger and more accented than others; e.g., in most pieces, there is a recurring pattern of a strong beat followed by one or more weaker beats.

In addition to forming concepts about tempo and beat, the child will begin to develop a concept of rhythm as it relates to *rhythmic patterns.*

Concepts of Rhythmic Patterns

Rhythmic patterns are the long and short tones of the music as grouped together. These patterns characterize such musical groupings as the "e-i-e-i-o"

— — — — ——

rhythmic pattern of "Old MacDonald" or the "happy birthday to you"

— — — — — ——

rhythmic pattern of "Happy Birthday." Some of the initial concepts about rhythmic patterns include:

1. Music has tonal patterns consisting of long tones and short tones.
2. A melody and word phrases contain several rhythmic patterns, e.g.:

Are you sleeping — — — —

Brother John — — —

Morning bells are ringing ‒ ‒ ‒ ‒ — —

Ding, ding, dong — — —

In experiencing tempo, beat, and rhythmic patterns, the child will gradually develop a clearer, more concise, and broader understanding of the concept of *rhythm* as it relates to music.

Concepts of Dynamics

One of the earliest of all understandings of music that the young child develops relates to the *dynamics*—the relative loudness or softness of music. Some of the basic understandings of dynamics include:

1. A piece of music may be relatively loud or soft.
2. The relative loudness or softness of a piece may change; i.e., a piece may become louder or softer.
3. Changes in the dynamic level of a piece can occur gradually or suddenly.
4. Loudness levels affect the mood of music.
5. Sudden loudness (accents) often causes an unsettling, jerky, or startling feeling and mood in our reaction to the music.

Concepts of Melody

Concepts about *melody*—the flow of tones of different pitches organized in a rhythmically meaningful way—also **83** form in early childhood. It is the melody or "tune" of a piece that usually helps the child to recognize it. It is the melody or "tune" the child sings or hums. Some of the basic concepts of melody include:

1. A melody is the tune we sing for a song. Each tune of a song has its own unique melody.

2. A melody has tones of varying pitches that go high, or low, or stay the same. For example, the tones of "Jingle Bells" begin by staying the same, and then they rise and fall.

Jin-gle bells, jin-gle bells, jin-gle all the way

3. A melody has tones of varying rhythms. Some tones of the melody's rhythm are longer than other tones (see the preceding illustration for "Jingle Bells").

4. Some melodies have words; some do not. A melody with words is called a *song*. A melody without words is called a *tune* (or a *theme*, *piece*, *composition*).

5. A melody has many *tonal patterns*—organized groups of tones that give the melody its unique characteristics, e.g.:

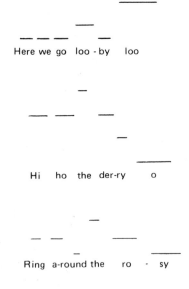

Here we go loo - by loo

Hi ho the der-ry o

Ring a-round the ro - sy

The young child, as a result of many musical experiences, will also develop concepts about *tone color*—the differences in sound due to the unique qualities of the sound. It is the tone color that enables the child to perceive differences between his mother's voice and a stranger's voice, the male and the female voice, the sounds of a guitar and a piano, and the sounds of an orchestra and a solo instrument. Some of the understandings the young child will begin to develop about tone color are:

1. Sounds in the environment differ from each other.
2. People's voices differ from each other.
3. Instrumental sounds differ from each other.
4. Voices, instruments, and environmental and electronic sounds may be combined to produce musical sounds.

Concepts of Harmony

Another basic element of music to which the young child will become exposed is *harmony*—the simultaneous sounding of two or more tones. When a guitar is strummed, it is harmony that is heard. When an adult chorus sings, it is harmony that is usually heard. Some of the child's early basic understandings about harmony are:

1. Two or more different tones may be sounded at the same time, resulting in harmony.

2. A melody may be sung or played by itself—as when a mother sings a lullaby to a child—or it may be accompanied by harmony—as when the mother uses an Autoharp or guitar to accompany her singing.

3. Harmony may be made by combining different voices or different instruments or by combining voices with instruments.

85

Concepts of Form

When the elements of rhythm, melody, harmony, tone color, and dynamics are arranged and organized into a total musical design that communicates aesthetic significance, the result is called the *form* of the music. The music's overall form or design is related in part to aspects of repetition and contrast in the music, as well as to the division of the work into various parts or sections. Thus, the form or design of a piece of music might be the following for "Jingle Bells":

Introduction
A. Verse ("Dashing through the snow . . ."
B. Chorus ("Jingle bells, jingle bells, . . ."

and the following for "We Wish You a Merry Christmas":

Introduction
Ⓐ Chorus ("We wish you a merry Christmas . . .")
Ⓑ Verse ("We wish you joy, we wish you good cheer . . .")
Ⓐ Chorus ("We wish you a merry Christmas . . .")
Ⓑ Verse ("Oh, bring us some figgy pudding . . .")
Ⓐ Chorus ("We wish you a merry Christmas . . .")
Ⓑ Verse ("We won't go until we get some . . .")
Ⓐ Chorus ("We wish you a merry Christmas . . .")

Notice that in both these examples, the tune in the chorus is different from the tune in the verse. In "We Wish You a Merry Christmas," the words for each verse are different, but the tune is repeated on each verse. The form for "Jingle Bells," then, is basically *AB* (two contrasting sections), whereas the form for "We Wish You a Merry Christmas" is *ABABABA* (two alternating sections that are repeated several times).

For the child, the concept of form develops slowly, since it relies upon developing concepts of melody, rhythm, harmony, dynamics, and tone color. Yet, even the young child can begin to develop certain understandings about form, such as:

86

1. A piece of music has a beginning, a middle part, and an end.

2. A piece of music may have an introduction that serves as a brief opening or prelude to the main section.

3. Some parts of a musical work may have clearly identifiable melodic material called *themes.* It is the theme we recognize when we identify a Sousa march or a song performed by a pop singer.

4. Some patterns or parts of a piece of music may repeat themselves after a contrasting section. For example, the "e-i-e-i-o" pattern in "Old MacDonald" and the "fa-la-la-la-la" pattern of "Deck the Halls" both repeat several times after a contrasting tonal pattern. In instrumental works, many sections of the music may be repeated after contrasting sections.

To summarize the discussion on the concepts of music, we note that:

1. Music consists of tones and silences organized into rhythmic and melodic patterns that communicate aesthetic meanings to the listener.

2. The basic ingredient of music is tone.

3. A tone has intensity, duration, pitch, and quality or timbre.

4. Combinations of tones are organized into the music's rhythm, melody, and harmony.

5. Dynamics and tone color influence the expressive qualities of music.

6. Form results when all the elements of music are organized into patterns or designs reflecting aspects of repetition and contrast.

As illustrated in the figure on page 88, these elements, when experienced through the interrelated processes of creating, listening, and performing, lead to an increasing
87 understanding of music and its aesthetic dimensions.

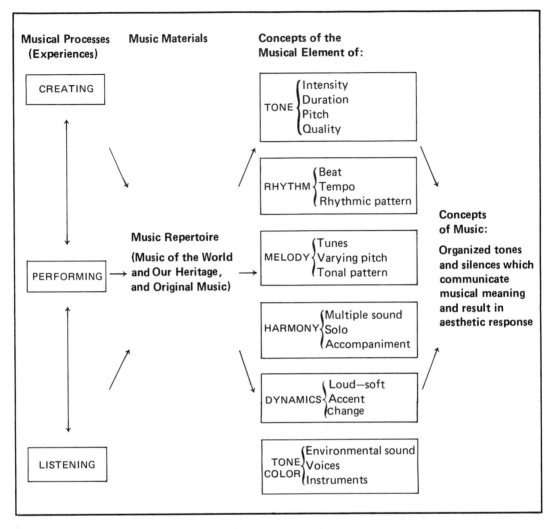

Musical Processes (Experiences)

CREATING

PERFORMING

LISTENING

Music Materials

Music Repertoire

(Music of the World and Our Heritage, and Original Music)

Concepts of the Musical Element of:

TONE { Intensity, Duration, Pitch, Quality

RHYTHM { Beat, Tempo, Rhythmic pattern

MELODY { Tunes, Varying pitch, Tonal pattern

HARMONY { Multiple sound, Solo, Accompaniment

DYNAMICS { Loud—soft, Accent, Change

TONE COLOR { Environmental sound, Voices, Instruments

Concepts of Music:

Organized tones and silences which communicate musical meaning and result in aesthetic response

Music—A Summary of Its Processes and Elements.

Summary

Experience with and knowledge about music are necessary prerequisites for all adults who wish to educate the young child in music. The three basic areas of experience—listening to, performing, and creating music—provide the activities to use with the young child. In these experiences, only quality music representative of world's peoples and culture should be used. This repertoire should contain a wide variety of music of different

88

styles, societies, and historical periods. Through experiencing music, the child will be guided to form concepts of tone, rhythm, melody, harmony, tone color, dynamics, and form, so that he can more fully feel and understand the aesthetic significance of the music and what it means to him. Such concept development is an ever-changing, growing, lifelong process and starts at birth. Specific ways to enhance concept development and musical response in the young child are provided in the remaining sections of this book.

Selected Readings

For those readers with only limited experiences in musical response and understanding, the following resources on listening to and appreciating music are recommended:

Baker, Richard, *The Magic of Music.* New York: Universe Books, 1975.

Britten, Benjamin, and Imogen Holst, *Wonderful World of Music.* New York: Doubleday Co., 1968.

Copland, Aaron, *What to Listen for in Music,* rev. ed. New York: McGraw–Hill Book Co., 1957.

Dallin, Leon, *Listener's Guide to Musical Understanding* (3rd ed.). Dubuque, Iowa: William C. Brown Co., 1972.

Dasher, Richard T., *Music Around the World.* Portland, Me.: J. Weston Walch Publishers, 1975.

Marple, Hugo D., *The World of Music.* Boston: Allyn and Bacon, Inc., 1975.

Music in World Cultures. Washington, D.C.: Music Educators National Conference, 1972.
A reprint of the October 1972 issue of Music Educators Journal.

Nadeau, Roland, and William Tesson, *Listen: A Guide to the Pleasures of Music.* Boston: Allyn and Bacon, Inc., 1971.

Randolph, David, *This is Music.* New York: McGraw–Hill Book Co., 1964.

The following texts will be helpful to those readers who wish to learn how to read and write music:

Austin, Virginia, *Learning Fundamental Concepts of Music: An Activities Approach.* Dubuque, Iowa: William C. Brown Co., 1970.

Colwell, Richard, and Ruth Colwell, *Concepts for a Musical Foundation.* Englewood Cliffs, N.J.: Prentice–Hall, Inc., 1974.

FOUNDATIONS OF MUSICAL GROWTH

Hargiss, Genevieve, *Music for Elementary Teachers.* Englewood Cliffs, N.J.: Prentice–Hall, Inc., 1968.

Kiely, Dennis K., *Essentials of Music for New Musicians.* Englewood Cliffs, N.J.: Prentice–Hall, Inc., 1975.

Nye, Rogert E., and Bjornar Bergethon, *Basic Music: Functional Musicianship for the Non-Music Major* (4th ed.) Englewood Cliffs, N.J.: Prentice–Hall, Inc., 1973.

Puopolo, Vito, *Music Fundamentals.*New York: Schirmer Books, 1976.

Part Two

EDUCATING THE YOUNG IN MUSIC

We have seen in Part One that the foundations of musical growth in the young child are based upon an understanding of the child and how he learns and on an awareness of the nature of music and the musical experience. Part Two now considers specific ways to implement a program designed to foster musical growth in our young. Emphasis is placed on "how-to-do-it" procedures, i.e., practical hints and recommendations needed to achieve the goals of music education for the young child. First, the home, school, and community environments as they relate to music responsiveness are discussed. Following this, several chapters are devoted to specific musical experiences for the young child in listening and moving to music, singing, playing instruments, and creating music. A summary is presented on how various musical experiences serve to develop concepts of music in the young.

Both the home and school musical environments are important to the child's musical development. (Photo courtesy of American Music Conference)

4

The Musical Environment

For the young child, *planned musical environment* is the key to his music education. It is this environment that maximizes the child's inborn capacity to respond musically, and which allows us to structure the child's experiences in a manner that is in harmony with his intellectual, physical, psychological, and musical potentials. In this chapter we turn to suggestions on organizing this environment so that the young child can undergo quality musical experiences. Specifically, we look at the home, the outdoors, the community, and the day-care center or preschool and see how each of these environments influences the musical growth of the young.

The Home

The type of home environment is vital to attaining musical growth in the young child. It is here where the child spends most of his first five years of life. It is the home that has major impact on the child's total growth **97** and development. The young child will have a storehouse of experiences to refer to in growing musically—if the home environment has provided him with frequent opportunity to listen to music of various styles; to use the radio, television, phonograph, and tape recorder for musical pleasure; to hear sounds in nature and the immediate environment; to experiment with sound-producing objects and instruments; to experiment with and use his voice; to hear others sing; to create tunes and rhythms with his voice and instruments; to observe and imitate objects and animals that move; and to move rhythmically to music. This experiential storehouse will serve as the basis for future musical growth. Thus, when we consider musical environment, we must start with the child's home.

The home musical environment and specific activities relating to listening, movement, singing, playing instruments, and creating music are discussed fully in the next few chapters. In general, this environment should contain many sound-making objects for the child's experimentation: rhythm instruments such as wrist bells, drum, rhythm sticks, and tambourine; recordings of music of various styles and cultures, and a good-quality phonograph. The emotional climate should be one of constant support, encouragement, and creative freedom.

Beginning at about one and a half to two years of age, it is best that the child be provided with a certain area in the home set aside for musical activities. This area should be a place where experimentation, banging, and noise making are permitted. An open-spaced area is advisable, wherein the child can move around with his instruments and dance. Although you should allow time for sound making in any area of the house, the child should also learn that at times, this activity will be inappropriate except in his music area. This place should contain a phonograph, instruments, sound-producing objects for experimentation, and miscellaneous props to stimulate creative movement, e.g., a scarf, balloons, a soldier's hat, paper streamers, hoops, rug squares, netting.

The home should contain one good-quality, three-speed phonograph. Accurate fidelity and a dust-free needle are essential. The phonograph and connecting wires should be positioned away from the child's curious hands. In addition to this phonograph, an inexpensive one for the child above age two is recommended in order to foster his own selection of recorded music and to induce early habits of listening to recorded music.

Several other pieces of music equipment and supplies are recommended for the home. These include:

- a cassette tape recorder, with recording tape
- a set of xylophone-type bells, with mallets (see p. 213)
- commercially made rhythm instruments (see pp. 205–211)
- some easy-to-make "homemade" instruments such as a drum, shaker, tambourine, sand blocks, and wood blocks (see pp. 219–231 for instructions on how to make these.)
- sound-producing implements such as pots, lid covers, spoons, wooden blocks, hollow pipes, coconut shells, and durable seed pods (see pp. 203–204)
- for the infant, several sound makers tied to a cord or cloth and suspended over the baby's crib and within his reach (see p. 152)

What are some of the activities you can do in the home environment to stimulate musical growth?

Activities

Specific suggestions in listening and movement activities, singing, playing instruments, and creating music are given in the next four chapters. In general, these activities include:

1. Sing frequently with or to the child.
2. Hold the very young in your arms or lap as you move rhythmically to music.

3. Read many nursery rhymes, poems, and stories to the child. Encourage him to repeat some words rhythmically; make up a chant or tune using the words.

4. Call attention to and compare the many sounds in his environment. If the child is old enough, discuss whether the sounds are loud or soft, short or long, and high or low in pitch.

5. Assist the child in making simple percussion instruments (see pp. 219–231). Encourage him to experiment with producing different sounds on these instruments.

6. Play many vocal and instrumental recordings for the child, illustrative of a variety of musical styles from many cultures.

7. Tape-record the child's musical efforts, and replay these sounds for him.

8. Encourage the child to imitate the way animals, objects, and people move. Urge him to use a wide variety of types of movement.

9. Learn to play a simple instrument, and play it for the child as you practice.

10. Carefully choose television programs for him to watch. Occasionally, view part of a public educational television concert (rock, jazz, classical, ballet), and explain to the child what is happening. Hold the child and move rhythmically to the music.

11. Have frequent family get-togethers in which the entire family engages in music making.

12. Take the child to family events (birthday parties, weddings, graduation parties) in which music plays a significant role. Let the child listen to and participate in the festivities.

The Outdoors

The outdoor environment—the street around the child's home, the nearby playground or park, the preschool yard—is an important area for musical learning. The outdoors provides countless opportunities for the young child to use and develop his sense of seeing, smelling, feeling, tasting, and especially hearing. He can listen to the sounds of trucks, cars, and motorcycles as they whiz by. He can hear the sounds of birds, dogs, cats, and people. The sounds of an airplane, the wind through the trees, a cricket, running water, the electric saw in a nearby lumberyard, and older children chanting as they jump rope can acquaint the young child with an endless variety of sounds.

The outdoors also provides opportunities for the child to be creative and musical. As he explores the slide, swings, or a hill and as he crawls, walks, and runs, tension is released, and he is freer to move, to notice things, and to create. It is often at outdoor play that the otherwise inhibited child will spontaneously begin to babble, chant his name, move freely like the butterfly or worm he sees, or pound rhythms on a hollow pipe with a stick. The freedom and space of the outdoors are conducive to eliciting a wide variety of creative and musical responses.

The outdoors provides an excellent experiential background for the child's musical response and concept development. As the child moves up and down on the seesaw or swings back and forth on a swing or rope, he is developing a sense of high and low and of rhythmic movement that later can be transferred to learnings about pitch and rhythm. As the child observes moving objects, he is obtaining experiential background for creative movement activities. As he hears environmental sounds, he is gaining more awareness of differences in sound and volume, tone color, pitch, and duration. As he plays with other children, he is learning some of the singing games and chants that are characteristic of his culture. The outdoors contains an immense reservoir of musical learning opportunities for the young child and should be used frequently.

The Community

Another part of the child's environment that shapes his response to music is the community. The community **101** and its people, its businesses and cultural institutions, and its values and attitudes have great influence on the musical growth and aesthetic values of the impressionable child. The extent to which a community is musically active and the quality and variety of its events greatly influence what the young child feels and knows about music.

Activities

Some recommendations for using community resources in the musical education of the young child are:

1. Take frequent "sound-hearing" walks on the main streets of the community. Listen for sounds of traffic, people's voices, building construction, equipment in auto repair shops, and airplanes and helicopters.

2. Visit various pet shops and the zoo to listen to animal sounds.

3. Take walks to different parks. Listen to the sounds of birds, crackling leaves and twigs, the wind, streams, and small animals.

4. Go to stores that sell musical instruments and records. Listen to the musical sounds and see the many different types of instruments.

5. Visit the airport and other transportation terminals. Listen to the sounds of the vehicles as they arrive and depart.

6. Attend musical events in the community (a children's concert, a summer musicale, a rock concert, a parade, a folk or square dance festival, a July 4th celebration). Try to sit close to the event, so that the child can see as well as hear. Keep him at the event only as long as his attention lasts.

7. Attend rehearsals of musical events. These rehearsals are often very worthwhile for the young child, since the audience is small, the child can move around, and you can leave freely when his attention wanes.

8. Ask permission to observe a high school music group in rehearsal, or an elementary school chorus or music class, or a preschool music period. One of the best

102

motivators for a young child is to watch older children making music.

The Classroom

An Aesthetic Environment

The musical environment is part of a total classroom environment in which there are many opportunities for the child to explore, create, and learn. Most day-care and preschool classes today have planned learning environments that are sensitively and aesthetically arranged to foster exploration and discovery. Attractive bulletin boards, wall coverings, children's artworks, plants and aquaria, child-sized tables, chairs, and shelves, and orderly and pleasant displays of books; science, math, and art materials; blocks, housekeeping and woodworking materials, and other materials conducive to learning are typical of a preschool environment. Here, learning centers or interest areas are established. These are specific locations planned to provide certain activities and experiences for the children. These usually include a housekeeping area, a block-building area, a sand-play and/or water-play area, a woodworking area, a book corner, a science–math table, an art area, and a music area. There is also space—usually in a large room or outside—for large-muscle activities. Each of these learning areas will reflect a sense of order and arrangement and a feeling of discovery and beauty. In addition, care should be taken to ensure that the room is visually attractive. Window curtains, off-white paint, plants and flowers, mobiles, attractive displays of children's artwork, decorator pillows, throw rugs, colorful bulletin boards, and orderly storage of materials will help in creating an environment conducive to aesthetic response.

A pleasant and aesthetic environment in the classroom refers to both visual *and* aural stimuli. Often teachers are concerned about how their rooms look but completely ignore the influence of sound and noise **103** levels. A pleasant aural environment is one in which loud noises are held to a minimum, talking is at a normal frequency, and the tonal level and sounds in the class are pleasing to the ear and indicate child participation in various activities.

Perhaps the principal means of providing an aural environment that encourages musical growth is to use recorded music in the classroom. By choosing records carefully and by playing them at selected times and at normal volume levels, you can help develop responsiveness in the children. Place three to five records, representing a wide variety of music, on the phonograph, and provide about one hour of listening time. These selections could be familiar children's songs or ones that you are planning to teach, folk songs, music from shows or the movies, ethnic music, classical music, music for holidays, religious music, and choral music. Avoid loud, rhythmical rock or march music for background, since this may distract from other activities in the classroom. Do not play the background music continuously, since this may make the children insensitive to all music. Rather, use selected times such as "indoor-activity time," snack period, and mealtime. If the children react to the music through singing or movement, this should be encouraged. It is hoped that this procedure will add much beauty to the aural environment of the classroom and cause children to seek musical experiences throughout the day.

Materials

What types of materials are needed for a classroom averaging between fifteen and twenty preschoolers? Generally, the following items are needed to implement a music program:

- audio equipment
- a large collection of records
- many instruments and sound-producing objects (see pp. 202–219)
- pictures and books about music
- song-books and other resources for the teacher

In addition, you will need an adequate supply of regular classroom equipment and materials, e.g., blocks, house-keeping materials, art supplies, balance boards, and slides, since these are often conducive to eliciting musical responses. Often, a child will sing as he finger paints, or play interesting rhythmic patterns as he knocks on the aluminum pipes of a slide, or make up a song about his boat as he immerses his arms in the soapy water tank. The better, more suitable, and more varied the overall materials and equipment in the classroom, the more opportunities for musical response in the children.

Several kinds of "hardware" are needed for the classroom, including:

- a good-quality, three-speed phonograph, preferably with at least two speakers
- an inexpensive small phonograph for use by the children
- an automatic cassette tape recorder with an ample supply of recording tape
- a listening center with a phonograph and built-in headsets, semienclosed booths or carrels for listening privacy, a cassette tape recorder, cassette tapes, and a viewer (all optional, but highly recommended)

As discussed on pp. 75–79 and 133–34, use musical recordings representative of the wide variety of music available in our culture. Exposing the child to this balance will serve to acquaint him with as wide a variety of experiences as possible and will help establish a musical frame of reference for the child to build on in later years. A list of recommended records is found in the Resources section of this book.

Many types of rhythm, melody, and harmony instruments are needed in order to provide the child with different experiences in listening to and producing sounds. Some recommended instruments appear on pp. 202–219. Besides instruments, include a wide variety of other sound producers such as lids from pots and pans, large metal spoons, hollow pipes, resonant pieces of wood, stainless steel mixing bowls, and music boxes. **105** Make available various drumsticks, mallets, metal strikers, and drum brushes for use in hitting these sound producers.

Large pictures and picture books about music, instruments, and dancers should be available for the children's use. In addition, no teacher should be without several teaching resources from which to plan the music program. Several song, finger play, nursery rhyme, and poem collections should be part of your professional library. Source lists on instruments, records, and suppliers should be centrally located. You should have several teachers' books on music and creative movement for the young. If the children are ages four or five, several teaching guides with accompanying records can prove invaluable as teaching aids. Begin to collect teaching resources to help in planning and implementing the music program for young children.

One frequently overlooked source of music equipment and materials is the parent. Many times a parent will have certain types of music at home that she is willing to lend or give to the school. This music may be of the parent's own cultural heritage, or it may be classical, jazz, or contemporary music. Often, with assurances that you will take care of the records, the parent will be more than willing to share her own musical tastes with the preschoolers. One word of caution: Aim for different types of music, not just rock music!

Unfortunately, the cost of adequately supplying the preschool with music equipment and supplies is often prohibitive. A good-quality piano, Autoharps, xylophones, rhythm instruments, tape recorders, phonographs, and records can quickly eat into the school's budget. Yet when purchasing this material, we should not necessarily buy the cheapest item unless the musical quality and durability are at least equal to the more expensive items. If we are sincere in our desire to develop sensitivity to beautiful sounds, then we must obtain material from which these beautiful sounds can emanate. The instruments, records, and audiovisual equipment must be capable of producing sounds that have tonal quality and beauty. Better-quality equipment will also last much longer. It is advisable to have fewer materials of better quality than lots of materials that are poorly constructed and have poor musical tone.

Nevertheless, there is a place for some materials of less than excellent quality. Such materials are useful for experimentation and can include an old piano on which the children are free to experiment, homemade instruments such as coffee-can drums, shakers, shoe-box banjos, and sand blocks (see pp. 219–231 for instructions on how to make some of these instruments); plastic ukuleles and guitars; plastic tonettes, flutophones, song flutes, and recorders; and old, discarded orchestral instruments. Remember, however, that these are only supplements to good-quality instruments and equipment.

Where can music equipment, materials, and records be purchased? Try various retail outlets and major music suppliers in your area. These are commonly listed in the phone company's *Yellow Pages* under:

Music Dealers	Phonographs
Music Instruments	Records
Music, Sheet	School Supplies (for
Piano	instruments, records)
Tape Recorders	

Adequate storage space for musical equipment and supplies is essential. Keep phonograph records in a dry, cool, and dust-free area, and store them on their ends, rather than piling them one on top of another. When not in use, place instruments carefully on shelves or in boxes. Empty wooden orange crates stacked in a corner of the room, or heavy cardboard cylinders attractively painted and placed against the wall often make good storage containers for larger instruments. Use shoe boxes or coffee cans for storing the smaller ones. Place each type of instrument in a separate container or storage area. This will make it easier to locate them and will teach the children basic classification skills relating to instruments, how they are made, and how they sound.

The Music Area

All preschool classrooms should have a music interest area—a location that invites the children to participate in music. First, find an open space in the room. If it is cramped, make the space larger by moving a table or chairs out of the way. What is needed is plenty of room for movement. It is best that this area be in the noisier, more active part of the room. You might place the "music corner" near the block and/or housekeeping areas, since this will stimulate creative movement and play between these areas.

The music area should be clearly defined. This can be done in several ways. Use a table or open shelf for a display of two to four instruments. You might place on this table a children's phonograph, a few records, a seed pod that rattles, a pot lid cover with a metal striker, a drum, and a small xylophone. Display pictures of instruments, singers, and dancers on a nearby bulletin board or wall. You might store the class phonograph, records, and other instruments in the area. Use a table or movable bulletin board to set the limits of this area and separate it from the adjacent interest areas. The music area, by the way it is arranged, should signal to the child: "This is a special place to listen to and make music."

Some suggestions for the use and care of the music area within the preschool classroom are:

1. Change some of the instruments on the music table about once every two to three weeks.

2. Cover the music table with heavy white paper, and outline the instruments that are on the table (see following). In this way, you can teach the children that the instrument, when not in use, must be returned to the proper picture on the table. As an example:

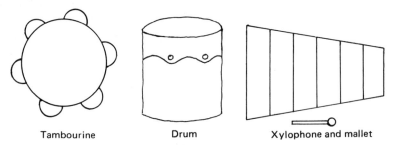

Tambourine   Drum   Xylophone and mallet

3. Have available a variety of instruments and records in this area, in case they are needed during a group music period.

4. If finding a space for your music area is a problem, then try to use the block area for music, since that too has a large space. If you are having a group music time in this area, be sure to cover the blocks in order to avoid distractions.

5. A scatter rug or masking tape in the form of a circle can mark the place where the children sit for group music.

When to Have Music

Three time periods can readily be identified in which music may occur: (1) during various activities in the child's day; (2) during a regular indoor play period (in a preschool, this is usually the "free-choice activity" period); and (3) in a regularly scheduled "music time."

THROUGHOUT THE DAY

Traditionally, music in many preschools has been a teacher-directed group experience in which all the children gather around the teacher and follow her directions. In fact, preschool music is one of the few activities in which all the children are expected to attend. It is usually teacher dominated and is often difficult for her to handle. Group music experience can be successful, but it is no substitute for the individual child's spontaneous exploration of sound and music. This is often not possible in a group situation where only a few children may get a chance to play the drum or create a song. Group music experience, by its very nature, does not focus on the individual. It often encourages conformity and discourages creativity. Although it still has some value in the preschool, it must not be the prime musical experience for the young child. Time must be allowed throughout the day for the child to interact with music. The musical experience cannot be limited to the fifteen- or twenty-minute music period.

Music can occur many times throughout the day as the young child carries out his daily activities. Music can permeate much of what the child does. It is an integral part of the child's life and an important part of the day-long instructional program of the preschool.

The alert adult takes advantage of the many daily opportunities to use music with the young child. The mother rocks her baby to the steady beat of a recorded folk song. The father repeats the "da-da-da" babbles of the infant and varies the pitches of these babbles for the baby to hear. The parent notices the one-year-old banging a steady beat on the drum and chimes in with a song that matches the beat. The adult plays the radio and dances with the two-year-old to the rock music. The mother swings her three-year-old on the swing and chants the child's name in rhythm with the swing's movements. The preschool teacher notices the four-year-old playing "soldier" and beats the drum to accompany the child's marchlike footsteps. As children rhythmically pound the clay or Play Doh or build castles in the sandbox, the teacher picks up the beat of the movements on a drum or rhythm sticks and chants about what the children are doing. As a child moves on the seesaw or bounces a ball, the teacher rhythmically chants "up and down" or "high–low" to correspond with the child's movements. As a child plays with a doll, the teacher encourages him to make up a lullaby to put the doll to sleep. As the child becomes fascinated with the sound he hears when he knocks against the metal water pipes, the teacher encourages him to hit other objects and discover their sounds. And as a child watches the butterfly flit from flower to flower, the adult encourages him to move like a butterfly and sings as the child moves. The adult who capitalizes on these everyday situations will promote musical growth in the child in the most natural way possible.

Your day-to-day, ongoing role in music instruction with the preschool child is primarily one of supporting, encouraging, and interacting with him. You can capitalize on the child's songful jabbering in the playground by joining in with him or by adding a drum beat to the child's rhythm. You can encourage the child as he role plays the part of his older brother or a television star strumming the guitar. You can hear the child's chant or rhyme and repeat it for him and for other children. You can encourage the child to find different ways of playing the tambourine. Once a feeling of warmth and support permeates the relationship between you and the child, then the child will readily seek you and other adults to share his experiences.

There are several times during the day when musical activities are particularly welcome. As mentioned on p. 104, it is a wise practice to play records for children when they are indoors. Use a wide variety of recorded music when they play, eat, or prepare for a nap, since this creates a beautiful aural environment and usually quiets the noise level in the classroom. In addition, sing chants, songs, and singing games either at home or in preschool when:

• it is time to awake from, or prepare for a nap;
• everyone is waiting for a snack or a visitor;
• you take the children for a walk or a bus ride;
• you talk to the children or read a story to them (chant-sing some of the words in the story);
• the children are playing outdoors;
• you take attendance (chant the children's names);
• the children leave school (sing a goodbye song).

Music can be used in many different ways throughout the day in support of various learning activities. It can enhance learning in language development, science, mathematics, movement education, social studies and social skills, and the other arts. Although the main objective of teaching music to the young child is to develop his response to the tonal and rhythmic organization of sounds, music can be an excellent means of promoting the child's total physical, social, emotional, and intellectual growth.

Music can help develop language response. It can be used to chant the names of people and objects in the environment. Chants and tunes can be used to describe actions, e.g., "Billy is sitting" or "Maria is hopping." It can invite conversation, as you chant and the child responds (see pp. 174–178). Names of animals, colors, shapes, objects, and utensils can be taught through

111

chantlike patterns. When singing many songs with actions, e.g., "The Hokey Pokey," "Looby Loo," "Where is Thumbkin?" "If You're Happy," the child learns to respond to language directions. Songs can help teach the child to use correct language patterns. There is much in common in the chanting of nursery rhymes and poems, the use of choral speaking, and the singing of songs. Work on proper singing skills, especially diction and breathing, can help develop proper speech habits. Musical instruments can be used to accompany the mood and actions of a story or poem. Some of the most successful parents and teachers of young children frequently use musical chanting instead of speech to communicate with the children. Music and language activities complement each other so well!

Music can help develop learning in science. Concepts of sound and vibration can be developed when paper scraps are placed on vibrating Autoharp strings; when all (or none) of the Autoharp bars are pressed down and then the strings are played; when a struck triangle is dipped into water; when the sounds of two different ukulele or guitar strings are compared; when the sounds and sizes of two separate resonator bell bars are compared; and when a child is allowed to experiment with various parts of the piano or guitar. There are many folk and nursery songs that can help teach the child about animals ("Old MacDonald," "Bought Me a Cat," "Baa, Baa, Black Sheep," "Mary Had a Little Lamb") or the weather ("Rain, Rain, Go Away," "Spider and Spout"). Songs about a wasp, a frog, or a beetle can be created by the child. He can be encouraged to move rhythmically in imitation of the movements of machines, animals, birds, and insects. Chants can accompany actions such as brushing teeth, drinking milk, washing hands, and combing hair, so that health and nutrition learnings can be made more meaningful and enjoyable.

Music can help develop learning in mathematics. There are many children's songs that emphasize counting, e.g., "Ten Little Indians," "This Old Man," "One Potato, Two Potatoes." Tapping rhythm sticks can be used to help the child count. Classification and size relationships can be emphasized using instruments.

112

Awareness of differences and similarities in sounds and in music will aid the child in developing logical thinking. Songs and music can be used to develop concepts of shape and size. Rhythmic movement activities can be used to develop spatial relationships. Tunes can be created by the child to help him learn about the days of the week and the months of the year.

Music can be used in movement education activities (see Chapter 5 for detailed discussion). Activities in gross-motor skills,—e.g., running, throwing a ball, skipping, swinging, moving on a seesaw, walking on a balance beam—can be accompanied by chanting or by rhythmic accompaniments. Fine-motor activities—e.g., painting, working with clay, cutting with scissors—can also be accompanied by musical chanting and rhythmic activities. Helping the child to sing, use instruments, and move to music are all important aspects of movement education. Many songs, finger plays, and singing games can teach the child the difference between his right and left hands or feet and ways to move (sideways, up and down, forward and backward). Since music and movement are so interrelated, they should be used together frequently throughout the child's day.

Music can help develop learning in social studies and social skills. Appropriate songs can be used or created to teach about family members, community workers, transportation, people in other countries, and holidays. Recordings of songs and dances of other peoples can provide insight into the nature of other peoples—their beliefs, customs, and feelings. Simple songs and chants can be created to describe the child, his clothing, his activities, and his accomplishments. In this way, the child's self-awareness and self-concept can be enhanced. Routines can be made more pleasant when a tune is played or a song is sung to clean up ("It's clean-up time, it's clean-up time"); to prepare to eat ("Let us go to eat our food"); or to gather together in a group. Directions and verbal encouragement can be sung to the child. Various recordings can be used as cues for the child to rest, look at picture books, or eat.

Music can help develop learning in the other arts.

113 As the child paints or draws, elements of repetition and contrast, rhythm, and line can be discovered. Recorded music can be played to set a mood for the child's art activities. Drawings, paintings, and pictures can be shown to the child to enhance the mood of a recorded piece. You can chant to the child's rhythm as he scribbles on paper or pounds on clay. In creative dramatics, rhythmic accompaniments or recorded music can be used as the child enacts a story or uses a puppet. Stories read to the child can be accompanied by instruments to highlight certain moods or actions. Songs about favorite storybook characters can be created. The child can be encouraged to paint, draw, make up a story, or create a dance movement to depict the mood and meaning of a recorded piece of music.

DURING INDOOR TIME

In the preschool or day-care center, music can also occur during the "free-play" or "free-choice" activity time. This is a period at least one hour long in which the teaching staff arranges the environment to encourage self-choice and active and creative participation by all the children as they choose one or more activities. Some children will choose art, some blocks or wheel toys, some water play, some books, some science or math, and some music. Music, then, should be one of the options during this free period. Encourage the children to enter the music area to listen to records on the children's phonograph or at the listening center, play the instruments displayed on the music table, create a song about their friends or the rabbit in the class, use instruments in their dramatic play taking place in the housekeeping area, sing their favorite songs, and use puppets to present a musical show. A parent, a volunteer, or you should stay in the music area or in the blocks or housekeeping or music areas to encourage, but not interfere with, the child-initiated musical activities. This may also be a good time to work individually with a child to develop musical skills and understandings. It is also an excellent time to integrate music with other areas of the preschool **114** curriculum (see pp. 111–114).

Though music for the young child most frequently arises out of the day-to-day activities of preschool living, it is also recommended that a regularly scheduled music period be held on a daily basis. The group music period is a time when all the children can gather together to participate in and learn about music. The benefits of such large-group instruction are that it builds group feeling and identity; provides a change of pace from the dominant child-initiated activities; helps prepare the children for learning how to be group members; allows them to learn certain group skills (waiting one's turn to speak, speaking clearly in front of a group, facing the audience when speaking); allows them to learn from other children; provides in some cases a more efficient way for the teacher to introduce certain learnings to children; and most importantly, it provides a suitable means of large-group learning and response, both of which are pertinent to such musical activities as singing, playing instruments, and creative movement.

Group music time should be an activity in which all the children above age three can participate. Preferably, it should be held at about the same time every day, so that consistency of routine is built. Some recommended times are at the beginning of the school day (if the children are alert), before or after mid-morning snack, after a story, and after the morning "free-choice" time. It is best to have music after a relatively quiet time, since most music times will be physically active. Group music should not be scheduled after outdoors, in the early morning (if the children are generally irritable or tired), immediately before lunch (children are often tired and hungry by midday), immediately before rest (music may tend to overstimulate the children), or immediately after nap (most children will be too listless and tired). Do not force all the children to be at group music time. However, do set up expectations that they need to be in the area when everyone else is. Convey the feeling that all children can participate effectively and enjoyably in **115** the large group experience. If you plan well and have "fun" activities, then all of the children will want to be there.

The group music period should start as early in the preschool year as possible. Do not wait until midyear to introduce this period. If you start it early enough, routines for group time can be set and developed so that by the year's end, no problems will arise in group management. At the beginning of the year, more parents are usually in the classroom, and they can help you in case problems arise in group management.

The group music period should never be too long. At first, try five to ten minutes. By midyear, aim for ten to fifteen minutes. The key to increasing the children's attention span during the music period is to provide for a variety of interesting, enjoyable things for them to do, including clapping and bodily movement, playing instruments, playing finger and singing games, and creating music. For all-day centers, two short music periods—one in the morning and one in mid-afternoon—are recommended.

Effective group management of the music period is necessary for its success. It is not easy to handle 15 to 20 three- and four-year-olds. Yet many preschool teachers do this very well. How does one manage such a large group? Some suggestions are:

1. Use a consistent signal (a bell, a guitar or Autoharp chord, a song, a chant: "It's music time") to call the children together.

2. Arrange the children in a semicircle or circle rather than in rows facing the leader. In this way, all the children can see and learn from each other. It also will make each child more accessible to the leader.

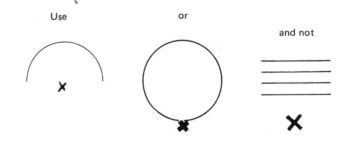

Use   or   and not

3. Besides the adult leader, have a second adult sit in or near the group. This person should be in a position to see all the children and assist the leader. A third adult (a parent, a volunteer) might also help. Other adults can sit in the group. Every adult should participate with the children, thereby modeling expected group behavior. Discourage adults from standing over or watching the children from a distance, since this may inhibit the children and does not show expected group behavior. If necessary, politely ask these adults to leave the room, and explain why.

4. Free the area from all distractions; e.g., cover the blocks and book shelf, if nearby.

5. Begin with a song involving the children's names, or how they look, or a "hello" song (see p. 175). Continue by alternating familiar activities with unfamiliar ones. End with a familiar and enjoyable activity.

6. Keep each activity, especially at the beginning of the school year, very short and very rewarding to the children. Only gradually expand the length of these experiences over a few months.

7. Alternate physical movement or interesting discussion–demonstrations with quiet listening activities. Remember: Children tire quickly if there is too much physical movement and get bored quickly by too much sitting and listening. Utilize many audio-visual experiences, especially pictures and puppets. Do not drag the lesson. Keep activities moving and well paced.

8. Frequently invite a child in the group to help you demonstrate, hold a picture, perform, or discuss a topic that arises during the music lesson.

9. Provide one or two children with alternative activities at the beginning of the music period if the teacher (and children) feel the children might not be ready for the group that day.

10. Minimize negative feedback and reinforcement during this period. Ignore potentially disruptive behavior if the total group is not affected. Separate children who might "set off" each other. Remove a disruptive child from the group and provide him with an alternative

activity that neither rewards nor punishes the disruptive behavior.

11. Praise the children who carry out routines expected of the group—i.e., waiting turns, sitting or moving without disturbing anyone, holding instruments in their laps until the music starts, not interrupting the speaker, speaking clearly and loudly.

12. Vary the voice level to attract attention and set the mood. Whispering or exaggerating the vocal tone often helps. Singing the directions to be followed also adds interest.

13. Be well-prepared and even overprepared. Have all the needed equipment and material next to you. Have lots of interesting activities planned in case your original plans go awry; be flexible. Be willing to discard ideas that do not work or expand on ideas that come from the children.

14. Frequently repeat group-time activities, since preschoolers respond well to repetition. Sing familiar songs and finger plays at every group music period.

15. Do not always blame the children when disruptive behavior occurs. The successful preschool teacher, with experience, will learn how to manage the entire group with little or no difficulty if she is aware of the children's needs and interests during this music time and can master the procedures for using music with young children.

Coordinating Efforts Between the School and Home

The education and care of the child enrolled in a preschool or day-care center call for cooperative efforts between the school and home. Neither one, working by itself, can educate the young child as effectively as when efforts are coordinated. If teachers and parents work closely together in planning for and implementing the educational program, then they are more likely to promote significant growth than in programs where teachers do one thing and parents, another. This mutual cooperation involves working together in both the home and the school—having parents observe their children in school, having parents become involved as volunteers and paid staff members in the day-to-day operation of the school, having teachers visit the homes of the children to provide resources and support for the parents, and having both cooperatively evaluate the efforts of school and home as they affect the child's education.

The mutual reinforcement of school and home efforts to educate the child in music can be accomplished in several ways. *The teacher can:*

1. Invite parents into the school to observe the children, especially as they engage in musical activities.

2. Provide parents with developmental guidelines on what they can expect their children to be doing at various ages and developmental levels (see Table 1 and pp. 19–27).

3. Ask parents to join in on planning sessions in music.

4. Encourage parents to work in the music interest area of the classroom to support the children's efforts as they partake in musical experiences.

5. Arrange for parent study groups and seminars in which the teacher and/or a preschool music specialist discuss and demonstrate ways of working with young children in music. Include work on singing with children, making and playing instruments, using records, and moving creatively and rhythmically.

6. Send notes home that summarize what you are doing in music and outlining the child's accomplishments and progress. Also phone the parents to report on the child's interests and achievements.

7. Send home the words and musical notation of new songs taught in the classroom, and encourage the parents to learn and sing these songs with their children.

8. Encourage parents and parent groups to learn how to play easy instruments such as the ukulele, Autoharp,

guitar, flutophone, tonette, or recorder, so that the parents can use these instruments in the home with their
children.

9. Invite a parent who can sing, play an instrument, or
dance to perform for the children. Encourage the parent
to share the music of her culture with the children.

10. Work with a group of parents to help them prepare
a song, musical drama, or dance for their children.
Holiday times are usually very appropriate for this type
of activity.

11. Ask parents to assist in the class music programs
that are being prepared for an audience.

12. Organize parent sing-alongs and music times. Use
activities and materials appropriate for their children.

13. Offer to help parents choose appropriate recordings
for their children. Make a list of suggested records,
songbooks, and instruments. Include information on
where they can be purchased and the price.

14. Establish a "lending library" system for records and
instruments.

15. Send music activity sheets to the parents, suggesting
ways in which they can provide more varied musical
environments for their children.

16. Tape-record a musical performance by the child, and
send this home on loan to the parent.

17. Arrange for home visits in which the teacher dem-
onstrates the uses of certain instruments with young
children. Also provide appropriate dittoed song sheets or
music books. List and demonstrate musical activities
that the parent can engage in with her child at home.

To foster mutual cooperation between the school and
home, *the parent can:*

1. Observe in the classroom, especially as the children
engage in "music time."

2. Offer to assist the teacher by working with a small
group, helping the teacher in the large-group music
period, and joining in on planning sessions.

3. Help organize the parents into groups to learn how to play or make simple instruments, learn appropriate songs and finger plays, and explore other ways to work with children in music.

4. Volunteer to perform for the children.

5. Seek others in the community who can enrich the preschool's music program.

6. Loan or give to the school various appropriate instruments or records.

7. Inform the teacher of significant progress or problems relating to the child's musical responses.

8. Seek advice from the teacher on any area relating to music, through a phone call, a note, or personal contact.

9. Invite the teacher into the home to share the family's musical experiences.

10. Help the teacher plan and carry out field trips designed to enhance musical learnings, e.g., a walk to the nearby elementary school to hear children rehearse or perform, a walk to the music store, a trip to a children's concert, a trip to the zoo to hear animal sounds, a walk to the park to listen for birdcalls.

The success of this effort to unite the home and school into common purposes and activities depends, then, on the mutual cooperation of the parent and the teaching staff. They must work together to achieve the coordination necessary to enhance musical growth in the young child.

Summary

A home environment that plans for and implements a program designed to foster musical responsiveness is essential. This environment should be emotionally supportive and have available many types of materials for the child to use in experimenting with sound, listening and moving to music, singing and playing instruments, and creating music. Use the outdoor and community environments to influence the child's responses. In the school environment, make available many types of materials: phonographs, tape recorders, listening centers, records, instruments, and teacher resource materials. Set aside an area in the room as a music center in which music materials are placed and in which special music activities can occur. Music should take place throughout the day, as the occasion arises. It can be integrated with many activities in language, mathematics, science, movement, social studies, and the other arts. Parents and the teaching staff should work as a team to plan for, implement, and complement each other's efforts in educating their children to the joys of music listening and music making.

Selected Readings

Many resources are available on providing the needed environment for home and school learning. Some worthwhile materials are:

Andress, Barbara, Hope M. Heimann, Carroll A. Rinehart, and E. Gene Talbert, *Music in Early Childhood.* Washington, D.C.: Music Educators National Conference, 1973, pp. 26–34.

Coleman, Satis, *Creative Music in the Home.* New York: John Day Co., 1938.

Home Play and Equipment. Children's Bureau Publication No. 238. Washington, D.C.: U.S. Department of Health, Education and Welfare, n.d.

Kritchevsky, Sybil, and Elizabeth Prescott, *Planning Environments for Young Children:Physical Space.* Washington, D.C.: National Association for the Education of Young Children, 1969.

Markel, Roberta, *Parents' and Teachers' Guide to Music Education.* New York: The Macmillan Co., 1972.

Marsh, Mary Val, *Explore and Discover Music,* New York: The Macmillan Co., 1970.
(See especially Chapters 2 and 3.)

Nye, Vernice, "Music in the Integrated Curriculum," in Nye, Vernice, *Music for Young Children.* Dubuque, Iowa: William C. Brown Co., pp. 107–204.

For more information on parent–teacher relations at the preschool level, consult the following excellent resources:

Adair, Thelma, and Esther Eckstein, *Parents and the Day Care Center.* New York: Federation of Protestant Welfare Agencies, 1969.

Hess, Robert D., "Parent Involvement in Early Education," in Grotberg, E. H., *Day Care: Resources for Decision.* Washington, D.C.: Office of Economic Opportunity, U.S. Government Printing Office, 1971, Chapters 9 and 10.

Pickarts, Evelyn, and Jean Fargo, *Parent Education.* Englewood Cliffs, N.J.: Prentice–Hall, Inc., 1971.

Project Head Start, *Parents Are Needed.* Washington, D.C.: U.S. Government Printing Office, 1967.

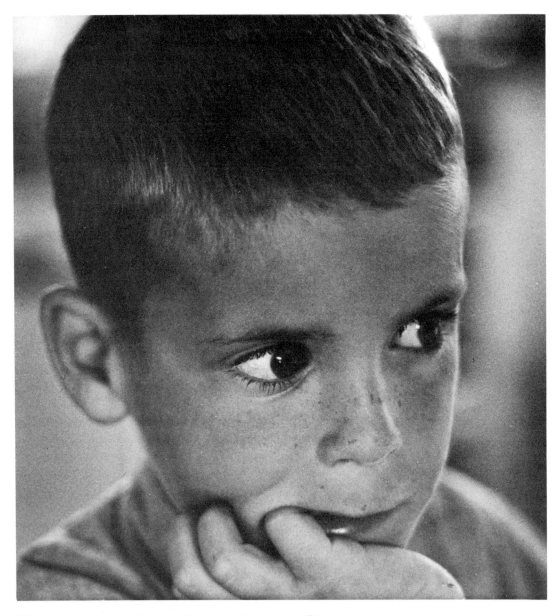

All music experiences involve listening to the music. (Photo courtesy of Hannah Lou Bennett, University Preschool, University of Hawaii, and Will Kyselka, photographer)

5

Listening and Rhythmic Movement

From birth, the young child hears sounds and music throughout his waking hours. He hears music on the radio or television. He hears his mother's voice as she talks and sings to him. He hears the sounds from his older sister's guitar. He hears door bells and people's footsteps. The child often reacts to these sounds through physical movement. In fact, his primary response to sound and music is through bodily movement. Listening and movement activities are basic to musical response and go hand in hand in fostering the musical development of the child. This chapter discusses the relationships between listening and movement activities and presents techniques to use in developing children's abilities to listen to sounds, to respond to live and recorded music, and to move rhythmically to music. Movement and listening skills are outlined, and suggestions are offered on how to promote musical growth through their use.

The Importance of Listening and Movement Response

Music is a nonverbal language that communicates feelings, emotions, and aesthetic meaning and beauty. It **127** does this through tonal and rhythmic patterns of sound.

In learning the language of music, just as in learning any language, the young child must listen to the language and its sound patterns before he is able to use it. Therefore, it is essential that the young child hear a great deal of music to provide a foundation for growth. As in language learning, the child will build his own understanding of the musical structure of tones and rhythms through a system of contrasts. He will hear differences in high–low (pitch), loud–soft (dynamics), tone quality (different sounds), and long–short (duration). As he experiences these contrasts, he will gain finer and finer discriminations. And as in language learning, the young child at first will perceive the sounds in a vague way; then, through listening, he will gain increasing control of his new language.

Activities involving listening are necessary for all musical response. Every musical experience involves listening, since the child must perceive the tonal and rhythmic organization of the sound whenever he sings, plays instruments, moves to music, and creates music. Listening is an integral part of *all* music activities and is the basis of all experience in music.

The young child gets to "know" music in probably the same way that an adult does—through listening to it, performing it, and creating it. However, one fundamental difference exists between the adult and the young child as they learn music. The adult has had many years of musical experience, and her conceptual framework is broader and in more depth than the child's. The adult tends to respond to music in a relatively reflective, thoughtful way. Adult inhibitions often prevent her from showing her response to music through physical means. The young child, on the other hand, has had limited musical experience. For him, the essence of music is expressed in his inner feelings toward what he hears and through active physical expression. The young child is actively engaged in responding to music, and it is through his own body that he shows how he feels and what he understands about the music. The young child's body, in a real sense, is his primary musical instrument.

Movement is the language of the body, and as such,

128 it is as important to the child's communication as is verbal language. Movement is the child's natural means of communicating, and finds an ultimate expression in his rhythmic movement to music. It is through listening and responding through bodily movement that the young child first gains his knowledge about music. Listening and rhythmic movement provide the foundations for musical growth in the young child.

Listening and Movement Skills

Listening and rhythmic movement to music involve two basic skills:

1. being able to listen to and focus on the music and sense its feeling and mood
2. being able to move parts of the body in coordination with the music

These skills begin to be developed in infancy when the child moves rhythmically to a song sung by his mother or to the lilt of a recorded waltz. They gradually become more refined as the child learns how to move his body in synchronization with the music's rhythmic flow. By the age of five, with previous experience, the child should be able to listen to a wide variety of music, think about and feel what he hears, and show this understanding through free rhythmic bodily movement.

Merely moving the body is not enough to show the various qualities of the music. When the child moves to music, we should guide him to move his body parts in several ways and in different combinations and to use space around him to express what he feels and understands in the music. His movements must show the music. Our role is to:

1. provide musical experiences that invite the child to move to the music;
2. help him move to the music in a variety of ways;
3. help him show through movement what he feels and understands about the music.

129

How can the child show his feelings and his musical understandings through bodily movement? In general, the child's movement can show:

- *mood*—by moving happily, sadly, and in other ways to the feeling aroused in him by the music
- *fast and slow and tempo change*—by varying the speed of the movement
- *loud and soft and dynamic change*—by varying the size and energy of the movement or by tiptoeing for soft music and stamping the feet for loud music
- *high and low pitch*—by moving at different high and low levels, as appropriate
- *long and short tones*—by sustaining the movement or by making it short and jagged
- *accent*—by using an accented, strong bodily movement
- *beat*—by moving steadily to the music's pulse
- *repetition and contrast (form)*—by repeating or varying certain physical movements or by resting on contrasting sections and moving only on the repeated sections
- *any change in the music*—by changing the style, direction, or level of the movement

The ability to show these musical aspects takes many years to accomplish but begins during the child's earliest years.

Few young children have the natural awareness of the many ways to move their bodies to music. The young child should be given the opportunity to move to music with complete freedom, but it also is suggested that you plan experiences in which he learns how to use his body to express music. This is best done by: (1) moving the child's body to the music (from birth to age two and older); (2) modeling and providing examples for him on ways to move (from about six months on); and (3) giving him verbal directions (from about age two on).

Skill in rhythmic movement to music usually follows many successful experiences in developing those skills. Obviously, the child cannot move to music very well until he has some control of his body. Efforts must be made at every developmental level to help the child gain increasing control and mastery of his body and muscles. For the infant, the movements will certainly be uncoordinated and nonrhythmical, since at this stage he is just learning how to use and control his muscles. Although he may wish to move to the music, he will have difficulty in directing his hands, fingers, and legs to move as he wishes. As he gains control, he will increase his skill and learn many ways to move his body parts to music. He will learn to move his head, his arms, his fingers, his legs, his hips, his thighs, his stomach, and his entire body. As he does this, he also will need to move his body parts in various ways in order to express what he hears in the music. He will learn to swing and clap his hands, pat his hands on his knees, move his hands up and down, and beat them on instruments as he listens to music. Given many experiences with moving his body—with and without musical accompaniment—the young child will attain more and more control and fluency in the use of body movements to express music.

There are three basic types of movement the child will use: (1) *locomotor (fundamental) movement*, (2) *nonlocomotor or axial (body) movement*, and (3) *a combination of locomotor and/or nonlocomotor movements*. Locomotor or fundamental movement involves moving the whole body from one place to another (examples: walking, running, hopping, crawling, creeping, jumping, sliding, skating, trotting, whirling, shuffling, swaying). Axial or body movement is nonlocomotor, since the feet remain stationary while other parts of the body move (examples: bending, twisting, bouncing, shaking, reaching, clapping). A combination of locomotor and nonlocomotor movements involves various motions that occur simultaneously, such as walking and clapping, hopping and shaking, and rising and then falling. Of the three basic types of movement, nonlocomotor movement occurs the earliest in the life cycle, followed by locomotor movement and then combined movements. Obviously, the timing of this sequence depends on the child's physical development and his increasing mobility and control of his muscular coordination.

131   One of your tasks in working with the young child is to help him learn to vary his movements. The child should learn to:

- move in different *directions* (go forwards, backwards, sideways, across, and circle about)
- use different *levels* (move low, high, and points in between, move while lying down, kneeling, falling, and leaping; and move under, above, and below)
- vary *dimensions* (use large or small movements)
- use different *qualities* of movement (move smoothly, sadly, happily, hurriedly, slowly, heavily, lightly, jerkily, flowingly, jaggedly, stiffly)
- move in different *ranges* (use a large or small space)
- use focus (move toward a certain spot or area while gazing at a certain point in space)

Certain physical movements to music are easier than others for the young child to accomplish. In general, the easier movements should be experienced before the more difficult ones are tried. Examples of these movements are:

- *Easier movements*: pounding, as when hitting a drum, using the entire arm; pounding, using the forearm; hitting the thighs with the hands (palm down); clapping one's hands; hitting one's body parts with the hands; moving the hands horizontally and vertically through space; walking in place; walking around the room
- *More difficult movements*: swinging the hands, swinging the body, making pushing motions with the body, moving the head rhythmically to music, moving on tiptoe, moving the fingers, marching, tapping the feet, bending the knees, running, hopping, jumping, galloping, skipping, walking or running and clapping at the same time

Exploring space for the child means helping him move his individual body parts in various positions. What can the child do when he lies on his stomach? How can he move his legs, his arms, his legs and arms together? Can he move when he lies on his back? Can he rock back and forth? What can he do as he sits? as he stands? How many ways can he clap or walk? Can he combine two or three movements? Can he move lightly, with strength, smoothly, or jaggedly? Your role is to help the child explore his potential for moving his body. As this is done, you can accompany the child's movements on a drum, tambourine, tone block, or piano. You can play the rhythm of the child's swinging arms or chant "walk, walk, walk, walk . . ." as the child moves around the room. From this initial exploration of the body stem the more refined and complex movements required in moving to music.

Types of Records to Use

Many listening and movement experiences with the young child will involve the use of records. In Chapter 4, the types of records suitable for the child were discussed. Remember that the basic guideline for selection is: *Use good-quality records representative of all types of music.* Use nursery tunes, classical music, rock and popular music, music for the theater and films, dance and march music, contemporary and electronic music, religious music, holiday music, and music of other cultures. Provide an equal balance of vocal and instrumental music. Be sure that most of the music used has stood the test of time, i.e., that it is music of lasting quality. Do *not* use music contrived especially for young children that is not part of our general musical culture. As a rule, nursery songs, folk music, and ethnic music are excellent. Avoid children's songs with such titles as: "We Learn Our Colors," "Let's Go Fishing," "Winnie and the Honey Bear," and "Mommy and Daddy," since these songs are written for children for nonmusical purposes and are not part of our recognized musical literature.

In general, it is best to use a majority of records that have strong rhythmic qualities (a definite beat, interesting rhythmic patterns, a moderate or relatively fast

133

tempo). Much of what you use should be "obvious"; i.e., it should evoke definite moods or responses and/or be highly descriptive. It should have potential for active physical response. The melody usually should be clearly outlined and songlike. Careful selection of the music to be used for the young child will reap benefits in increasing his attention span in listening to music and promoting his desire to hear a wide variety of music.

In selecting music for the child, be guided by the maxim that it is best to start with what is familiar to him. Generally, this means starting with rock music, nursery and folk music, and music of the child's cultural heritage. Rock music, in particular, is useful, since it is the popular music of our day, and almost all young children (perhaps unfortunately!) are exposed to rock music almost from birth. Rock music elicits response from children of all ages because of its obvious beat and repeated rhythmic patterns, its simple, songlike melodies, and its frequent use of repetition. This music, often so alive and rhythmical, is an excellent first choice for music activities aimed at encouraging the child to move freely to what he hears. But be careful of the rock music you choose! Renditions by the Beatles, Elton John, Neil Diamond, and the Jefferson Starship, among others, often represent pop or rock music of a higher quality than the constantly loud, pounding music of many less artistic rock groups. Try to play only the best examples of a given style, including rock music. Remember, too, that rock music is only one small part of our musical heritage. Our job is to expand the child's awareness of *all* kinds of music, rather than to limit his listening experiences only to music with which he is familiar.

When selecting records for the child, be sure that they have excellent tone fidelity and reproduction, with no warps or scratches. The selections chosen should be relatively short, lasting no more than two to three minutes. One exception to this is recorded background music, which may be played in its entirety. An excellent quality of performance is desirable. If recorded songs are used, the performance should be artistic, and the performer's diction, tone quality, and rendition should be exemplary (see p. 192).

134

Basic Experiences

Five types of listening and movement experiences are recommended for the young child:

1. exploring sounds
2. listening to live music
3. listening and moving to recorded background music
4. adult-directed listening and movement experiences
5. child-initiated listening and movement experiences

All five experiences need to begin during infancy and continue throughout childhood. A balance of all five experiences is recommended in order to achieve an effective listening and rhythmic movement program for the child.

Exploring Sounds

One of the earliest and most basic listening experiences for the young child is his exploration of sounds—where they come from and how they are made. Beginning in infancy and continuing through early childhood, you should guide the child to look at the sound source, attend to it, and eventually, to make sounds using a wide variety of objects and implements (see pp. 203–204). Our role is to provide many sound-making materials, to help the child make sounds with these materials, and to develop his ability to identify similarities and differences in sound.

Some of the many sound sources that should be used frequently with the young child are:

- *wood objects*: tables, chairs, poles, blocks, pencils, tongue depressors, rulers, kitchen utensils, toys, broom handles, crates

135 • *rubber objects*: balls, tires, inner tubes, rubber bands

- *paper objects*: boxes, toilet tissue cylinders, aluminum foil, sandpaper, newspaper, construction paper, ice cream containers, cups, magazines
- *glass objects*: drinking glasses, soda bottles, jars, bottles (with supervision)
- *foods in cardboard, metal, plastic, and rubber containers*: sugar, coffee, bread crumbs, beans, grains, seeds, rice, popcorn, condiments
- *plastic objects*: bottles, buttons, combs, boxes, cups, straws,food containers, toys
- *materials in the outdoors*: pebbles, stones, dirt, sand, leaves, twigs, water, seed pods

In each case, the child should be given many opportunities to make sounds by hitting, dropping, or shaking the objects. Of course, careful adult supervision is necessary in experimentation with objects such as glass or pointed or sharp instruments.

Experimentation with sound also should include

Various objects can be placed in covered containers, and when shaken stimulate recognition of sounds for the child. (Photo courtesy Family Services Center, Honolulu, Hawaii, and Paulette Geiger, photographer)

experiences with all types of instruments (see Chapter 5). As soon as the infant is able to grasp a small rhythm stick, rattle, or wrist bells, give him many opportunities to see what happens when he shakes, hits, or drops these instruments. Guide him to pluck or strum the strings of an Autoharp, to make sounds on the xylophone, to tap the tambourine on his crib, to hit the tambourine with the wrist bells, to rub a notched rhythm stick on the edge of a coffee can, to experiment with a set of melody bells. Complete freedom of experimentation is recommended as he tries various means of producing sounds on these instruments.

One frequently overlooked sound source that is important to the listening experience are sounds made by the body and body parts. These include experiences in making sounds with the mouth (saying "sh," clicking the tongue, humming repeating nonsense syllables as "da-ba-da-ba-doo," and hissing) and body parts (hitting the thighs or chest, clapping, tapping the feet, snapping the fingers, rubbing the palms of the hands, and hitting the fists against the floor). Give the child many opportunities to listen to and make these sounds.

ACTIVITIES FOR SOUND DISCRIMINATION

Many gamelike activities can be suggested that are useful for developing sound discrimination in the child above age two (for listening activities for children below age two, see this chapter).

1. Ask the child to listen to a sound and to imitate it with his voice.

2. Tape some common sounds in the environment, e.g., a door slamming, a pencil dropping, a foot stamping, hands clapping. Play each sound, and ask the child to make the sound.

3. Ask the child to identify sounds you make that are hidden from his view. For example, hide behind a screen and snap your fingers, click your tongue, tear some paper, or tap a pencil, and ask the child to identify the sound.

137 Also use rhythm instruments in this game after the

child has had many experiences in playing and listening to these instruments.

4. Fill small containers of the same size with sound-making materials (rice, pebbles, beads, marbles, buttons, seeds). Have two containers for each material used. The child must find the two containers that can be matched by their sounds.

5. Play "The Muffin Man" game (this song and directions for the game are found in the Appendix). Vary this game by having "It" speak, or sing any song. Also use the singing game "Who is Tapping at My Window?"

6. Provide the child with many experiences with other instruments, e.g., visit the instrument section of the music store, watch a school's instrumental group perform, attend a children's concert or parade.

7. Play a piece of music, and have the child point to the picture that shows which instrument he hears.

Live Music

Recorded music is a convenient way of bringing variety to the young child. Yet there is no substitute for live performances. When the child can see as well as hear the music being performed, his experience becomes more real and meaningful. Thus, give the child from birth to five many opportunities to see and hear music being performed. This experience starts in the home, where the young child is offered many experiences in seeing and hearing family members sing, play instruments, and move to music. You also should seek out many live performances by amateur and professional musicians in the community (see pp. 101–103), children and teachers from other preschool classes, college music students, and performing groups and soloists from elementary and secondary schools. Take the child to live musical performances, including marchers in a parade, a high school band rehearsal, a rock group performance, a church choir, an elementary school recorder group, and a children's concert given by a symphony orchestra. Depending upon the resources available, the child should be given many opportunities to hear and see the music and instruments of other cultures.

Background Music

Listening to background music, as selected by the adult, is the young child's first recorded listening experience. The infant's first experiences with music are often through recorded background music. He is frequently exposed to this type of music when he hears us play the phonograph, television, tape recorder, and radio. Our role is to choose carefully the types of music to be played and the most appropriate time for it to be played. The child's response will range from inattention to active response. If responses occur, then we should notice these, capitalize on the child's interest, encourage his response, and help the child learn from his experience. Further discussion on background music is found on p. 104.

Adult-Directed Experiences

Adult-directed listening and movement experiences usually follow experiences with background music. In these, the child is asked to listen to certain selections of music and to respond under your guidance and supervision. During infancy, this might mean playing a Strauss waltz and moving with the child in your arms or encouraging the child to move to its rhythmic flow. Or this experience could mean playing a march for the four-year-old and asking him to use tone blocks to highlight the 1 2 3 4 pattern of the beat. In adult-directed experiences, you play an active role in focusing the child's attention on the music. The basic sequence of steps is:

1. *Introduce the recording.* Set the stage by saying to the infant, "Let's listen to some music," or by telling **139** the preschooler something about the music and what

musical aspect to listen for. (Examples: "I have a piece of music to play. Listen to it, and see if you can tell me what you hear," or "Today's record has some very interesting sounds. Listen to the music, and see if you can hear the voices of people. What are they singing about?")

2. *Play the record*, as the child listens.

3. When the record is finished, *discuss the answers* to the questions posed in step 1, or if you are working with the infant, say something about the music. (Example: "That music was very loud," or "I see the music makes you want to dance.")

4. *Repeat steps 1, 2, and 3*. Again ask the child to listen for something in the music, and play the record. Let the child respond by sitting and listening, moving to the music, playing instruments, or discussing the music. Stop the music, discuss, and repeat steps 1, 2, and 3 again and again, as long as the child's interest and response continue.

Reminder: Minimize talking: The more listening and movement response by the child, the better. The aim is to involve the child directly with the music on an emotional, physical, and aesthetic level rather than stressing factual knowledge about it.

Child-Initiated Experiences

Child-initiated listening and movement experiences involve having the child himself seek to listen to music and respond accordingly. These experiences, when records are involved, begin between ages two and three or as soon as the child can be taught to handle and operate a phonograph. Initially, you should guide and supervise this experience. Gradually you can teach the child to use the phonograph by himself. As he plays the record, he may just sit and listen, or he may respond through movement or by playing a rhythm instrument to the music. Reinforce the child positively (reward him) with a smile, physical contact, or positive verbal comment whenever he seeks recorded listening experiences on his

A phonograph should be made available for children so they can play records of their own choices. (Photo courtesy of Family Services Center, Honolulu, Hawaii, and Paulette Geiger, photographer)

own. Encourage him to respond in a variety of ways to the music. This type of listening experience is really the ultimate goal of recorded listening activities with children, since it stresses the ability to seek one's own musical pleasure and aesthetic satisfaction through music.

Rhythmic Movement Activities

When the child moves in response to music, three types of movement are possible: (1) formal or structured rhythmic movement; (2) informal rhythmic movement; **141** and (3) creative rhythmic movement. All three types of

movement are important to the musical education of the
child.

Formal or Structured
Rhythmic Movement

In this type of movement, you model the movement
patterns for the child, or give specific directions for the
movement, or define it specifically in the title or words
of a song. Examples are taking the infant's hands and
clapping with him or swinging him to the music's beat;
having the child follow your movements as you clap,
jump, or swing to the music; telling the child to walk,
hop, or march to the music and providing the model for
such movement; and using action songs and games that
provide specific directions in their words, such as "Ring
Around the Rosy" and "The Hokey Pokey." In formal
rhythmic movement, the child's response may be made
through imitation of your specific movement. Or it may
be made by following your specific verbal directions. You
might say: "Can you clap your hands like me?" or "Let's
see you march in place as the music is played," or "On
the part of the game that goes 'all fall down,' we must
all fall to the floor like this . . ." Since the young child
learns a great deal from imitation, this type of movement
experience is very important in eliciting the child's
musical and movement response.

Formal or structured movement to music is also an
important means to help the child expand his alternatives for moving parts of the body. You might play some
music and say: "Let's twirl like a dancer. Let's jump like
a grasshopper or rabbit. Let's skate on ice. Let's move on
our roller skates. Let's bounce like a ball or jumping
beans. Let's squirm like eels or worms or snakes." You
may wish to work on leg movements. You might ask
the child to imitate you as you stamp with one foot,
walk on tiptoes, click your heels together, bend your
knees, tap your toes, and kick. You can guide the child
in practicing hand and arm movements in time to the
music. You could say, "Can you do what I'm doing?" as
you swing your hands, stretch and reach, move your

142

hands stiffly, pull and push, lift, throw, punch, wave, shake, pat your hands on your shoulders, slap your lap or knees, and move your hands in a circle, windmill fashion. In each instance, lead the child in making a wide variety of movements to the rhythm and mood of the music being played. This type of formal, structured movement will enhance the child's ability to move in a less structured, more creative way.

Informal Rhythmic Movement

Movement of this type allows the child to be creative within limits suggested by the music or words. The directions for the movement are left somewhat open, giving the child freedom to interpret within set limits. In informal rhythmic movement, you can give the child directions for the basic movement to be used but allow him freedom to interpret within that context. Although the child's movements may still be somewhat limited, you do encourage him to move more creatively than in formal rhythmic movement. There are many types of informal rhythmic movement activities, including:

1. *finger plays*, in which the child moves his fingers and hands to act out the stories in songs (examples: "Where is Thumbkin?" "Spider and Spout," and "Hickory Dickory Dock")

2. *action songs*, in which the child responds by appropriate movements to the words of the songs but not by definite prescribed patterns of movement. (For example, there is plenty of opportunity for originality in the movement for "This Old Man" and "He's Got the Whole World in His Hands.")

3. *impersonation and dramatization songs*, in which the child can act out characters or stories in the songs (examples: "The Mulberry Bush," "Old MacDonald," and "Lazy Mary")

4. *singing games*, in which the child moves and plays the appropriate game to the words of the songs (examples: "London Bridge," "The Farmer in the Dell," and "A Tisket, A Tasket")

143

5. *mimetic play or imitative movement*, in which the child imitates things and objects that move with the movement in rhythm to the music

6. *free rhythmic activities using locomotor movements*, in which music is played for walking, running, hopping, and other basic movements, and the child is free to be creative within the prescribed movement patterns

7. *playing rhythm instruments*, in which the child creates rhythmic patterns on instruments within the overall framework of the music

In using rhythmic movement, you might say: "How many different ways can you march to the music? Can some of you hold flags, play instruments, or be toy soldiers?" or "Can you walk like a big, fat elephant?" or "Let's see how you iron your clothes with doing 'The Mulberry Bush,'" or "Can you act out the story of the clock and the mouse in 'Hickory Dickory Dock'?" Thus, in informal rhythmic movement some guidance is given, but the child is free to move within the overall structure.

Many songs and finger plays that describe or imply physical actions should be sung to or with the young child to encourage his movement response. Songs such as "Row, Row, Row Your Boat," "Open, Shut Them," "Rockabye Baby," "Where is Thumbkin?" "The Noble Duke of York," "Paw Paw Patch," and "I'm a Little Teapot," among others, are excellent for inducing informal, nonstructured movement. As you or some children sing the song, the other children can move rhythmically to the music as they act out the words.

One very important type of informal rhythmic movement activity for the young child is the *singing game*. By the age of two, most children can begin to learn such simple games as "Ring Around the Rosy" and "The Mulberry Bush"; and by ages three or four, almost all children can learn most of the simple singing games used in early childhood education programs, such as "The Hokey Pokey," "London Bridge," "Looby Loo," and "The Farmer in the Dell." Some suggestions for using singing games with the young child are:

144

Singing games such as "London Bridge" stimulate rhythmic responses to music in the child. (Photo courtesy of Keiki Music School, Honolulu, Hawaii)

1. Know thoroughly the directions of the singing game beforehand. Write any difficult directions on a card that you hold as you teach the game.

2. Use only those singing games that require basic movements already familiar to the child; e.g., do not teach "Skip to My Lou" as a singing game until the child knows how to skip.

3. Teach the game in context with the music and song. The child should learn both the music and the required movements at the same time rather than learning the physical movements first and the music afterwards.

4. Do not always follow the prescribed directions for a singing game. Ask the child for ideas on what actions to do for "You do the hokey pokey" or "Here we go looby loo." In general, it is better to help the child devise his own game actions than to teach him prescribed motions. In this way, he will learn to use motions that correspond with the music and to move with the music.

5. It may be necessary to "walk" through the game and/ or practice the physical movements at a slower tempo *after* the child has responded to the music several times.

6. Encourage the child to move to the music's beat at all times. For example, the child should not just walk to "The Farmer in the Dell." He should clap and then step to the beat of the music as he performs the actions of the game.

7. After learning the singing game, it is often helpful to sing the words of the game while seated, and then sing and clap to the beat. In this way, the rhythmic feeling for the song can be felt, and the words and singing skills can be stressed.

Another important activity recommended to foster rhythmic movement is the use of *imitative movement* or *mimetic play* to music. In this activity, the child is asked to imitate certain objects, people, and events that are already familiar to him and to express this to a musical accompaniment. The child can imitate:

- the movement of animals and insects such as alliga-tors, butterflies, kangaroos, elephants, chickens, don-

146

keys, rabbits, snails, fish, geese, cows, ants, owls, horses and ponies, monkeys, snakes, crabs, frogs, lions, bears, ducks, mice, cats, dogs, bats, and goats, among others

- how people move when they work, play, and tend to household tasks
- objects relating to water such as boats, waves, waterfalls, dripping faucets, and buoys
- various elements in nature such as clouds, the wind, rain, snow, a misty fog, a storm, plant life, and plant growth
- specific activities or events that are meaningful to the child such as waking up in the morning, riding in the school bus, horses galloping, a band marching, snowflakes or raindrops dancing, birds running on the lawn; dogs, squirrels, or lambs frolicking; woodpeckers tapping on a tree; a carpenter hammering on wood; moving on the swings, digging at the beach, pushing a heavy wagon, driving a car, picking fruit, jumping rope, wading through mud; pretending to be leaves blowing in the wind, a spider weaving its web, and a bud growing in the warm sun.

Imitative movement activities can occur either by having the child first imitate objects or things that move and then adding musical accompaniment (a drum, tambourine, piano) to his actions or by playing some music and having the child imitate the movement in time to the music. Initially, the child who is two or older should learn to imitate the movement, and then you can add musical accompaniment. Once the child is able to do this, then music can be played prior to his movements. He can then learn to synchronize his movements with the music. At the preschool level, both techniques should be used, with increasing attention to movement to the music *after* it is heard.

Creative Rhythmic Movement

Creative rhythmic movement is another important bodily movement activity. It involves having the child use his body to interpret his feelings and thoughts about the music in his own way. No one tells him how and when to move; he moves as an expression of what he feels and knows as he listens. In one type of creative movement, the music is played and the movement follows it. The title of the music is not given to the child, nor are any directions given other than: "Move to the music and show in your body how the music makes you feel." You encourage the child, but do not suggest any movements. The desired response is a free, creative movement, stimulated by the music alone. In another type of creative movement, the child may be asked to express, through dramatic pantomime, an idea or story such as showing how he gets up in the morning, or how Goldilocks explored the house of the Three Bears. As the child acts out the story, you add improvised music, usually with a drum, piano, or rhythm instrument. The music and its rhythm are adjusted to the child's movements and serve to reinforce the child's creative rhythmic response.

Creative movement to music is a skill that can be developed from infancy. It begins when you move creatively to music with the baby in your arms or when the infant observes how you move creatively to recorded music. It continues as you encourage the baby to move creatively and with freedom to the songs and recordings he hears. By the time the child is two or three years old, he should have had many such experiences.

In general, there is some need for adult direction in developing creative movement skills in the child. However, there is a "fine line" between facilitating the child's own unique responses to the music and molding the responses into patterns that are yours and not the child's interpretations. Initially, you should encourage lots of child-initiated movement, whereby the child moves and you then improvise an accompaniment to fit the movements. This technique is especially useful for children between one and a half and four years of age and for older children who are inhibited or who lack movement experiences. Then use songs and singing games, whereby the child creates movement to fit the words and mood of the song (see pp. 144–146). You can also use various percussion instruments—e.g., the drum, tone block,

148

tambourine—to play rhythms; then invite the child to move to these rhythms in any way he sees fit.

To help the child move creatively to music you can use stories or events that stimulate the child's imagination. Ask the child to be a snowflake, or a circus clown, or a galloping horse. Or ask him to show in movement how Red Riding Hood walked through the woods, or how the Big Billy Goat Gruff crossed the dangerous bridge on his way to the pasture. After many experiences with moving to music with a story as a guide, it is then best to play music in which the child imagines his own story, based upon the mood and character of the music.

Your role in facilitating creative movement to music in the child aged two and above can be achieved by knowing how and when to ask certain questions. Each question should serve to help the child discover more about his own movement skills and how he can express his feelings and thoughts about the music through movement. Sample questions include:

- Can you move your hands in another way? Can you move only your head? Can you move your body higher? Can you push with your body?
- Can you lie on your stomach and move your hands to the music? What can you do with your head? your hips? your feet?
- Can you walk to the music? Can you move your head (or your hands) to the music as you walk?
- How can you show that the music is getting louder? How big can you grow? How small can you be when the music is soft?
- Can you move to the music like a snake? a rabbit? a frog? How would a beautiful fairy princess move to the music? If you were an airplane (a boat, a car, a rocket), how would you move?

Specific Ideas for Creative Movement

Some other suggestions for developing creative movement responses in the child are:

149

1. Provide opportunities to listen quietly before asking the child to move. Never ask him to move immediately during the first hearing.

2. Prepare for creative movement by having the child move rhythmically as he sits and listens. Help him move to the music by clapping, moving his hands and feet, moving his fingers and other parts of the body, and moving his entire body. Try to have him feel the rhythmic flow *before* he attempts to move creatively.

3. Motivate and stimulate, but try not to be too specific. Say: "Maybe this music reminds you of some animal or some bird," rather than saying: "Let's see if you can be an elephant to this elephant music."

4. Continually compliment the child on how he moves all his body parts, how he shows how he feels about the music through his movements, and how he moves in time to the music. Say: "I see the rhythm of the music in your feet," or "You are moving your body just as the music tells you."

5. If the music is very long, only play and move to one short section at a time.

6. To stimulate creative response, ask the child if he can hear where the music gets faster or slower, where it gets louder or softer, where it climbs up or slides down, and where it repeats or stops.

7. Use paper streamers, scarves, kerchiefs, and balloons to stimulate creative response. Use paper bag masks to help the shy child.

8. Frequently ask the child to close his eyes, listen to the music, and imagine what the music is trying to say.

9. Use words, descriptions, and pictures to stimulate imagination.

10. If working with a preschool class, divide it into two groups. Ask one group to watch the second group as it moves and to observe how the children move creatively to the music, using their whole bodies.

11. During a creative movement experience, also work on developing movement skills in using body parts, in walking, running, and hopping to music; and in varying movements by using different levels, directions, focus, quality, and range (see p. 132).

150

Specific Listening and Movement Activities

The nature and frequency of listening and movement experiences that you provide for the child from infancy through one and a half or two are very important to his musical and language growth. Many of these experiences should occur often throughout each day. In general, these experiences include:

- listening to and experimenting with many different types of sounds in the environment
- listening to various human voices as they speak, hum, chant, and sing
- listening to a wide variety of recorded and live music
- moving to music

For Infants

For the infant from birth to six months, some recommendations are:

1. There is need for only a few music materials or instruments during the first two months of life, since the infant sleeps most of the time. Have available several rhythm instruments, many sound-producing objects, a phonograph, and a varied collection of records.

2. Handle the infant's distress or discomfort by holding the child gently and rocking him in your arms or in a rocking chair or cradle. Rock him to a steady beat. If singing to him, make the song's beat conform to the rhythmic rocking. Also pat his back to the beat of the song.

3. Sing or hum frequently to the baby as you put him to sleep. Use lullabies, folk songs, nursery songs, and any other songs you know. Use your singing voice in connection with awakening or quieting the infant in order to develop a good feeling and a sense of security in connection with the human voice.

4. Talk to the infant as you feed, dress, or change him. Use a friendly tone of voice. Make up chants about the

151

infant and what you are doing with him, e.g., sing: "You are taking a bath," or "Now it's time to eat."

5. Talk and sing to the infant at close range as you play with him. Make funny sounds. Sing "la-la-la" and other patterns. Encourage older children and adults to talk, chant, and sing to him.

6. Let the baby see you as you talk or sing to other people or read to older children.

7. When approaching the baby, call and sing his name and tell him you are coming and what you will be doing (examples: "It's time to change your diaper" or "Here is your toy"). Start before he can see you or before you enter the room, and continue until you reach him. Walk naturally and not quietly, so that the sound of footsteps will let him know you are approaching.

8. Provide on a daily basis recorded music in the baby's environment. Play music for him in the early morning, at nap time, when he is bathing, when he is ready for sleep, and when feeding him.

9. Sing nursery songs with actions. Take the baby's hands, and have him join in with simple movements.

10. Rock and bounce the child to recorded music as he faces you. Sing or chant "la-la" with the music. Rock the infant on your knees as he lies on your stomach, facing you.

11. Play music or sing for the infant. Place him on his back on a sturdy blanket. Using two people at opposite sides, pick up all four ends and gently swing him side to side to the music. Make sure the child can see you.

12. Hang a musical mobile within reach of the baby's hands. Place various sound-producing objects on the mobile. Show the child how he can produce sound by touching the mobile with his hands or feet. The mobile should be sturdy and fastened securely to the crib or to a rope strung across the crib, the playpen, or a portion of the room. It should produce sounds the infant likes. If possible, it should be attached to elastic so that it can be moved in different ways (sideways, bouncing up and down, swaying). *Important reminder*: Beware of possible hazards of some instruments. Make sure they cannot be swallowed; check them for sharp edges or splinters.

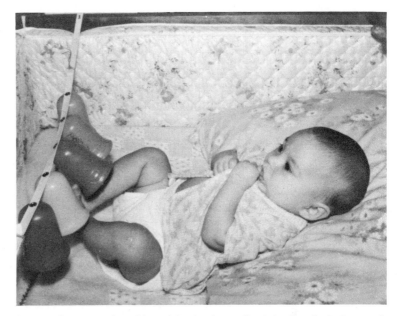

Suspending sound-making objects above the infant's crib fosters early musical responses. (Photo courtesy of Joseph and Katherine A. O'Reilly)

13. One of the best sound-making instruments for the infant is the small jingle bell or wrist bell. Suspend a bell or series of bells within the infant's reach. At times, lower it so that his waving or kicking motions can hit the bells and make them ring. Also use different types of small bells, all of which are available in toy shops and are relatively inexpensive. Ring one bell at a time, and let the infant handle it and make it sound. Put two bells together and ring them for a new sound. Sew a series of bells on a piece of cloth, and let the infant hold and shake the cloth.

14. Attach some small bells to elastic or cloth and put these around the infant's wrists or ankles, so that when he moves, the sounds from the instruments will be heard. Place the bells on the child's wrists or ankles; then place them on both wrists and ankles. Use bells of different pitch so that the sounds he makes will differ as he moves different parts of his body.

15. Place the infant on his back. Shake a bell seven to ten inches from his eyes, to the left and then to the right **153** of his head. Use other sound makers such as brightly colored rattles with low tones, different colored rattles with high tones, rattles with faces painted on them, and squeaky rubber toys. Shake the bells and rattles loudly and softly. Repeat the activity, with the baby lying on his stomach, or sitting in a carrying seat, or held sitting on your lap, or held over your shoulder.

16. When ringing a bell or rattle, place this against the cheek or arms of the child, so that he feels the vibrations of sound. Also use a triangle, tuning fork, cooking pots, and covers of pots or cans.

17. Place a small instrument in the child's hands so that he can feel the texture and shape of it. Help the child move the instrument to produce sound.

18. Hold the child very still. When a sound is made by another person or when a phone rings or a plane passes by, move the child and turn him to face the sound source, or simply give the child a slight lift in your arms.

19. Make different sounds by knocking on wood, cans, and other material. Acknowledge the source of sound by showing the child the object, smiling and showing pleasure at the sound, and becoming more animated. Say or chant: "That was a _____," or "Listen to the _____." Touch the child's arm, head, or face as you say or chant this.

20. Listen with the child to music on the phonograph or the radio. When the music starts, rock or move to its beat and rhythm. When it stops, stand very still. Hold the child as you do this, or have him watch you.

21. Sing and hum tunes, with your head and lips against the baby's head so that he "feels" the song. Occasionally turn the infant and encourage him to look at your mouth and touch it.

22. Sing to the infant. Encourage him to touch your mouth. Occasionally put his hand over your mouth so that the singing stops. Then let him watch your mouth as you sing again.

23. Help the child hold an instrument and shake it so that he feels his own movement with sound.

24. Pick up the infant and hold him. Hit various objects in the home and outdoors as he listens and watches (see list of sound sources for experimentation, pp. 135–136).

154

25. Obtain small tins and spice cans filled with rice, beans, buttons, and other small objects, and secure them with hard-to-open lids. Shake each can for the infant, and then let him handle and examine it. Frequently change the objects placed in the cans.

26. Talk and sing to the infant during everyday activities so that he becomes familiar with your voice. Encourage other family members to do the same.

27. Call and sing loudly, then softly, to the child. Use high and low pitches.

28. Notice which instruments and sounds the child prefers. Use these more often than other sound makers.

29. Tape-record familiar voices or sounds, and play these on the tape recorder for the infant.

For Ages Six Months to Two Years

Most of the activities already suggested for the infant from birth to six months of age should be continued from ages six months to one and a half or two years. In addition, depending upon the developmental level of the child, consider the following recommendations:

1. Place a rattle in the infant's hand. If he does not spontaneously move, hit the rattle, and then help him by gently tapping or moving his arm at his elbow. Move his arm so that the rattle is about six inches from his eyes. Show him the rattle and help him move it. Encourage him to explore the rattle with movement. At first, use easy-to-grasp, thick-handled rattles; later use thinner handles and other easy-to-hold instruments. Repeat this activity many times, using bells, rhythm sticks, and other instruments.

2. When sound is heard, bring the child close to its source in order to touch and see it. For example, take him to the telephone when it rings. When airplanes and trucks are heard, go to the window with him, point, and say: "Look at the airplane (or truck). It goes ____." When the television, phonograph, or radio is on, bring the child close to it to touch and hear it.

155

3. Place a record on the phonograph, and dance to it. Walk to the phonograph, touch it, talk about it, listen to the music, and continue to dance. Then pick up the infant and dance with him in your arms.

4. Play a wide variety of musical selections on the phonograph or tape recorder for the child at times when he is most likely to be awake. The adult should not be in sight of the child so as not to distract him, since at this age, especially between six and ten months, he is more interested in human faces than in sound.

5. Listen to music with a definite beat, and dance with the child as you carry him. Bounce the child on your knees or lap, rock him in a sitting position, and snap and clap your hands to the music as the child sits with you.

6. Encourage the child to join in rhythmic movement with you. Tap his arms, clap his hands, and shake with him. Hold him in a standing position so he can bounce to the music's rhythm.

7. Place a wooden box, a pan, and a pail in front of the infant. Play repeated rhythmic sequences on all three objects, such as:

PLAY: box pan   pail pail

as the child follows. Let the child experiment with these sound-producing objects. Often repeat this activity, using other sound makers.

8. Provide many crib toys that hang within the reach of the infant, including instruments that make sounds when shaken or hit, e.g., bells, tambourines, rattles, maracas.

9. Take the infant around the house and outdoors, and expose him to as many different sounds as possible.

10. Move to the rhythm of things you see (a dog eating, a boy riding a bicycle), and encourage imitation by the child. Also imitate for the child how he eats, drinks, and plays.

11. When it's raining and you are in the car with the infant, sing "Rain, Rain Go Away" or 'It's Raining, It's

156

Pouring," and rock the child to the beat of the windshield wiper.

12. Play and sing movement games and finger plays like "Row, Row, Row Your Boat," "Open, Shut Them" and "This Little Piggy Went to Market" as you move the child's body parts to the game.

13. Play rhythm instruments to the beat of songs and recorded music. Encourage the child to join in with you.

14. Using sounds the child likes, make these sounds when sitting or standing behind him. When he turns, show him how to make these sounds.

15. Take the child into the kitchen to see, hear, and smell cooking and frying, the gurgling dishwasher, popcorn popping, and water running in the sink.

16. Give the child a box full of small, unbreakable objects as he sits in the high chair or at the table. Encourage him to drop the objects, listen, and see where they fall.

17. Use toys that rock and make sounds, such as rolypoly clowns, Japanese rocking dolls, rocking horses, and other toys that go back and forth into an upright position after they are moved sideways. You can also use music boxes.

18. Clap your hands and then clap the child's hands. Play "pat-a-cake" as you keep a steady beat with the child.

19. Listen to quiet sounds, e.g., the ticking of a clock or watch, water running in a pipe, the flow of bathwater, the clicking of the light switch, the wind and rain, keys jingling.

20. Have the child bang coffee cans on their tops, insides, and sides, using big and small spoons of metal, wood, and plastic.

21. Have the child touch objects that visibly vibrate when they sound, such as the telephone, bells, tuning forks, cymbals, two pot covers hit together, triangles, strings on the guitar and Autoharp, and most metal objects.

22. Move about the house with the child as he creeps,

157 crawls, and walks. Encourage the child as he knocks or rubs on the wood, rugs, walls, metal, paper, furniture, and cushions, and as he listens to the sounds he makes.

23. Hide behind a sofa or chair, and make various sounds to attract the child to find out what is making the noise.

24. Let the child use lots of "blowing things," such as paper horns, whistles, tonettes, straws, and recorders.

25. Place the child in a swing, and sing a song to the beat of the swing's movement.

26. Chant to the child about things and events in his environment, using a variety of melody patterns.

27. Request "clap," "sing," or "dance" when music is being played, but do not use gestures. If there is no response, use a gesture, and repeat the word for the child.

28. Speak to the child with extra emphasis on words and inflections. Use a variety of vocal inflections (see pp. 178–183 for specific listening activities as they relate to singing).

Planning and Implementing Activities

In planning experiences in listening and rhythmic movement for the young child, consider the following:

1. Some movement should occur during *every* musical experience. Sometimes it may be the main activity, such as listening to records and moving creatively to the music, or learning a singing game, or moving like soldiers or lions to the music. At other times, movement will have a relatively less important role in the experience, such as singing songs and clapping their beats, or tapping rhythmic patterns on instruments. Nevertheless, rhythmic movement is an essential activity during every activity in music and, as such, should occur on a daily basis.

2. The young child tires quickly as a result of movement. Plan to alternate movement with quiet activities to be done when the child is seated.

3. Every time there is a movement activity, plan to work on some movement skills, even though the emphasis will be on the musical response. Work on ways to move the body and its parts, use various types of movement, and use space in a variety of ways (see pp. 129–133).

4. Always prepare the child for movement by first having him listen to the music and respond to it as he is seated (by clapping, hitting his thighs, tapping his foot). After this response, then he can rise and move rhythmically to the music.

5. Try to encourage movement to recorded music at least two to three times a week.

6. Plan frequent experiences that encourage the child to move to both familiar and unfamiliar songs.

7. Try to introduce the child to at least one new recording a week. If in a preschool, plan on at least two to three weekly group music periods that involve listening to recorded instrumental and vocal music and responding to it.

8. Group music periods in preschool that focus on listening and movement will take longer than activities devoted to singing. Remember that recorded selections generally take longer to play than songs sung by the children. Allow time for setting up the phonograph, finding the album, and placing the needle on the correct record band each time a piece is played.

9. Plan to involve the child in the music as soon as possible. You will quickly lose his attention if you allow him to sit too long as you prepare the phonograph or play the music.

10. During a group music time, where movement to records may be the focal activity, also include some singing, creating, and playing instruments. Vary the activities as much as you can.

11. Use a variety of music in your listening time. Remember that there is much value in listening and moving to many different styles of music.

When presenting recorded music to a preschool group, you will need to set some standards for listening. Above all, you must set an example of how to listen to
159 music. Sit with the children as the record is played, and

listen to the music. If you feel like moving to it, do so as you remain seated. Show that there is much in the music to listen for by sitting quietly and attentively as the music is being played. You should also discuss with the children why everyone should listen quietly to the music and the need to respect other listeners. You, other adults, and the children should all show that your full attention is on discovering what the music is trying to communicate. Since there is much to listen for and respond to each time a piece of music is heard, you should be a musical learner, side by side with the children.

An adult-directed, listening–movement experience using recordings cannot be presented simply by playing the record for the child. You have certain responsibilities. You must be familiar with the music. This means that you have listened to it several times and noted the musical aspects—the beat, tempo, melody, tone color, mood, and other elements—to which you hope the child will respond. Before playing the record for the child, you need to determine its suitability and to plan some approach and activity that will motivate the child to experience and discover the various musical elements in the piece. You must hear and feel what is in the music before guiding the child to listen to it.

Activities in Rhythmic Movement

Certain procedures and activities are recommended in using rhythmic movement activities, whether they take place in the home or school. These suggestions include:

1. Encourage the child to take off his shoes. This will allow for a freer type of movement.

2. Set certain limits on the space to be used. Define the area of the movement.

3. Have a clear and open space. Move chairs to the side, and shift other furniture.

4. Encourage complete freedom of movement in which the child listens and moves freely to the music with

little or no structuring. Alternate this with times where you help the child in his body movement and in his synchronization of the movement with the music. Do not stop a child from experimenting with movement, even though it does not fit into your plan.

5. Frequently compliment the child on his efforts. Be specific with your praise ("You are moving your body so well to the music's beat," or "It's nice to see how well you are moving up and down to the music."). Reinforce responses that are unique and different.

6. Emphasize the need to stop when the music stops or pauses.

7. Often have the child clap or sway to the music's beat and tempo, so that he concentrates on the music's rhythmic flow before moving creatively around the room.

8. Accept the child's responses rather than spending time on drilling or practicing prescribed movements.

9. Do not refer to pieces of music as suited only to specific movements, such as saying, "This is running music," or "Can you play the tone blocks to this galloping music?" Use the same music for different movements to avoid such associations.

10. Encourage the child to add instruments or props (flags, hoops, cartons and boxes, pictures, netting, elastic, ribbons, scarves, cloth, balloons, paper streamers, bean bags, balls of varying sizes, tissue paper, cord, and rope) to accompany movement.

11. Replay many recorded selections several times during the year. The more exposure to the music, the more the child will get to know the music and its particular qualities.

12. Provide frequent (daily, if possible) and short listening periods, rather than infrequent, longer periods. The child will not learn to listen to and enjoy recorded music if it is played only once a week.

13. Try to find a way of letting the child express an individual response to what he has heard. For most children, this response will be through movement. For many, it will be through playing instruments. For a very few, it will be through discussion.

161

14. Do not interrupt a listening experience by questioning or discussion. Do not talk during the listening experience, except to point out briefly a specific aspect of the music (example: "That's the piano you hear," or "Oh, the music is starting to get faster").

15. Have a listening corner (center) with records, a phonograph, and earphones for individual listening. Provide time for quiet listening and the free selection of recordings.

16. Plan a concert of favorite records. Invite other children and parents to attend.

17. Plan many "favorite record" days or a concert of favorite records. Invite other children and parents to attend.

18. Encourage the child to find, cut, and paste pictures of musical groups and instruments from old magazines.

In the preschool environment, listening and rhythmic movement activities can be somewhat chaotic unless the teacher works on certain procedures and routines. Some of these include:

1. Have the children spread out, rather than gather in clustered groups. Space should be ample enough, so that when the children spread their hands, they cannot touch anyone else.

2. Stress certain rules, such as: (a) no one is to touch or bump into anyone else when moving; (b) all children must be quiet when moving, so that the music can be heard; (c) everyone must move only within the defined space; and (d) everyone must move when the music starts and stop when the music stops.

3. To help solve problems of space, you may need to decide on and limit the direction of the movement ("move in your own space only," "move in a line," "move within an imaginary circle").

4. All the children do not need to move at once. At times, it is valuable to have others watch as some move. Yet involve all the children. Those watching could be

162 evaluating, looking for specific movement patterns, clapping to the beat, playing instruments, or watching a particular effort by one or more children.

5. Ask the children not to face one direction or look at the "audience." Encourage them to move in all directions.

6. Consider the length of the piece and the child's attention span when planning to use a recording. If needed, only play excerpts from the music. Adapt directed listening experiences to the child's previous experiences, attention span, and interests.

7. Always give specific and clear directions when attempting rhythmic movement activities.

8. Compliment those children who make up their own interpretations rather than copying other children's movements.

9. Do not single out or comment on movements while the children are in motion, for this may stimulate imitation. Similarly, do not call attention to the child who has trouble moving to the music.

Activities for Repeated Hearings of Music

The enjoyment of music is partially derived from familiarity. This is dependent upon repeated meaningful hearings of the music. You should find interesting ways to repeat the music, so that the child will become more interested in it through repeated hearings. Some ways to vary the listening experience include:

1. Hold the child and move with him to the music.
2. Clap, stamp, and tap to the beat of the music.
3. Stand or become bigger when the music becomes louder, and sit or become smaller when the music becomes softer.
4. Move to the mood or accents in the music.
5. Point to pictures of instruments heard in the music.

163 6. Add a rhythm instrument accompaniment.

7. Have one child or group move to one section of the music and another child or group move to a contrasting section.

8. Raise hands every time the music gets loud, or increases its speed, or pauses; or raise hands when you hear a drum, or a female singer, or a loud accent.

9. Use visual aids such as marking the beat, rhythm, or other rhythmic or melodic characteristics on the chalkboard, e.g.,

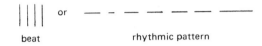

beat   rhythmic pattern

10. Ask specific questions that focus on the musical elements; e.g., "What did you hear while you listened? How did it make you feel? Did you like the music? Can you tell why? Was it fast or slow? loud or soft?"

11. Occasionally play the piece and follow it with a contrasting selection. Compare the two pieces.

Improving the Child's Rhythmic Response

The ability to move to music involves coordination of the mind, ear, and muscles. Although the child will want to move to music during infancy, he normally will not be able to coordinate his movements with what he hears until at least age three. Many children will not develop this coordination until several years later. There always will be a few children who will have trouble moving to the rhythm of the music and will not follow the beat or respond to the prescribed patterns of rhythm set forth in the music.

Activities

Some suggestions for improving the rhythmic coordination of young children from birth to two are:

1. Frequently hold the child and move rhythmically to the beat of the music.

2. Rhythmically bounce the child on your lap or knees as the music plays.

3. Hold the child's hands or feet and move them rhythmically to the music.

4. Play pat-a-cake with the child as you clap rhythmically to the music.

5. Push the child on a swing or in a rocker as you sing a song, with the beat matching the child's movements. Also swing the child in the air as you sing.

In order to improve the rhythmic coordination of young children aged two to five, repeat many of the activities just suggested for children from birth to two. In addition:

1. Have several children join hands together with you and swing rhythmically to the music.

2. Face the child, take his hands, and move them in a rowing motion to the music's rhythm.

3. Have some children form a line of "cars," join hands to the elbows, and play "train" as their arms move together to the music.

4. Ask the child to walk or hop. Add a rhythm instrument accompaniment to his movement. Ask the child to play a walking rhythm on the instrument. Join in with him.

5. Hold the child's hands and march or walk with him to the music's beat.

6. Play some easy rhythmic patterns on the rhythm sticks. Ask the child to match them. If he has problems, ask him to play his own patterns, and then join in with him. Encourage him to keep together with you.

7. Use many activities designed to develop rhythmic concepts (see pp. 260–262 and pp.264–266).

8. Use many pieces of music that are neither too fast nor too slow. Adjust the song you sing to the child's rhythmic movements.

165

By assisting each child in reaching his potential for listening and responding rhythmically to music, you will be making significant headway in helping the child achieve aesthetic satisfaction and growth in musical experiences.

Summary

All musical experiences involve listening to music. The young child's feelings and understandings about the music he listens to are shown primarily through physical movement. Give the infant and preschooler many opportunities to make and listen to sounds within the environment and to listen to both live and recorded music. Provide activities to foster each child's ability to move rhythmically to this music. Pay attention to movement skills and how the child uses his body to express what he hears. Choose a wide selection of recordings, action songs, singing games, finger plays, and instrumental experiences. Rhythmic activities should provide a balance of structured, informal, and creative movement experiences. Careful planning and specific teaching procedures are important for fostering each child's ability to listen and move to a wide variety of music. If successfully done, listening and rhythmic movement activities will be two basic modes of expression that will develop each child's potential to respond aesthetically to music.

Selected Readings

Each of the following texts contains valuable information on listening experiences and rhythmic movement with children:

Barnett, Elise Braun, *Montessori and Music*: *Rhythmic Activities for Young Children*. New York: Schocken Books, 1973.

Listening and Rhythmic Movement

Cherry, Clare, *Creative Movement for the Developing Child*, rev. ed. Belmont, Calif.: Fearon Publishers, 1971.

Clark, Carol E., *Rhythmic Activities for the Classroom*. Danville, N. Y.: The Instructor Publications, 1969.

Fleming, Gladys Andrews, *Creative Rhythmic Movement: Boys and Girls Dancing*. Englewood Cliffs, N. J.: Prentice–Hall, Inc., 1976.

Gerhardt, Lydia A., *Moving and Knowing: The Young Child Orients Himself in Space*. Englewood Cliffs, N. J.: Prentice–Hall, Inc., 1973.

Saffran, Rosanna, *First Book of Creative Rhythms*. New York: Holt, Rinehart and Winston, 1963.

Sheehy, Emma, *Children Discover Music and Dance*. New York: Teachers College Press, Columbia University, 1968.

Smith, Robert B., *Music in the Child's Education*. New York: The Ronald Press, 1970, pp. 69–92, 119–136.

Singing is a joyful activity for all children. (Photo courtesy of Hannah Lou Bennett, University Preschool, University of Hawaii, and Will Kyselka, photographer)

6

Singing

Besides listening and rhythmic movement, another essential experience that all young children should have in their music education is singing. This chapter emphasizes how the young child can be educated musically through singing. It reviews the origins of singing response in the child, describes what types of vocalizations and songs to use, provides specific suggestions on how to develop singing responses and vocal skills, recommends ways to teach songs, and offers many other "how-to-do-it" ideas for singing with the young child.

The Young Child Sings

The voice is the child's primary musical instrument. This instrument is uniquely personal and expressive. It is always with him, whether he plays, watches his parent work in the kitchen, or walks in the park. The child's singing voice will be his own instrument for life, and as such, needs careful nurturance and development from the beginning of infancy.

The child learns to sing from birth (see pp. 55–65 for detailed discussion). Many of his first vocalizations, including the cry and the coo, are musical, since they are rhythmic tones of varying pitch and intensity. The basis of all singing, as well as spoken language, originates in these earliest vocalizations. As the infant grows, he gradually begins to gain control of, and to experiment with, his voice. He imitates certain vocal sounds he hears in his environment. He uses rising and falling vocal inflections. He makes different vocal sounds. He babbles and soon learns to say some words. He makes speech sounds on various pitch levels (musical babbles"). By age two, he begins to sing tonal patterns and make up chants. And in one or two more years, he can sing songs he has created and that he has learned in preschool or from his parents and friends. By age five, the child has made considerable progress in learning how to use his vocal instrument.

The young child vocalizes throughout the day. As an infant, he experiments by cooing, gurgling, and babbling. He makes musical sounds in his crib, at lunchtime, and before nap. A year or two later, he sings as he washes, dresses, prepares to eat, plays, climbs, and rides in a car or bus. He sings short tunes that he has created about his pet dog or his doll. He sings nonsense syllables as he builds with blocks. He chants rhythmically as he pounds the clay. He sings "Jingle Bells" at a family Christmas gathering. For the young child, singing is a meaningful activity in his life. He sings because he wishes to express himself and to convey ideas and moods, and he sings for the sheer enjoyment of the activity.

Young children differ in their ability to sing. Some infants will be more vocal than others. Musical babbling (see pp. 58–59) begins at different ages and varies from one infant to the next. Some children will create tunes by age one and a half; others may not sing until at least age three. Some will be able to sing in tune by age two; others will not master this ability until age four or later. Some will rarely open their mouths when they sing, and if they do, the words and tones of the song will be muffled and/or inaccurate. Some may sing vigorously, but the tones will be chanted on one or two pitch levels, with only occasional attention to the rise and fall of the melody's pitches. Some children will sing most of the tones correctly, but will have difficulty with the rhythm or the pronunciation of the words. Others will be able to sing quite well by themselves, but will not be able to match their pitches with that of the group. Some will be able to sing well with a group, but will refuse to sing by themselves. And some will able to sing well with both the group and alone. Despite the differences in children's abilities to sing, it seems evident that *all children can learn to sing at their own rate of development* (see pp. 55–65 for further discussion of developmental stages in singing). How you can help develop the potential of every child to sing is the objective of this chapter.

Singing: A Learned Behavior

Learning how to sing, like learning language, is a long process that begins at birth (see pp. 55–65). The young child must hear singing in his environment. He must sense that it is an enjoyable, rewarding experience for both the singer and the listener. He must experiment with making vocal sounds and with using various vocal inflections in these experimentations. He must learn to remember tones and groups of tones and then be able to match these with his voice. He must learn to remember the words of songs and their appropriate pitches. He must learn how to use the chest and head registers of his voice, expand his vocal range from only a few tones to eight or more tones, and sing with a variety of dynamics and expression. Learning how to sing is not a single, automatic task; rather, it involves a complex set of behaviors that require the adult's encouragement and guidance.

The young child is influenced greatly by adults and the way we sing. If we sing well, with expression, clear pronunciation, good tone production, accurate pitch and **173** rhythm, and good breath support and posture, then the child probably will do the same. If we show in our manner that we are interested in and enjoy singing, this will influence the child's attitudes toward singing. Our role in developing the singing response of the young child is to provide models for singing well, to encourage spontaneous vocalization when it does occur, to expand the child's song repertoire by singing and playing many songs for him, and to teach the child how to sing a wide variety of songs appropriate to his interests and ability.

Songs for the Child

The song repertoire for the young child should aim for a balance between the child's own songs and those of the culture. The younger the child is, the more difficult it will be for him to learn other people's songs. For him, song repertoire begins with his own songs—the chants, tonal patterns, and short tunes he creates during the day. These songs become the nucleus of the young child's repertoire. However, as the child matures, you can teach him more and more songs to complement his own creative vocal expressions.

The *chant* is one of the most important types of songs utilized in early childhood. This song, resembling a "speech-song," consists of nonsense syllables, word patterns, and rhymes repeated on one, two, or three tones. The young child, beginning at about age two, makes up chants about what he does and what he sees. Typically, the chant sung by the child consists of two or three different tones, repeated in sequence, such as:

Hel-lo mom-my! You can't catch me. La-nee, la-nee boo-boo. I am 3 years old.

These traditional "children's chants," whose tones are common to many children all over the world, are characterized by the descending minor third (bracketed in the above examples) and the use of tones 3, 5, and 6 of the major scale. Chants such as these should provide the **174** "backbone" for singing experiences in early childhood.

You should chant frequently with the child, asking him to:

Repeat what you say, using "la" or "oo:"

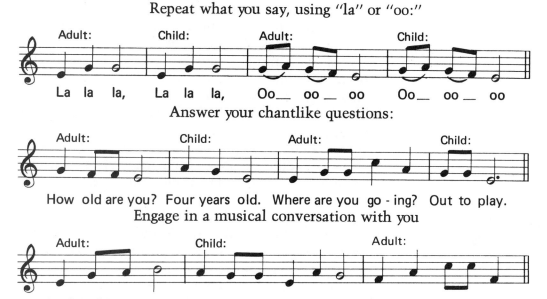

La la la, La la la, Oo__ oo __ oo Oo__ oo __ oo

Answer your chantlike questions:

How old are you? Four years old. Where are you go - ing? Out to play.

Engage in a musical conversation with you

Let's build a house. I want to build a farm. That's a good i - dea.

Some common chants or chantlike songs include: "It's Raining, It's Pouring," "Rain, Rain, Go Away," "Ring Around the Rosy," and "A Tisket, A Tasket." Several chants appropriate for young children are found on pp. 287–296 of the text.

Besides the chant, what other songs should be used with the young child? As already stated, the music and songs we use should reflect our musical heritage. Nursery and Mother Goose songs, seasonal songs, simple folk songs, hymns and spirituals, lullabies, humorous songs, action songs, popular songs, and songs from various cultures are recommended. "Contrived children's songs" about the robin redbreast, the names of the months, or the witch on the broomstick should be avoided. If a song is to be used to teach about a policeman's job, or how to cross the street safely, or how to name the colors, it is best that the words of the song be recited to the child as in a poem and that the child be encouraged to *create his own tune* to the words. In this way, the creative potential of the child can be developed (see pp. 240–242), and the

175

child need not be exposed to contrived songs designed to educate the young in nonmusical learnings. Some recommended songs suitable for the young child are found in the Appendix of this book.

When selecting songs, keep in mind that many traditional songs that have been passed on from one generation to another have been used successfully with young children for many years. They are traditional songs simply because children like to hear and sing them. Many nursery and Mother Goose songs, work songs, religious songs and spirituals, and "fun" songs provide ample material for the young child's song repertoire. In addition, songs from the child's own ethnic and religious background and children's songs from other cultures should be sung. A few contemporary songs, such as those from *Sesame Street*, or "You Are My Sunshine," "Love Makes the World Go 'Round," or the refrain from the rock song "Joy to the World" will add variety to the child's repertoire.

Echo songs, question-and-answer songs, and cumulative songs are very popular with preschool children. Echo songs such as "Are You Sleeping?" are useful for helping the child listen and then sing on pitch. Question-and-answer songs such as "The Muffin Man" encourage independence in singing. Cumulative songs, in which there are many verses sung to the same melody,—e.g., "This Old Man," "Alouette," and "Bought Me a Cat"—enable the child to repeat the melody many times as the different words are sung.

Children aged four and under are egocentric, i.e., their world and their activities focus around themselves. They have little interest or facility in communicating with others, and they are still being socialized. Singing and other musical activities for this age are best implemented when they appeal to each individual child at his own level, using his own body movements and songs relating directly to his own interests and needs. Thus, at this age, songs involving the children's names, body parts, family, clothing, and food are usually very popular.

Many songs have one or two words that may be difficult for the child to understand. Some "purists" object to altering any words of a song to suit the learner.

176

Other educators often change all the words of a song to suit the situation. Perhaps no "hard-and-fast" rules should be set. In a song such as "Round and Round the Village," it is acceptable to change the word *village* to *city* or *schoolyard* or *table*. Similarly, adding verses to "Skip to My Lou," such as "Run, run, run around," or "Hop, hop, up and down," can extend the general character of the song. However, it is objectionable to change all the words of a song to fit a science or social studies learning, since the emotional–aesthetic meaning of the original song may be altered significantly. For example, singing "Let us go to brush our teeth" to the melody of "London Bridge" essentially destroys the song's original intent. An original tune or chant to accompany the walk to the bathroom for toothbrushing is preferable to using the tune of a familiar song.

What are the characteristics of songs to be used with the young child? The songs should exhibit at least some of the following attributes. They should:

- have aesthetic value, convey moods, and have inherent beauty (examples: "Twinkle, Twinkle Little Star," "Hush Little Baby," "He's Got the Whole World in His Hands")
- have frequent repetition of the melody, words, and rhythmic patterns (examples: "This Old Man," "When the Saints Go Marching In," "Skip to My Lou," "We Wish You a Merry Christmas")
- have words that are understandable and easy to remember (examples: "Go Tell Aunt Rhodie," "Happy Birthday," "If You're Happy")
- be short and simple (examples: "Ring Around the Rosy," "Mary Had a Little Lamb," "Kumbayah")
- have definite and easy-to-remember rhythms (examples: "The Hokey Pokey," "Hickory Dickory Dock," "Go In and Out the Window")
- have relatively limited vocal ranges (not more than an octave, as from C to C, or D to D), and tunes that are easy to sing (examples: "A Tisket, A Tasket," "The Muffin Man," "Where is Thumbkin?")

- be fun to sing (examples: "The Bus Song," "Spider and Spout," "Shortnin' Bread")
- have a variety of moods, with some songs being fast and peppy, some slow and moody, some lilting, and some marchlike

Songs with accompanying body movements, or with nonsense syllables, or with stories about characters or animals are definite favorites for most young children.

Songs appropriate for the young child are available from several sources. There are a number of songbooks that contain collections of songs for the very young. Most kindergarten and first-grade songbooks from elementary school music series have many songs suitable for preschool-aged children. Folk-song books are another source of quality songs. Many parents and preschool teachers have a large repertoire of easy songs that may be used with the young. Some songs heard on radio or television can also be used. And, of course, one of the best sources of songs is the child himself. These are the songs that he has learned in the home, from his parents and older siblings, or from radio and television. These are the songs that he has created in his play. These are the songs that have the most meaning for the young child in his life.

Helping the Young Child to Sing

How can you help the young child develop his ability to sing pitches and rhythms accurately? Some suggestions for working with the child from birth to one year, six months (Stage 1, "The First Vocalizations," and Stage 2, "Vocal Experimentation and Sound Imitation"—see pp. 56–61) are:

1. Frequently sing to the infant. Allow him to touch your face as he listens. Move rhythmically with him as you sing.

2. Have older children and adults sing to the child at different times. The infant should be given the opportunity of hearing many types of voices: women's *and* men's.

3. Play many recordings of songs for the infant, including folk songs, art songs, operatic selections, pop songs, choral music, and ethnic songs.

4. Encourage happy, spontaneous sounds by making funny noises, gently bouncing or tickling the infant, laughing and chuckling, and playing simple "peek-a-boo" games.

5. Allow the child to hear voices with specific intonations and with a variety of emotions.

6. Imitate the infant's joyful sounds as soon as they are made.

7. Tape-record the infant's vocalizations, and play these back for the infant.

8. When the child babbles and vocalizes, show pleasure. Smile, repeat his sounds, and fondle him.

9. If the child is making sounds, do not interrupt him.

10. Encourage the child to imitate your babbling by playfully producing sounds you have heard him make. At first, use the labial consonants *p*, *m*, and *b*, combined with the open-mouthed "ah," e.g., "pa-pa," "ma-ma," and "ba-ba." Do not use two consonants in a vocalization, as "ma-ba," or "pa-ma." Syllables should be limited to two or three per vocalization.

11. Emphasize vocalization of double-consonant sounds. Use words that can be produced as double consonants, such as *mama*, *dada*, *bye-bye*, *oh-oh*, and *no-no*.

12. Encourage all spontaneous vocalizations by patting the child and repeating his sounds.

13. Use and repeat many chants that describe the activities of the child, such as:

Tom-my is tak-ing a bath. Jean-nie is play-ing with a doll.

14. Chant many poems and rhymes to the child, emphasizing their rhythmic flow and feeling. Use exaggerated rising and falling vocal inflections. Also let him hear many questions (rising inflection) and statements (falling inflection).

Some suggestions for working with the child from one year, six months, to age three (Stage 3, "Approximation of Singing"—see pp. 61–63) are:

1. Continue to sing to the child, and play many song recordings for him.

2. Continue to chant many poems and rhymes.

3. Sing familiar poems and rhymes on one pitch, and then on two or three pitches. For example:

Good morn - ing to you, and how do you do? (or)

Hump - ty dump - ty sat on a wall.

4. Chant familiar language patterns; e.g., "you are walking," or "my name is Billy." Again, stress the rhythmic patterns, and exaggerate the vocal inflections. Sing these patterns on one and then two pitches. Also chant the names of people and objects in the environment.

5. Frequently engage in singing nonsense or fun syllables, such as "beep-beep, got a jeep," "ting-a-ling-a-ling," and "bi-pi-dee-bop."

6. Use familiar, traditional playground and jump-rope chants, such as:

You can't___ catch me   Jump high, jump low.

7. Imitate the sound of the wind, a ghost, a bird, an airplane, a siren, an auto horn, or the familiar musical

180

Singing logo of the NBC radio and television networks.* For example:

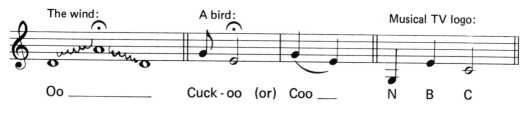

The wind: Oo _____

A bird: Cuck-oo (or) Coo ___

Musical TV logo: N   B   C

Have the child imitate these sounds.

8. Encourage the child to call from far away, sustaining the vowel. Use "hello—" and "Where are you—?

9. Use many echo games, with the adult (or child) singing a tonal pattern and the others in the room echoing.

10. Use many tone calls (repeated patterns from songs). For example, sing "ding, ding, dong" ("Are You Sleeping"), or "jingle bells," or "e-i-e-i-o" ("Old MacDonald"), or "this way and that way and . . ." ("Did You Ever See a Lassie?").

11. Begin to teach the child many songs with a limited tonal range and with "catchy" tunes or tonal patterns (examples: "Ring Around the Rosy," "Jingle Bells," "Mary Had a Little Lamb," "He's Got the Whole World in His Hands," "Michael, Row the Boat Ashore").

12. Reinforce the pitches of a song on the piano or bell-like instruments (see pp. 211–214).

13. Use a tape recorder to let the child hear himself and to record progress.

14. Play the "elevator game," with the hands and body going up and down while singing "la" to different pitches. Stop at different "floors" to correspond with changing pitch levels.

15. Use a ladder, steps, step bells, bell-like instruments turned vertically (see pp. 211–214), and drawings of a ladder or steps on the chalkboard. Move up and down as the pitches go high and low.

16. Have the child cup one ear as he sings. This will help direct the child's attention to his own singing.

Some suggestions for working with the child ages three to five (Stage 4—Singing Accuracy: Limited Range," and Stage 5, "Singing Accuracy: Expanded Range"—see pp. 63–65) include:

1. Continue singing many songs to the child, and play many song recordings for him. Also continue the frequent chanting of poems and nursery rhymes. Chant about his daily activities.

2. Continue the singing activities begun between ages one and a half and three, including imitating vocal sounds in nature, echoing tonal patterns, calling from afar, learning simple songs within a limited range, accompanying his songs on melody instruments, and playing the "elevator" and "ladder" games. Do these activities frequently.

3. Encourage the child to continue creating his own chants and songs.

4. Persuade the child to sing lightly so that he may listen more attentively to the tune.

5. Encourage the child with complimentary remarks and smiles, noting what he is doing well.

6. In a group situation, let a child who is having difficulty in singing sit next to or between children who are accurate singers.

7. Contrast singing with speaking by speaking the words of a poem, and asking: "Did I sing it or speak it?" Repeat this procedure, sometimes singing, sometimes chanting, and sometimes singing.

8. Use up-and-down movements of the body and/or hands to indicate high and low pitch.

9. Rather than having the child match your pitch, let him start first and then sing with him.

10. Have one child listen to another child sing.

11. Sing softly into the child's ear to focus attention on the pitches and rhythms.

12. Avoid grouping the children in formal music periods until at least age three and a half and preferably, not until age four. If you group the children in a singing experience, do not insist that they all sing. Some children need to listen to the songs over a long period of time before they feel free and confident enough to sing.

13. If using accompaniments, make them very simple. Never play them louder than the children's singing.

14. As the child learns to sing, frequently join in with him, matching his pitches. It is important for the child to experience his pitches being matched with tones of another person.

15. Gradually introduce new songs for the child to learn. Continue having him sing his own vocal compositions.

Singing with the Child

There are many times when you will sing with the child. This may occur when a new song is being taught, or when you lead a group of children in singing, or when you wish to reinforce the child's singing with your own voice. When you start a song for the child, you will need to consider both the vocal range of the child and various ways to start the song, so that the child can join in at the proper time.

Like adults, young children have different vocal ranges in which they sing most comfortably. Most young children begin to sing in the range from D up to G above middle C. A considerable number of children will begin to sing at middle C or B and B-flat below middle C, and even fewer at A or even B above middle C. By the age of five, this vocal range usually expands from middle C up eight scale tones to third-space C.

This means that if you are singing with the child, the pitches should be in the range that the child sings most comfortably. Unfortunately, many adults teach songs to children using pitches that are *too low* for the
183 child. If you cannot read music, try to sing as high in

pitch as possible, as this will probably be in the young child's vocal range. Never sing in a range that is too low, even if your voice is low pitched. If you are a male, then sing to the child in a light, tenor voice. The child will quickly adapt his pitches to the vocal pitches of a man after several experiences.

most comfortable
range

One common problem in singing with a group of young children is that some adults frequently do not help the children begin the song on a pitch that is comfortable for the majority. Many adults "grab" the starting tone out of the air, without regard for the children's vocal range. This practice invariably results in having the group sing too low and inaccurately. It fosters insecurity in developing a sense of pitch relationships in the song. It also causes poor group singing, since the song may be half over before many of the children adjust to, and then match, the song's pitches. You should *always* prepare the children for singing a given song by providing the starting pitch of the song beforehand. This can be done by following these steps:

1. Find the key and the key note (DO or the song's key signature). If the musical notation is not available, or if you cannot read music, then select a tone above middle C (usually D, E, F, or G is a good choice).

2. Sound the key tone on a pitch pipe, a bell set, the piano, or a string instrument.

3. Then find the starting tone of the song (it is often *not* the key tone), and sound this tone on the same instrument as before.

4. Hum the starting tone, or sing it with the first word of the song. Have the children imitate.

5. Sing the first phrase by yourself, or play it, to establish the tempo and a feeling for the song's pitch relationships.

The tempo and rhythm should be set by counting
aloud—"1–2–3–4 . . .ready, go"—in the desired tempo or
by showing the beat with an up-and-down hand motion,
with the hand moving noticeably to show when everyone
is to sing; or by using a harmony instrument (Autoharp,
ukulele, guitar, piano) to play an introduction; or by
singing or playing the last phrase of the song as an
introduction.

As an example of how to start a song, let us consider
"London Bridge":

LONDON BRIDGE

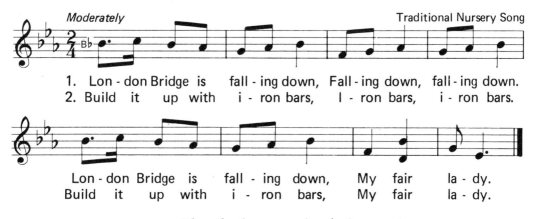

1. Lon - don Bridge is fall - ing down, Fall - ing down, fall - ing down.
2. Build it up with i - ron bars, I - ron bars, i - ron bars.

Lon - don Bridge is fall - ing down, My fair la - dy.
Build it up with i - ron bars, My fair la - dy.

1. Play the key note ($E\flat$) on an instrument.

2. Then play the starting tone ($B\flat$).

3. Hum the starting tone ($B\flat$). Have the children
repeat.

4. Sing the first word or words (London bridge . . .").
Have the children repeat.

5. Sing or play an introduction, or say "1, 2, ready go,"
and lead the group with hand movements for the beat or
by playing an accompaniment.

If the musical notation is not available to you, or if you
have difficulty reading music, you would start the song
on D, E, F, or G. In this case, you should start on one of
the higher tones (F or G), since most of the tones of the
song are lower in pitch than the starting tone.

185 When singing with the child, keep several things in

mind. Set an example of proper singing habits (see below). Never dominate the child's voice; rather, sing softly enough so that you can hear his voice. If he begins the song and you join in, try to match his pitches, rather than having him conform to your tones. Frequently mouth the words while he sings, so as to encourage good diction and independence in his singing.

Developing Vocal Skills

Singing is a complex skill that involves learning how to use several physical mechanisms relating to voice production and listening to and matching pitches and rhythms. Unfortunately, we often forget that we need to develop in the child certain vocal skills in order to improve the quality of the singing tone. The aim is to develop a singing tone that is free from rigidity, natural, effortless, true to pitch, resonant, emotionally colored, steady, smooth, and under control. We hope to develop proper singing habits and increasing mastery over the singing voice. This can be done by emphasizing skills related to singing, i.e., correct posture, good diction and clear enunciation, an open throat, resonance, proper attacks (starts) and endings, and adequate breathing. We also hope to teach the child to sing so that the meaning and emotional content of the song are understood and expressed. We want to help him to expand his vocal range and to sing with freedom and abandon, avoiding tenseness and strain. Proper development of these skills will have a direct effect upon the child's ability to sing well.

Correct posture is one skill necessary for singing well. You will need to set an example by sitting or standing straight, but not tensely, when singing. Keep the body erect, relaxed, and alert. Hold the head naturally, looking forward instead of down or up. Encourage the child to sit up tall without stretching and with his spine straight. When standing, you and the child should have your bodies straight, with the weight placed forward, toward the toes. When sitting, you and the child should sit slightly forward, as if witnessing a surprise or an unusual event. Show pictures of singers who show correct singing posture to the child. You can point out and praise the child who exhibits correct posture by saying: "Look how nicely you're sitting when you sing. No wonder you sing so beautifully!" or "Do you see how Randy is sitting? He must sing very well, since he sits so tall."

Clear enunciation and diction are vitally important in conveying the song's meaning and aesthetic significance. To develop this skill, you will need to set an example of correct diction and enunciation in both singing and speaking. Use the lips generously in the pronunciation of words, with initial and final consonants uttered distinctly. Minimize the hissing sounds of "s" and "z" and the nasal sounds of "m," "n," and "ng." In singing, sustain the vowels and not the consonants. Play a "silent movie game," with you or the child mouthing words with no sounds and the other person(s) guessing what words were said. Mouth the words of familiar songs, with the other observer(s) guessing the songs' titles. Use mirrors to show the child different positions of the lips, teeth, and tongue when various vowels and consonants are spoken and sung. Show the child pictures, films, and videotapes of other children singing and clearly pronouncing the words.

Singing with an *open throat* is another necessary skill for effective singing. Encourage the child to keep his mouth open wide as he sings and speaks. The jaw should be moved loosely up and down. Two fingers can be inserted in the mouth when singing so that the child can feel how his mouth should be when singing. Praise him when his singing is neither excessively hushed nor loud. Work for a tone that is light and free. Discourage shouting.

Proper breathing technique is another important skill involved in singing well. Again, you will need to be a model by using a controlled, continuous, inaudible flow of breath from the diaphragm when you sing. Of course, controlled breathing will be enhanced by good posture. Take an easy and deep breath before each phrase

187

of the song, with no breath in the middle of the phrase. Ask the child to raise his hand every time you breathe when singing. Encourage him to move his hands in a rainbow-shaped arc to feel the song's phrases. Have him place his hands on his diaphragm to feel the breathing. Compare proper breathing skill with the expansion and slow contraction of a balloon.

Still another skill to develop is the ability to *sing with meaning and spirit.* Again, you will need to act as a model for the child. You should "look the part" when singing happy or sad songs. Express the meaning of the song's text and the flow of the melody and the rhythm in your vocal quality, face, and entire body. Encourage the child's physical movements to the rhythmic flow of the music.

Teaching a New Song

Several methods can be used in teaching a new song to a child or group. In the *whole-song method,* you sing the entire song several times. With each rendition, the child responds by moving his body, or by playing instruments, or by joining in on a phrase, or by listening to the words, or with other appropriate activities designed to make the rehearings meaningful. Then, at a certain point, ask the child to try to sing the entire song. In the *phrase-by-phrase method,* you first sing the entire song and then sing one phrase at a time. Then ask the child to repeat each phrase after you sing it. Repeat certain difficult phrases. Finally, after each phrase is learned, sing the entire song. In the *combination whole-song, phrase-by-phrase method,* you use the whole-song method and ask the child to join in on the easy phrases. Work separately on the more difficult phrases until each phrase is learned. Most songs should be taught by the whole-song or combination method, since almost all songs suitable for the young child are relatively short and generally have **188** no more than four phrases.

One excellent technique for teaching a new song to the child is to play a recording of the song for several days before actually "teaching" it. Use the recording at nap time, during snack time, or at playtime. You could also play the tune on the piano or sing it several times as the child engages in his everyday activities. The child often will "absorb" the song after several hearings, and when the song is actually introduced, he will learn the song more quickly.

Before teaching a new song, you should prepare to sing it accurately and musically. It is best to memorize the song. Practice singing it expressively, using some facial expressions and even hand movements. Sing the song lightly, rather than using a heavy voice. Remember to pitch the song in the child's vocal range and to practice proper singing habits as discussed in this chapter.

When teaching a new song to the young child, you will need to provide some *motivation*. Depending upon the age and prior experience of the child, you might set the mood or establish the background of the song by telling the story of the song as told in the text. You might read or chant the song's words or show pictures relating to the story or its central character(s). You may relate the song to the child's past experiences. Avoid introducing a song this way: "Now I want you to sit still. I have a new song for you. Now listen!" or "Here is a lovely song I want you to learn. It is about a mouse who runs up the clock. Let me say the words. . . .Now say them after me." Rather, a new song should be introduced with enthusiasm, as if you were presenting a child with a surprise. Say: "Here's a song I hope you'll like. It's about a clock that says 'hickory dickory dock.' Listen to the song and see what animal went up and down the clock as it rang 'hickory dickory dock.'" After singing the song once, ask the child or children to join in on the "hickory dickory dock" and discuss what the mouse did. If you wish the child to learn the song and sing it enthusiastically, you too must be enthusiastic about the song and its words, pitches, rhythms, and

meaning.

Activities for Repeated
Hearings of Music

When first presenting the song, ask the child to listen to it in its entirety as you sing it, or as it is sung by the parent, another child, a visitor, another adult, or as it is played on an instrument or recording. Following the song's performance, you can ask brief questions about the song in order to get the child's reactions and involvement. Then you can repeat the song several times, so that the child can listen to it before singing. During these repeated hearings of the song, the child can be encouraged to:

- move in a variety of ways (clap, stamp, pat the knees, wave the hands) to the song's rhythmical elements
- rhythmically chant the words
- talk about the song's mood, tempo, or dynamics
- create a rhythmic accompaniment, using rhythm instruments and/or body rhythms, e.g., clapping, snapping, clicking of the tongue, smacking the lips
- dramatize the story in the song
- hum or whistle parts of the tune
- mouth the words as the adult sings
- discover and move in the appropriate locomotor movement, i.e., a walk, run, skip, that might reflect the song's rhythm or meter
- substitute other words for some of the song's words or make up new words for the melody
- listen to you play harmonic accompaniments on the Autoharp, ukulele, piano, or guitar
- evaluate how well the song was sung and suggest ideas for a better interpretation
- move hands up and down to the song's beat and meter, with a stronger downward movement on the first or accented beat
- raise hands every time the singer breathes or at the beginning of every phrase
- move hands in a rainbow-shaped arc to the phrases
- listen for the number of phrases

• alternate the singing of phrases between you and the child (or between the girls and boys)
- sing the song by himself

Following some of these activities, use judgment on when to ask the child to sing. Generally, most children will be able to sing after hearing the song from three to six times. The song can then be sung, as you help the child to sing the words, pitches, and rhythm correctly and to sing expressively. Encourage and reinforce proper singing habits relating to posture, breathing, diction, and musical interpretation (see pp. 186–188). Guide the child to evaluate his own performance.

Once a song is taught, it should be repeated at subsequent times in order for the child to become more familiar with it. Usually the child will learn to appreciate the song more fully with repeated hearings and familiarity. When using the song after its initial presentation, repeat many of the activities outlined above. Use different rhythm instruments or bodily movements. Work on singing the song more musically. New verses can be taught or created. Use the song to introduce and develop such concepts of music as its tempo, dynamics, beat, pitch, and rhythm (see Chapter 9). And most importantly, sing the song just for the fun of it!

Using Song Recordings

Many adults who work with young children often ask: "What can I do if I don't sing or if I'm afraid to sing by myself? Can I still teach the children how to sing?" Of course you can! There are many excellent recordings of songs suitable for young children (see Appendix B). Adults who have difficulty in singing can still do an excellent job, because they use records or tape recordings of the songs. And even if you *do* sing well, it is often advisable to add variety to the singing experience by using records.

Phonograph records and tape recordings of songs are important assets in developing musical responses in young children. They assist the adult who cannot read musical notation or who has a limited song repertoire, thus providing a wider variety of songs than otherwise possible. The song recordings are often done more musically than when performed by a nonprofessional. They usually have tasteful instrumental accompaniments and are sung by trained adult singers and children. They provide other examples of singing voices besides the one that the children hear so often. They also free the adult to do other musical activities besides singing when she leads the group.

What are some criteria for selecting a recording of a song for use with young children? The recording should be of excellent tonal quality, with accurate reproduction and good fidelity. The rendition should meet the same aesthetic and musical standards as if you were singing it; i.e., it should be sung expressively, with the words being clearly enunciated and easily understood, and with the accompaniment appropriately and musically performed. The singer's voice should be pleasant and simple. Highly affected operatic voices and loud, unmusical renditions by pop singers should be avoided. Wherever possible, use recorded children's voices. The recording of the song should be long enough so that the listener(s) has time to learn the song and grasp its musical content.

You should be familiar with what is on the recording before playing it for the child. The recording should serve as a rendition of the song and not as a substitute for teaching it. You must still be responsible for teaching the song and guiding musical response. The approach to use is the whole-song method described previously, although you may wish to teach the song phrase by phrase with your own voice after the recording is played. Since the words of the new song are sometimes hard to follow on a recording, you may have to review the words with the child once the recording is played a few times. If the song is unfamiliar, replay it several times before the child is asked to join in. During each rendition, encourage the child to respond rhythmically to it in order to sense the tempo, beat, and rhythmic flow. Once the child joins in, ask him to sing softer than the recording so that he can keep the same tempo as on the recording. Later on, in order to encourage independence in singing, have the child sing the song without the aid of the recording.

Some Other Suggestions

There are many "tricks of the trade" that will help you do a better job of teaching and leading songs with either a group of children or an individual child. Some suggestions are:

1. Prepare the environment for singing. Have adequate ventilation, comfortable seating, a minimum amount of distraction, and an absence of outside noises. Avoid extended singing experiences when the weather is very warm and dry. Allowing the child to sit on the floor is acceptable, provided that he is encouraged to sit straight, with proper posture for singing.

2. Avoid tiring the child. Since singing involves a considerable output of physical and mental energy, do not have singing experiences after outdoor play or vigorous indoor activities. When singing, have the child change his sitting posture after a prolonged period of sitting.

3. Discourage repressed, hushed singing and loud, forced singing.

4. Do not sing lively songs too fast or slow songs too slowly.

5. Occasionally provide musically tasteful accompaniments on the piano, guitar, ukulele, or Autoharp to support the singing.

6. Avoid too much singing at one sitting, since this may bore the child, especially if there is little variety in the songs. Alternate singing with listening, movement, instrumental, and creative experiences.

7. Frequently review songs and singing activities already experienced. These will become favorites through repetitions in meaningful and enjoyable situations.

8. Always try to set an example when singing. Sing with an expressive tone, good diction and enunciation, adequate breath support, and an open mouth and throat. Continually stress and reinforce singing skills and proper singing habits.

9. When leading group singing, face the children, even if you are playing the piano. Eye contact is essential.

10. Make singing a cooperative experience by singing *with* the children, not *to* them.

11. Minimize your talking about the song. Get into the music as soon as you can. Do not spend an undue amount of time on drill or on clarifying word meanings. Let the music speak for itself!

12. Be flexible enough to move on to other activities if the singing activities planned for the day are not successful.

13. Change the starting pitch of a song, when necessary, to a more comfortable vocal range for the child or group.

14. If you use an instrumental accompaniment or a recording, make sure it is soft enough so as not to obliterate the young child's or children's voices. The accompaniment and/or recording should enrich, enhance, and aid the singing, not dominate it.

15. When singing, always allow time for requests made by the child or children. Frequently review favorite songs.

16. Encourage the children to sing individually for the group. Encourage them to sing songs learned in a group setting and in other settings.

17. Singing activities should occur throughout the day. Have the children sing greeting and good-bye songs, chant as they play indoors and outdoors, and engage in musical conversations.

18. Occasionally have the children sing for other adults and children in the preschool, in the home, and in the neighborhood.

19. Tape-record the children's voices to develop skills in self-evaluation and to record progress.

194 20. If you are preparing a preschool music lesson focusing on singing, try to alternate the singing of familiar songs with the learning of new songs. Begin and end the lesson with familiar songs.

21. Enrich singing activities by having the children move rhythmically to the song's rhythmic flow, play rhythm instruments to highlight certain musical elements (see p. 209), dramatize the story or characters within the song, create other stanzas, listen to how you accompany the song on an instrument, learn how to play part of the song on a melody instrument (see p. 215), and make up new words for the text or a new tune using the original text. Also, have the children identify a song sung by "la" or played on an instrument, or have them raise their hands when you sing or play the tune incorrectly.

22. Do not always sing with the children. Often mouth the words, but do not sing. This will allow you to hear the children's voices and will provide you with insight into their progress.

23. Use a variety of accompaniments. Often play an accompaniment without the melody. Also provide many opportunities for the children to sing without any accompaniment.

24. Most preschool-aged children are able to learn at least one new song per week. Aim to expand the children's song repertoire to between thirty and fifty songs per year.

25. Sing with a purpose. All singing activities should be fun and enjoyable, but do more than just sing. Guide the children to learn about music and their musical experience as they sing.

26. Develop for yourself a repertoire of songs appropriate for young children, so that you can use a variety of songs in different situations. It is always helpful to have a few songs "up one's sleeve" when the children are getting restless waiting for lunch or for a bus or when tension needs to be released.

27. To add variety to singing experiences, ask friends to tape-record some songs for the children to hear, or ask other adults or older children to help teach some songs.

195

Summary

Singing is one of the basic musical experiences of early childhood. The process originates in the first vocalizations of infancy and continues from the infant's earliest experimentations to his musical babblings, and from his self-created chants to learning simple children's and folk songs. The song repertoire for the young child consists of two main categories—his own songs and tonal patterns that he creates and songs from our musical heritage. Techniques for helping the child to sing can be started during infancy and continued throughout early childhood. In singing with the child, consider both the child's vocal range and ways to start a song. Model for the child the vocal skills related to proper breathing and posture, clear enunciation of words, having an open throat, and singing expressively. When teaching a new song, either by using your own voice or by playing a recording, consider how to musically and actively involve the child each time the song is performed. Every singing experience should aim at developing each child's potential to respond to music in an enjoyable and meaningful way.

Selected Readings

There are many books that contain suitable songs for young children. However, there are no books currently available that deal exclusively with singing techniques and methods with the child below age five. Some children's songbooks have brief introductions to the topic, and texts on music for young children usually devote a section to singing. Some recommended sources include:

Christy, Van A., *Foundations in Singing.* Dubuque, Iowa: William C. Brown Co., 1965.

Gould, A. Oren, and Edith J. Savage, *Teaching Children to Sing.* Dubuque, Iowa: Kendall/Hunt Publications, 1974.

Matthews, Paul W., *You Can Teach Music.* New York: E. P. Dutton and Co., 1953, Chapter 4.

Singing   Mursell, James L., *Music and the Classroom Teacher.* Morristown, N.J.: Silver Burdett Co., 1951, Chapter 6.

Nye, Vernice, *Music for Young Children.* Dubuque, Iowa: William C. Brown Co., 1975, pp. 87–105.

Sheehy, Emma D., *Children Discover Music and Dance.* New York: Teachers College Press, Columbia University, 1968, Chapter 4.

Young children love to play musical instruments. (Photo courtesy of American Music Conference. Head Start program)

7

Playing Instruments

Playing instruments is one of the principal means of music making and is enjoyed by children of all ages. Instruments are fun to handle and play and are an easy way to make music. They stimulate musical response and encourage the child to learn about the science of sound. Experiences with a wide variety of instruments teach the child the importance of the proper care, use, and techniques of playing instruments. They can be used for providing sound effects for stories and poems. They can reinforce the mood in a creative movement experience. They can highlight the rhythmic flow of poems and language patterns. They can even be used to teach mathematical counting patterns or develop classification concepts. Instruments can be used, then, in a wide variety of ways. This chapter outlines the various types and uses of instruments for educating the young child. Instructions are given on how to play and make some instruments. Many suggestions are provided on how to handle situations in which playing instruments is the main activity. The aim of this chapter is to show how playing instruments contributes to the overall musical **201** response of the young child.

Types of Instruments: How to Play and Use Them

Any type of instrument has value in the musical education of the young child. He can learn about music through experiences with everything from the simplest rhythm sticks to the more complex orchestral instruments. He can learn about music by plucking a string on a guitar, Japanese koto, or violin. In every case, the child should be encouraged to listen to the instrument, touch it, and experiment with making sounds and music on it.

The instruments to use with the young child are limitless. Nevertheless, it should be recognized that children below age five usually will have great difficulty in playing most instruments other than simple rhythm or melody instruments. This difficulty is caused by the limited fine-motor development of children between birth and five years of age. Yet approaches such as the Suzuki Talent Education Program (see p. 278) have shown that even two- and three-year-olds can play simple tunes on such instruments as the violin, cello, and piano. And there are many examples of musicians and composers who began their study of musical instruments at age three or four. Despite these examples, it is felt that for *most* children, the formal study of an instrument such as the piano, violin, flute, or guitar should be delayed until age six or later and should commence only after the child has had a rich and varied experience in listening and moving to music, creating music, singing, and playing many types of simple rhythm and melody instruments.

In general, there are several types of instruments with which the young child should have experience:

- *Sound makers* found in the home and in the environment, e. g., pots and pans, seed pods, cans filled with dried beans or popcorn, flat stones
- *Rhythm instruments:* percussion instruments that are hit, pounded, struck, shaken, or rubbed, such as the rhythm sticks, triangle, and wrist bells and a variety of "ethnic" instruments such as steel drums from

202

Trinidad, the ipu gourd from Hawaii, and large drums from Central Africa and India

- *Melody instruments:* instruments on which tunes may be played, such as the melody bells, xylophone, piano, tonette and recorder, and a variety of "ethnic" instruments such as West African xylophones, the Southeast Asian bamboo flute, and the Japanese shamisen (a three-stringed lute)

- *Harmony instruments:* instruments designed primarily for harmonic accompaniments, such as the Autoharp, ukulele, guitar, and banjo

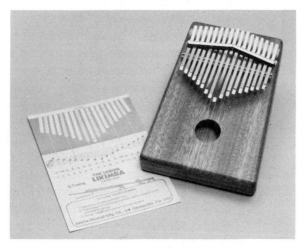

The likimba—an African instrument. (Photo courtesy of M. Hohner, Inc.)

- *Orchestral and band instruments* and other quality instruments of the "adult" world, such as the violin, trumpet, organ, saxophone, accordion, harmonica, the sitar (a long, hollow-necked lute) from India, the Japanese koto (a thirteen-stringed zither), the Balkan gusla (a bowed, stringed lute), the wooden flute from the highlands of Peru, the likimba (an African instrument), and countless other "ethnic" instruments from all over the world.

Sound Makers

Sound makers made out of objects found in the home, school, or outdoors are often the child's first instru-

203

ments. The infant will discover that a spoon, when hit on the crib, produces an interesting sound. The two-year-old will find a stick and bang it repeatedly on the metal pipes of the slide. And banging pots and pans is fun for all children. Almost any object in the child's environment can serve as an instrument to make sounds.

For infants, various objects found in the house can be strung together, so that they produce a novel sound when hit or shaken. Small pieces of wood or ordinary wooden clothespins are excellent for this. Also use bottle caps, empty spools, small spoons, keys, small metal lids from frozen juice cans, and other kitchen utensils. Care should be taken that the child does not swallow these "instruments." In addition, safety precautions are advisable to make sure that wooden materials are not splintered and that metal objects are not rusty or sharp edged.

Small baking powder, cocoa, or spice cans or boxes (preferably made out of wood and not cardboard), when filled with various small objects, become excellent sound makers for the young child. Ideally, the cans with removable lids are best. At first, only two cans should be used—one with rice or other small objects and one with small stones or other larger, heavier objects. A quick shake of each will catch the child's attention. If the child wants to, he can open up the cans to see what is making the sound. At times, he should shake both cans simultaneously and perhaps shake them fast and slowly to vary the rhythms and sound qualities. At another time, use a third or even a fourth can filled with small objects (popcorn, dried beans, tiny pieces of wood, buttons, marbles) to add variety to the child's "orchestra." Of course, the child should be supervised during this activity to prevent him from placing the objects in his nose, ears, or mouth. Other types of experiences for infants with sound and instruments are outlined on pp. 151–155 of the text.

Homemade instruments are also useful for the child's instrumental experiences. Suggestions on how to make these instruments are found on pp. 219–231. These instruments should serve as an important part of the instrumental program for all young children.

There is a large variety of rhythm instruments suitable for the young child. These instruments include the:

coconut shells

cymbals

drums

finger cymbals

gong

jingle bells and wrist bells

jingle sticks

ethnic rhythm instruments

rhythm board

rhythm sticks

sand blocks

shakers and maracas

tambourines

tone blocks and wood blocks

triangle

Coconut shells

Coconut shells can be used to highlight the beat or accents of music and are especially useful in fast, light, and "galloping" music. They can effectively imitate the "clip-clop" of a horse. Hold one shell in each hand, with the open part of the shell facing the palm of the hand. Strike the shells together in a horizontal motion. One shell can also be hit with a mallet or rhythm stick. Use two paper cups hit together on the closed ends to imitate the sound of coconut shells.

Cymbals may be used for accents, climaxes, and special effects. They are also excellent instruments for illustrating vibration and tones of long durations. Hold

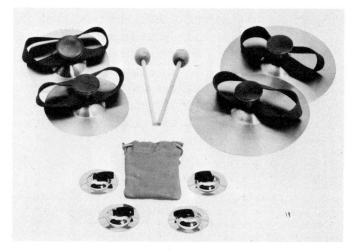

205 Cymbals and finger cymbals. (Photo courtesy of M. Hohner, Inc.)

one cymbal in each hand and strike them together by moving one hand up and down, in a vertical direction. Once hit, they must be allowed to vibrate by turning each cymbal slightly away from the player's face. Cymbals can also be played by holding one horizontally and tapping it lightly with the tip of the other. One cymbal can also be held horizontally and tapped lightly with a metal beater or mallet.

Drums come in various sizes and shapes. All kinds of drums, including hand drums, tom-toms, and toy drums, are suitable for experimentation by the young child. Drums serve to highlight the music's beat, accented beats, and the mood of slow, "heavy" music. They are especially effective in "drum talk" and in sending rhythmic messages (see p. 269). In order to play the drum, strike the drumhead quickly in a bouncing motion with a felt mallet, a drumstick, the fingertips, the knuckles, or the palm. To make varied tones, hit the drumhead in the center or on the rim and elsewhere.

Finger cymbals are small, delicate cymbals that can be used for sound effects or to highlight the beat of a slow-moving piece or music that is fast and light. They are also valuable for illustrating tones of long duration and to show vibration. Play them in the same manner as the cymbals, except strike them lightly instead of clashing them. One cymbal can be played by lightly hitting it with a mallet, stick, or small metal object.

The gong is used for special effects in the music. It can serve to imitate the ringing of bells or may be played at the musical climax of a piece. It is an excellent instrument for illustrating both tones of long duration and the meaning of vibration. Play the gong by striking it in a bouncing motion with a felt mallet or a metal striker.

Jingle sticks, jingle bells, and wrist bells. (Photo courtesy of M. Hohner, Inc.)

Jingle bells and *wrist bells* are excellent instruments to accompany music that is fast, light, and excited. They can be played on the beat or accented beat. To play the bells, shake them vigorously and sharply. Silence them by placing the hand over them.

The jingle stick has jingle bells or metal caps loosely placed on a flat stick. The bells or caps vibrate when the stick is tapped or shaken. The instrument has a similar function to the jingle or wrist bells. Hold the stick in one hand, and tap briskly against the palm of the other hand in such a way that the jingles are free to vibrate. Also, sharply shake the stick, or hit it against the body.

The rhythm board, a notched wooden board resembling a small washboard, is useful for highlighting the beat of the music and for providing special sound effects. It can be used to accent the rhythms of dance music from Latin America. Play it by rubbing a stick across the notches with a motion away from the body.

Rhythm sticks are useful for tapping the beat or melodic rhythm, for rhythmic echo games (see p. 268), for illustrating tones of short durations, and for highlighting the mood of fast, light music and marches. Hold one stick in each hand, and strike the upper portions together. Or hold one stick steadily, and strike it near its tip with the second stick. Or hit both sticks together in a crisscross fashion, or hit them on the floor. When the rhythm sticks are notched, rub them on each other in a motion away from the body. Chopsticks may make effective and quieter substitutes for rhythm sticks.

Rhythm sticks

Sand blocks are useful for highlighting soft, swishing music and for accompanying a fast rhythm. They can be used effectively for special sound effects, such as illustrating the movement of a train or sliding down a hill. They are played by rubbing (not hitting!) the sandpapered sides of two blocks together in a vigorous, shuffling motion.

Sand blocks

Shakers and *maracas* can be used to accompany fast and light music. They are particularly effective for Latin–American dance music. The sounds of different kinds of shakers and maracas can illustrate differences in tone qualities. They are played by sharply and briskly shaking the instruments at face level or above.

207

The tambourine is one of the most versatile of all rhythm instruments. It can highlight pronounced rhythms, light and fast music, and a strong, accented beat. It is particularly effective for Latin–American dance music and is a useful "shaking" instrument for sound effects. There are several ways to play the instrument. Shake it sharply, stiffly, and briskly in the air. Hold it in one hand, and move it against the heel or fingers of the other hand or against various parts of the body. Hold it steadily and strike it with the palm or fingers of the other hand. Beat it with mallets made out of felt, rubber, or wood.

Tone blocks and *wood blocks* are excellent for highlighting the steady beat or accents of music and for illustrating a definite rhythm and tones of short duration. They can be used effectively for sound effects and for illustrating the clip-clops of a horse, the ticking of a clock, or the dripping of water. Play the blocks by striking them lightly in a bouncing motion with a stick or a wooden or rubber mallet. Hit the tone block near the open slit and by its hollow end. If the tone block is notched, rub or scrape it with a motion away from the body.

The triangle is especially effective for highlighting the beats of slow, soft music, for light accents, for special effects (a clock, the ringing of bells), and for illustrating vibration and tones of long duration. Hold it by a string or handle, and strike it lightly with a metal beater, either inside or outside the instrument. Prolong the tone by jingling the beater on the inside of the triangle. Stop the tone by touching the instrument with the hand.

In addition to the standard rhythm instruments found in most preschool classes, children should be given experience with at least some of the following ethnic instruments: maracas from the Caribbean area and Mexico; American Indian drums and rattles; the Latin–American guiro (a long gourd played by rubbing a stick along the instrument's notches); steel drums from Trinidad; Chinese tone blocks and wood blocks; the Hawaiian ipu (a large gourd drum that is hit with the palm or heel of the hand or that is pounded on a wooden board or floor); Spanish castanets; the tabla (drum) from

Tone block

Wood block

Guiro

208

India; the South American wood block (shaped like a bottle and hit with a stick); the claves (a pair of small, cylindrical wooden sticks struck together while held in cupped hands); wooden slit drums from Fiji, Tonga, Tahiti, and Samoa; Chinese glass or brass wind chimes; Polynesian split and fringed bamboo sticks, such as the Hawaiian pū ˈili; and drums from the Middle East and Central and West Africa.

Traditionally, "rhythm bands" have been an important part of preschool music programs for young children. These bands were characterized by the adult's arranging the children according to rhythm instrument groupings, playing a recording, and conducting the children by pointing at them to play their instruments at appropriate times. What normally resulted was a bedlam of uncoordinated banging that was neither musical nor conducive to musical learning. The instruments were usually treated like toys, to be banged and misused. The rhythm band has *no* place in a program designed to enhance musical growth, since it most frequently is overstimulating, uncreative, and unmusical.

What, then, can be done with rhythm instruments? They have many uses in promoting the music education of the young child. They can be used to:

- experiment with sound
- encourage improvisation of rhythmic patterns
- accompany the beat of a song or recording
- play strong and weak beats
- echo rhythmic patterns, where you play a pattern and the child repeats it on his instrument (see pp. 267–268)
- highlight dynamics, by adding, deleting, or changing instruments when the dynamics of the music change
- emphasize the music's mood, by using instruments such as the triangle for soft, bell-like passages and cymbals for very loud passages
- add sound effects to accompany a poem, story, rhythmic movement, and creative dramatics
- show that the tone color of a recording changes, by playing one type of instrument when a woman sings

209

or the strings play and another type of instrument when a man sings or the brass instruments play

- highlight certain words of the text, such as having the tone blocks play on "clap, clap," the cymbals play on "*pop* goes the weasel," and the triangle play on "ding, ding, dong" or "twinkle, twinkle"
- develop classification concepts by sorting the instruments into how they are played, or how they sound, or from what materials they are made

Once the child has had many different experiences with a variety of instruments, you should guide him to compare the instruments' sounds, what they are made from, and how they are played. Gradually, the child will learn to classify the instruments on the basis of certain musical attributes, such as:

1. *Clicking instruments made from wood:* rhythm sticks, tone blocks, wood blocks, coconut shells

2. *Ringing or jingling instruments made from metal:* jingle and wrist bells, jingle sticks, triangle, gong, tambourine

3. *Rattling or swishing instruments:* sand blocks, rattles, maracas

4. *Booming or thudding instruments:* many kinds of drums

5. *Scratching or scraping instruments:* notched rhythm sticks, notched tone blocks, rhythm board

Some additional suggestions for using rhythm instruments include:

1. Guide the child to listen more closely to the sound qualities of the rhythm instrument by asking: "Does the sound click or ring? Is it long or short? Is the sound loud or soft? Can you make soft (loud) sounds on the instrument? Is the sound high pitched or low pitched? Can the instrument be played as well fast as it can be played slowly?"

2. No child should be forced to play an instrument. Encourage every child to play a variety of instruments.

3. Before using a rhythm instrument to accompany a song or a musical composition, prepare the child by having him:

- listen to the music at least two or three times
- move to feel the beat, rhythm, phrase, or any other aspect of the music that is to be highlighted
- make believe he is playing the instrument in the appropriate manner and at the appropriate time to the music

If he can do these activities, he is then ready to add an accompaniment on his rhythm instrument to the music.

4. If using rhythm instruments in a group, generally use no more than two or three different instruments at the same time. An exception to this is when you are helping the children to compare and classify sounds from a wide variety of instruments.

Melody Instruments

There are various types of melody instruments appropriate for the young child to experiment with and play, including the hand bells, piano, resonator bells, step bells, tuned glasses, and xylophone-type instruments (tone, melody, and song bells and the marimba).

Hand bells are individual bells that can be rung. Usually the chimers inside the bells are of different sizes, resulting in tones of different pitches. They are rung sharply and briskly, like dinner bells. One type of hand bell set, called the Swiss melodé bells, has eight bells tuned to a scale. Each bell is numbered from one to eight and is a different color, thus making it easy for some young children to play a tune using number or color symbols.

211

Swiss melodie bells. (Photo courtesy of Sally Gale)

The piano is often found in both homes and preschools. Experimentation on the piano with sound and melody should be encouraged. In addition, the piano is useful in that it shows that playing different keys results in tones of different pitch and that the low-pitched tones are on the left of the keyboard and the high-pitched tones on the right. The piano is also an excellent instrument for the child to play in order to describe monsters or giants (use adjacent low-pitched tones called "tone clusters"), an elephant walking (use alternating low-pitched tones), and birds chirping (use high-pitched, softly played tone clusters). An old piano or a baby grand can be opened, so that the child can pluck the piano's strings and experiment with more unusual sounds that can be produced on the piano.

Resonator bells are individual bells with wooden resonating chambers below each metal bar. The set of bells can be arranged consecutively, as on a xylophone, or each bell can be removed from the set and played separately. Play the bells by striking them in a bouncing motion with a rubber-tipped mallet. The tones of these bells are usually excellent in quality. The separate bells

212

are very useful for isolating certain tones in a melody or tonal pattern, e.g., playing the "e-i-e-i-o" pattern from "Old MacDonald." They are also conducive to creating melodies, using only a few tones of varying pitch. They are important additions to any music education program for the young child.

Resonator bells. (Photo courtesy of Ludwig Drum Company)

The step bells are inexpensive xylophone-type instruments in which the metal bars are arranged on an elevated frame, similar to steps. Although the tone quality of the step bells is not as clear as the quality of tones produced on resonator bells or xylophones, the

213 Step bells. (Photo courtesy of M. Hohner, Inc.)

instrument is very useful, since it shows the child visually that some pitches are low and some are high. When a melody is played on this instrument, the child can see that a melody can move up, down, or stay the same in pitch. The step bells are a "must" in any early childhood program designed to foster musical growth.

Tuned glasses usually consist of bottles suspended on cord from a wooden or metal frame and filled with varying amounts of water (see also p. 230). When tapped with a mallet or stick, different pitches emerge. Besides encouraging creativity and learnings about melody and pitch, these glasses also enable the child to see that different pitches result when the length of the vibrating air in tubes is different.

The xylophone (a pitched instrument with attached metal bars on a frame) and the *marimba* (a pitched instrument with attached wooden bars on a frame) are relatively common and inexpensive instruments. Play them by bouncing a small mallet on the instruments' bars. *Tone, melody,* and *song bells* and the *glockenspiel* are similar to the xylophone in construction and in the manner in which they are played. All these instruments are very valuable in providing the child with experiences in pitch, melody, and creativity.

Several other melody instruments can be used with the young child, including the *tonette, flutophone,* and *recorder.* Although the child will not have the physical coordination to play these wind instruments, he can be encouraged to experiment by blowing through them to make various whistling sounds. "Montessori instruments," developed by the noted Italian educator, Maria

214   Tonette. (Photo courtesy of the author)

Montessori, and "Orff instruments," originally designed by the German composer and educator Carl Orff (see p. 278), can also be used with the young child for melodic experimentation and creativity. These instruments are types of xylophones and marimbas and can be used in the same way.

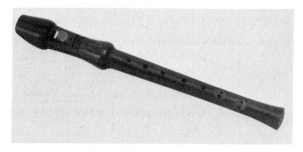

Recorder. (Photo courtesy of M. Hohner, Inc.)

All melody instruments are useful in helping the young child develop concepts of pitch and melody. As the child experiments by playing various tones or by watching as you play a tune, concepts about high and low pitch, repeated tones, and melodic contour (the shape of the melody) begin to emerge. These instruments invite the child to create tonal patterns and melodies. Several melody instruments visually show the child that bars that are longer sound lower in pitch than bars that are shorter. The bars of the instruments can also be played at the same time, resulting in harmony. These instruments are fun and educational for all children to hear and play.

The first experiences on a melody instrument, as on any instrument, should be experimental. Encourage the child to find out for himself how to hold and play the instrument. Let him discover the sounds it makes, different ways of making these sounds, and the various moods that can be created. Later on, show the child how the instrument is played in a musical way. Help the child produce a good tone quality on each instrument, and guide him to play it at various times during the day.

Some suggestions for using melody instruments **215** with the young child include:

1. Allow plenty of time for the child to experiment with and create his own tunes on the instruments. This experimentation should be part of every musical experience with these instruments.

2. The child can be invited to play a pitch or tonal pattern and then sing it back. You can also play a pitch or pattern for the child, and then sing it with the child.

3. Let the child learn about the science of sound from the construction of the instrument. For example, use the piano to guide the child to discover the piano's strings and their varying sizes, the vibration of the sounding board, and the use of the pedals.

4. Use melody instruments to establish the pitch of songs (see pp. 183–186).

5. Ask the child to find and play low- and then high-pitched sounds and loud and then soft sounds.

6. While singing with the child, play the tune on the melody instrument in order to show him the song's pitches. Also play the instrument at certain times to emphasize a particular musical idea (a repeated tone, a stepwise movement of the melody, a tonal pattern that repeats).

7. Have the child find pitches on the instrument that are near each other, and then far apart.

8. Show the child how to play simple tonal patterns from familiar songs, such as the "jingle bells" pattern, the "e-i-e-i-o" pattern from "Old MacDonald," the "ding, ding, dong" pattern from "Are You Sleeping?" and the "nick, nack, paddy whack" pattern from "This Old Man."

9. Sing a tonal pattern to the child. Have the child try to play it back on the instrument. At first, use lots of repeated tones or two tones that are far apart in pitch.

10. Play an easy pattern on an instrument, or sing it. Then encourage the child to try to play it back on his instrument.

11. Use the instrument for special musical effects to enhance a song and as sound effects for a story or creative dramatization.

12. Encourage the child to use the instrument to play tunes he already has heard or sung.

13. Invite the child to improvise on the instrument and to create tonal patterns, melodies, harmonic sounds (for the xylophone-type instruments, he will need two mallets), and introductions or endings to songs.

Harmony Instruments

One or more harmony instruments, including the *accordion, Autoharp, banjo, guitar, mandolin, piano,* and *ukulele,* are valuable additions to a music education program for the young child. Although few children until age six or later can discriminate harmony in music, playing these instruments does allow the young child to experiment with listening to and producing two or more tones sounded simultaneously. These instruments provide a way of adding variety to songs through harmonic accompaniments. They are also another means of helping the child build concepts about the science of sound.

The Autoharp is an important harmony instrument to use with children. (Photo courtesy of Sally Gale)

The Autoharp, banjo, guitar, mandolin, and ukulele are particularly useful in exposing children to understandings about vibration and pitch and the length, thickness, and tautness of strings as related to pitch. Place a piece of paper on the vibrating strings of an Autoharp to give the child visual experience with the meaning of vibration. Tighten or loosen the strings on the strummed instruments to show how pitch can vary according to how tight the string is; i.e., the tighter it is, the higher the pitch is. Place and move the fingers up and down on the frets of the ukulele or guitar to show that the longer the vibrating string, the lower the pitch. And compare the thickness of the strings on these harmony instruments to illustrate the principle that the thicker the string, the lower the pitch.

As with melody instruments, introduce the harmony instruments by having the child discover various ways to produce sounds. Later on, after much experimentation, you can play these instruments in a musical way and use them to accompany songs. The harmony instruments are generally too difficult for the young child to play, although most three-and four-year-olds can be taught to strum the Autoharp or ukulele to the beat of the music as you finger the harmony. In using the Autoharp, you can also show the preschooler how to press the chord bar and strum to get "pleasant-sounding" chords. Have the child strum chords on the strummed instruments and listen for the richness of the harmonic sounds.

Other Instruments

Orchestral, band, and such other instruments as the organ, harmonica, and those played around the world have a definite and important role in the musical education of the young. Few children below age five have the technical facility to play these instruments, but they still can be played for the young child. Identify the distinctive tone qualities of instruments such as the flute, violin, trumpet, double bass, harp, organ, trombone, and others. Help the child hold some of these instruments and try to make tones on them. Take apart some of the instruments and show the parts to the child. Play a tone on an instrument, and ask the child to sing it back or find it on the piano, step bells, or xylophone. When the child sings, play the instrument to reinforce the tune.

Pictures and recordings of various instruments will help the child visually and aurally recognize some of them. Many recordings of ethnic instruments are currently available. However, there is really no substitute for experiencing the "live" instrument. This experience can be had by:

- taking the child to a store where instruments are sold
- letting the child watch an older child or adult at her music lesson
- arranging for a visit to a nearby elementary or secondary school to watch the youngsters practice their instruments
- asking a local musical group, a musician, or a music teacher to perform for several children
- asking friends, parents, or older siblings who can play these instruments to demonstrate them for the child
- taking the child to see a parade, or hearing professional musicians rehearse, or watching an ethnic or dance festival

Making Instruments

The young child can be assisted in making many instruments from materials commonly available in the home or preschool. Most young children find this activity very rewarding. Making instruments is educationally valuable, because it combines learnings in art, science, mathematics, and music. The actual construction of the **219** instrument is usually not a musical experience and should not be a substitute for daily experiences with musical sound. Rather, it should be only one of the many worthwhile experiences the young child has in his daily life. Some easy-to-make instruments include the:

BANJO

Materials: cigar box without a top, cardboard, rubber bands.
Instructions: Place rubber bands over cigar box, tightening them on bottom. At one end of box, insert small piece of heavy cardboard under rubber bands. Press different "strings" to produce more tones.

BEATERS (DRUMSTICKS, MALLETS)

Materials: Wood doweling (or spoons, shoehorns, broom handles, knobs, sticks, or pencils), cotton, elastic, twine, cloth, rubber bands or cord.
Instructions: Wrap material around tip of wood. Secure with rubber bands or cord.

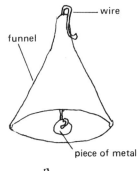

BELL

Materials: Metal funnel, small and heavy piece of metal, wire, hammer, and nail.
Instructions: Make hole in small piece of metal. Place wire through metal and secure. Put wire through funnel hole and tie so that metal will strike funnel when shaken.

BONE CLICKERS

Materials: Boiled shank bones, cord or heavy yarn.
Instructions: Boil and dry shank bones. String. Hit them together, or scrape them against each other.

CHIMES: NAIL OR SILVERWARE

Materials: Nails of different weights and lengths or table silverware, string, dowel or long stick or coat hanger.

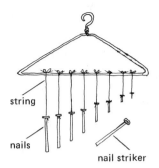

string

nails

nail striker

Instructions: Make small holes in dowl or stick, about 1 inch apart. Cut string into varying lengths. Tie the largest nail to the longest string, the shortest nail to the shortest string, and so on. Place the strings through the holes and tie, or tie the strings evenly spaced on the coat hanger. Also use silverware suspended from strings.

Note: Large metal chimes may be made in a similar fashion. Use plumber's lead pipes. For Japanese wind chimes, use bamboo pieces cut to different lengths.

CHIMES: SHELL

Materials: Large clam shells, drill or nails, string, dowel or long stick or wooden coat hanger.

Instructions: Drill small hole in each shell, or use hammer and small nail to make hole. Place string in each shell and tie. Hang each shell by its string from dowel, allowing some space for vibration. Shake or place in wind.

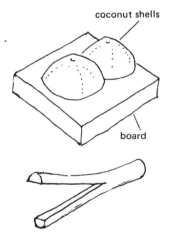

coconut shells

board

CLAP BOARD

Materials: Two halves of coconut shell, large wooden board.

Instructions: Place board on lap. Clap shells on board with open parts either facing upward or toward board.

CLAPPER

Materials: 12″ stick or dowel, sharp knife, sandpaper.

Instructions: Cut an 8″ long wedge in the stick. Sand. Hit stick against the palm or on a hard object.

COCONUT SHELLS

Materials: Ripe coconut, hacksaw, scraper or putty knife, sandpaper.

Instructions: Buy coconut at grocery store. Remove outside husk. Drain the coconut milk. Cut coconut in half with saw. Scrape out meat. Dry. Smooth the shells with sandpaper. If desired, paint or shellac. Strike halves together.

221

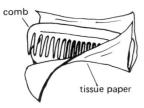

comb

tissue paper

COMB HARMONICA

Materials: Man's comb, tissue paper, tape, glue or staples, scissors.
Instructions: Cut piece of tissue paper to fit around both sides of comb, and cover the comb's teeth. Secure paper to comb. Hum with lips over the fold, and move comb back and forth.

CYMBALS

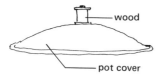

wood

pot cover

Materials: Old pot covers (or shortening-can lids, pie tins, or large biscuit-can lids), small pieces of wood (or spools or drawer pulls), hammer and nails.
Instructions: Nail the wood, spools, or drawer pulls to the center to serve as handles. Clash the "cymbals" together.

DRUM

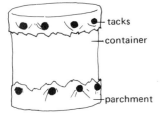

tacks

container

parchment

Materials: Inner tube rubber or goatskin or drum parchment, large cans or ice cream containers or oatmeal boxes, tacks or laces, paint or construction paper. *Note:* Animal parchment for drums can often be obtained free of charge from repair departments of some music instrument stores.
Instructions: Soak goatskin or parchment in water for about thirty minutes. Take goatskin or rubber and lace tightly over container. Tack. Decorate container.

DRUM, BLEACH BOTTLE

Materials: Large plastic bleach bottle with top, masking tape, stick or spoon.
Instructions: Screw top on bottle. Secure with tape. Decorate bottle. Strike with stick or spoon.

DRUM, BONGO

222 *Materials:* Two shortening or coffee cans with plastic lids, small piece of wood, tape, hammer and nails.

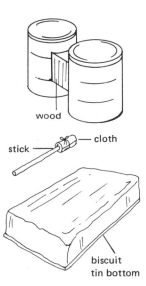

wood

stick — cloth

biscuit
tin bottom

Instructions: Remove the plastic tops. Place wood at center and side of can. Nail can to piece of wood and then nail the second can to the other end of the wood, so that the wood is in between both cans. Tape the plastic tops to the cans. Decorate.

DRUM, TIN

Materials: Large ship-biscuit tin, cloth, string, stick.
Instructions: Remove can top. Turn the can over. Cover the tip of stick with cloth, and secure with string. Strike the tin.

DRUM, TOM-TOM

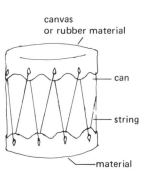

canvas
or rubber material

can

string

material

Materials: Coffee or shortening can or wooden buckets or pails, natural rubber or plastic, heavy string or cord, sticks.
Instructions: Remove both ends of can. Cut two circular pieces of the canvas or rubber material to about 1 inch more than circumference of the two openings on the can. Punch holes ½ inch from the edge of the material about every 2 inches. Place the material tightly over the can opening. Lace the holes with string or cord, and tie to material at the opposite end of can in a crisscross fashion. Play with sticks.

DRUMSTICKS (HARD SOUND)

Materials: Two small rubber balls, two pencils or sticks, glue.
Instructions: Make holes in balls, insert sticks, and glue in place.

DRUMSTICKS (SOFT SOUND)

Materials: Two spools, two sticks, scraps of soft fabric, glue.
Instructions: Insert sticks into end of spools. Wrap several layers of fabric around spools, and tie them in place.

223

FLUTE, CARDBOARD

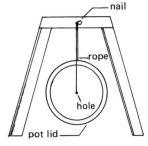

Materials: Cardboard tube from paper towels, waxed paper, Saran Wrap or toilet paper, scissors, waxed paper, rubber bands.

Instructions: Cut four small holes, about 1 inch apart, on one side of cardboard tube. Cover one end of tube with waxed paper, and secure with rubber band. Blow into open end of tube, and move fingers over holes to obtain various tones.

GONG

Materials: Lid from oil can, or hub cap, or iron skillet, or any large metal lid, or horseshoe; rope or string, stick, cloth, nail and hammer.

Instructions: Nail a small hole near edge of drum lid. Suspend the lid, tying string from hole to a beam, frame, or branch. Place cloth around tip of stick and secure. Hit stick on lid.

HARP

Materials: Wood or heavy cardboard, saw, rubber bands.

Instructions: Make a triangle or rectangle from pieces of wood or heavy cardboard. Make slits for rubber bands. Place and tie rubber bands in slits. Pluck the "strings."

HORN

Materials: Large plastic bottle, scissors.

Instructions: Cut off the top end of a plastic bottle, leaving the handle and small opening. Blow through the opening.

HUMMER

Materials: Cardboard tube from paper towel roll, rubber bands, waxed paper, scissors, adhesive tape.

Instructions: Cut a round hold approximately 3 inches long and 1 inch wide about 3 to 4 inches from one end

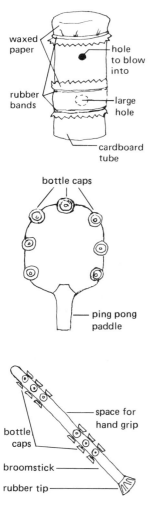

waxed paper

hole to blow into

rubber bands

large hole

cardboard tube

bottle caps

ping pong paddle

space for hand grip

bottle caps

broomstick

rubber tip

nail

can

stick

of the tube. Firmly cover the tube with waxed paper, securing it with two rubber bands. Also cover with waxed paper the end of the tube closest to the side hole. Secure the waxed paper with tape. Place tape around the open end of the tube, leaving a small hole. Hum into the open hole. The sound will be magnified by the waxed paper over the holes. Also tap the tube lightly when humming to obtain a drumming noise.

JINGLE STICKS AND PADDLES

Materials: Jingle bells or bottle caps, a 6-inch piece of flat wood, old broom handles or dowel or wooden paddle or rice scoop, cup hook, pliers, nails, paint.
Instructions: Screw cup hook at each end of bell. Tighten and close hook with pliers. Paint stick and saw to correct size. Fasten bells to ends of wood. Or tack or nail bottle caps loosely around rim of wood.

LAGERSTICK FROM AUSTRALIA

Materials: 3 to 4-foot broomstick, bottle tops, nails, rubber chair tip.
Instructions: Nail bottle tops around broomstick for its full length. Leave space in middle for hand to grip it. Place rubber chair tip on bottom. Hit stick on wooden surface.

MARACAS

Materials: Plastic lime or lemon, or pill boxes, or spice cans, or typewriter ribbon boxes, or frozen orange-juice containers, or baking powder cans; plastic tops from cans; pencil or stick about 9 inches long and 1 inch wide; pebbles or beans or rice or "B-B shot," or popcorn or small seashells; tape, hammer and nails, paint and/or construction paper.
Instructions: Make a hole in bottom of container. Push stick through hole so it fits tightly. Tape. Place small objects in container. Nail plastic top to the stick. Tape the top to the container. Paint and/or decorate the can.

225

MARACAS, PAPIER-MÂCHÉ

Materials: Large light bulb, pencil or small stick, papier-mâché, paint.

Instruction: Securely tape end of light bulb to a pencil or small stick. Cover bulb with several layers of papier mâché (made by dipping newspaper strips in a wheat paste mixture and molding the strips in many thicknesses around the bulb). Dry thoroughly. Hit against wall or floor to break bulb. Paint. Shake.

MARIMBA

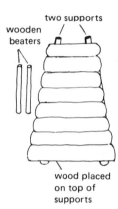

two supports

wooden beaters

wood placed on top of supports

Materials: Two similar-sized large wooden sticks or dowels, several small pieces of wood (varying in diameter), nails or cord.

Instructions: Place parallel to each other, about 3 to 5 inches apart, two large wooden sticks or dowels. Take small pieces of wood, and place them on top of the two dowels, as if making a footbridge. Nail or tie the sticks to the two main dowels (the supports). Hang the instrument over a carton, bucket, washtub, or on a tree limb. Strike the wood with sticks or mallets.

RATTLES

Materials: Pebbles or beans or rice or corn, containers (plastic bottles, Band-Aid boxes, small milk cartons, pill or spice boxes).

Instructions: Collect and sort objects according to their sizes. Place similar-sized objects into each container, and seal. Paint, or glue construction paper on containers. Shake.

RATTLES, PLATE

Materials: Small paper plates or aluminum pie plates, hole puncher, colored yarn or plastic lacing, small pebbles or rice or dried beans or popcorn.

Instructions: Punch holes about 1 inch apart around rim of two plates. Fill with small objects. Lace plates together with yarn or lacing. Decorate or paint outside of plates. Shake.

RATTLES, SEED

Materials: Seed pods, metal or plastic containers.
Instructions: Collect seed pods. Shake. Or open seed pods and place seeds in containers. Cover with lid. Shake.

RHYTHM BOARDS

Materials: Plastic, wooden, or metal washboards, nails, bells or bottle caps, thimbles, spoons, or metal.
Instructions: Nail bells or bottle caps to various parts of a wash board. Play board with thimbles, spoon, or metal, using a scraping motion.

RHYTHM STICKS

Materials: ½-inch dowels or broomsticks, saw, paint, sandpaper.
Instructions: Cut dowels into lengths of about 1 foot. Sand edges. Paint. Play. Use different circumferences to obtain different tones.

ROLLING PIN, MUSICAL

Materials: Rolling pin, large-headed nails, stick, hammer.
Instructions: Hammer nails at equal spaces on one side of rolling pin. Use stick to skim along tops of nail for sound. Also use stick to beat the rolling pin.

SAND BLOCKS

Materials: Two 3-inch by 2-inch by 1-inch wooden blocks, wooden handles or small pieces of wood or drawer pulls or spools, sandpaper or emery cloth, glue or staples.

227

Instructions: Glue or staple sandpaper or emery cloth to the 3-inch side of block. On opposite side, glue spool or handle. Rub. Experiment with sandpaper squares of different degrees of coarseness.

SHAKER, CHOCALLO (LATIN–AMERICAN INSTRUMENT)

Materials: Cardboard tube from paper towels or metal soda or soup cans, heavy construction paper, tape, paint, small objects.
Instructions: Cover one end of paper towel tube or can with construction paper. Tape. Place pebbles, rice, beans, or other small objects into tube. Seal the other end. Paint tube. Shake.

SHAKER, GOURD

Materials: Small, dry gourd with natural handle, saw, scraper, small objects, shellac or paint.
Instructions: Cut open the gourd crosswise, near its bottom. Scrape out seeds. Put in coarse gravel, rice, or pebbles. Glue the two sections together. Shellac or paint. Shake.

SHAKER, LID

Materials: Two smooth-edged frozen orange-juice can lids, flat piece of wood, nails, hammer.
Instructions: Fasten two lids not too securely onto a flat piece of wood. Shake.

SHAKER, METAL

Materials: Stick or dowel, pop bottle caps, nails, hammer.
Instructions: Nail some caps loosely to the end of stick.
228 Shake.

SHAKERS USING OBJECTS IN NATURE

Materials: Leafy branches or sticks or twigs of various sizes, or blades of coarse grass, or water in containers.
Instructions: Shake these objects, either in the air or against other objects.

SHOE BOX PLUCKER

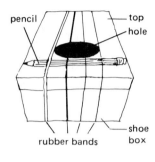

Materials: Sturdy shoe box, various sized rubber bands, pencil.
Instructions: Cut 2-inch oval hole on top of box. Stretch rubber bands lengthwise around the box. Place pencil at one end of top of box, near hole, to create a bridge. Strum and pluck. Move the pencil to get different tones.

TAMBOURINE

Materials: Aluminum pie plate or sturdy paper plate, or old rim, or plastic band or embroidery hoop; six to eight bottle caps with corks removed, nails or brass paper fasteners, hammer, wire, tempera paint.
Instructions: Make a large hole on one side of the plate rim to serve as a hand hole. Punch or hammer hole through bottle caps, and place nails or fasteners in holes. Punch or hammer corresponding holes, evenly spaced, in rim of plate or the elastic band. Bend nail. Put wire or string through holes and twist ends of wire together around the nail. Allow space for caps to vibrate. Leave the caps loose enough to vibrate. If necessary, place caps in pairs, so that more sound will result. Shake or tap. Another way of making a tambourine is to take two aluminum pie plates and sew or staple them together. Punch several holes on the rims. Tie small bells to the rims in such a way that they hang freely.

THUMB PIANO

Materials: Heavy paper bucket, small piece of scrap wood, tongue depressors of varying lengths, glue or tape.

229

tongue depressors

hole — wood

bucket

Instructions: Cut a hole about 3 inches in diameter in the bottom of the bucket. Glue or tape the tongue depressors on top of the wood. Place bucket on a wooden floor or table. Vibrate the depressors with the fingers.

TRIANGLE

Materials: Spoon or horseshoe or large spike or welding rod, string, nail.
Instructions: Suspend metal objects from a length of string. Make striker from a spoon or nail. Strike.

TUNED GLASSES

Materials: Three to eight small jars, bottles, or glasses of the same size; water, spoons or small wooden mallets.
Instructions: Fill bottles with water to different heights. Cover tops. Place on a wooden board or table. Gently tap the bottles. Tune the bottles by adjusting the water levels.

TUNED JUGS

Materials: Large bleach bottles or large bottles.
Instructions: Blow over the openings of the containers. Raise the pitches by adding water (less air will vibrate). Adjust the water levels to tune the containers. Cover tops when not in use.

WOOD BLOCKS

Materials: Saw, pieces of wood 3 inches by 2 inches by 1 inch, sandpaper, paint or varnish, mallet.
Instructions: Cut wood into blocks that are easy to hold. Sand until smooth. Paint or varnish. Strike with mallet.

WRIST BELLS

Materials: Jingle bells, narrow elastic cut to fit the child's hand, thread or heavy string.

Instructions: Thread bells onto elastic or heavy string. Tie at end. Place on wrist and shake.

XYLOPHONE

Materials: Small metal tubes cut in various lengths, hacksaw, wooden frame.
Instructions: Place tubes over two narrow wooden boards. Use pipe or hard rubber mallet to strike tubes (see also instructions for making the marimba earlier in this section).

Storing and Caring for Instruments

All instruments—whether they be "homemade" instruments, rhythm sticks, the flute, the accordion, or the zither—require certain skills for playing them. In general, skills are needed in caring for, holding, and producing tones on the instruments.

Instruments should be presented with the dignity and value of a rare violin. Immediately help the child to learn that an instrument is to be cared for, handled carefully, and valued. An instrument, from the simplest rhythm stick or old piano to the most valuable trumpet or violin, is to make music—*not* to be used as a toy or as a weapon. Discourage uncontrolled banging. Show the child that instruments are for producing sound. It is your responsibility to convey these feelings through your own actions with these instruments and by reinforcing proper care and use of these instruments. Work on skills such as learning how to handle and use all instruments in a way that will not damage them, learning to use them as instruments that produce a variety of musical sounds and not as toys to play with or objects to bang, and learning to put away and store the instruments when finished with them.

Each type of instrument should be stored in a separate container. Keep large drums in a special place on a shelf or in a box. Stack rhythm sticks vertically in a large coffee can or jug. Place finger cymbals in small boxes. Store sand blocks and tone blocks in separate shoe boxes. Store melody and harmony instruments in different containers from rhythm instruments. Avoid jumbled assortments of instruments, since this does not teach the child the need to classify instruments according to their sound, what they are made from, and how they are played.

The first experiences with instruments should be supervised. These experiences should focus on free experimentation on the instruments. Encourage the child to touch and make sounds on the instruments. Ask the child to make a variety of sounds in as many ways as possible. Invite him to hold the instruments in unique ways in order to produce interesting sounds. However, if he misuses the rhythm stick by hitting another child or by placing it between his toes, or if a drumhead is used as a canvas for scribbling, then you should not accept this behavior. Encourage throughtful and imaginative experimentation; discourage the careless use or destruction of the instrument. If the instrument is not being handled properly, despite your attempts to guide the child, then you should take it away. The child needs to learn immediately that instruments must be used to produce interesting musical sounds, and not for nonmusical experiences. Respect for any instrument will develop when the child senses your respect for, and enjoyment of, the musical values of that instrument.

Managing the Group Situation

When instruments are used with a group of children, chaos can result unless you consider routines and rules for distributing, handling, playing, and collecting the instruments. Some suggestions for using instruments in a group situation include:

1. Teach the children how to quietly distribute the instruments. If there is a small group, then the children

can line up by the box or container where the instruments are stored and select which one they want to play. Another technique is to have one child distribute the instruments.

2. Allow some time for experimentation with the instrument. Young children want to play their instruments as soon as they can. Recognize this. Give them a signal (a hand raised, a piano or ukulele chord, a drum beat) when the experimentation must stop.

3. Reinforce the rule that the instruments are to be handled carefully to make musical sounds and are not to be used as playthings or weapons. Do not hesitate to take the instrument away if a child does not follow the routines or abuses the instrument.

4. Establish the rules that: (a) no one is to play an instrument when anyone is talking; (b) no talking is to occur when the instruments are being played; and (c) the instruments are not to be played until the music begins or the adult gives a cue. Have the children place their instruments on their laps or on the floor when they are not being played.

5. Rotate different instruments within a given period or over a series of experiences, so that every child is given an opportunity to play all instruments.

6. In collecting the instruments, either have each child place his instrument into the appropriate storage area, or have one child walk around the room with a container in which the children are to place their instruments.

Some Other Suggestions

A few other recommendations for using instruments with the young child include:

1. Introduce only one instrument at a time.

2. If you wish the child to play an instrument to accompany a song or recording, use familiar music. This

233

will let the child concentrate on coordinating what he plays with what he hears.

3. Aim at having the child use the instrument as an enrichment for the music. The instrument should never be played as loud as the music to be accompanied.

4. Set up a music table or music area where several instruments are made available for any child to play and practice (see also pp. 107–109 for detailed discussion).

5. Expect a crudeness and lack of precision whenever a child first learns to play an instrument. The process of learning how to play, rather than the final rendition, is most important.

6. Every child should be allowed to experiment with and learn how to play several instruments. Playing them should not be reserved for only those children who do it well.

7. Encourage the child to listen to and evaluate his own playing.

8. In planning musical experiences for the child consider alternating the playing of instruments with singing, listening to music, creating music, and moving rhythmically. Try to integrate these musical experiences.

9. Always have some instruments available in every musical activity. Even when the emphasis is on singing or rhythmic movement, it is useful to have some rhythm instruments and a xylophone or step bells readily accessible in case the occasion arises to use them to reinforce the rhythmic or melodic experience.

10. Instruments seem to perk up an otherwise dull or unrewarding musical experience. But remember: They are only one of the principal experiences in music and should be used in balance with singing, listening and moving to music, and creating music.

Summary

Playing instruments is one of the basic musical activities for all young children. A wide variety of instruments should be experienced, including sound makers from the environment and rhythm, melody, harmony, band, orchestral, and ethnic instruments from other cultures. The first experiences should be experimental, with the child discovering the different sounds possible on each instrument. The child should learn how to handle the instrument and how to produce sounds on it. The instrument should not be regarded as a plaything; rather, it should be viewed as a sound producer. The child can also learn to make various instruments on which he can play. The instrumental experience in a group should be well planned to allow for experimentation and musical response. Your role is to guide the child to use the instrument in a variety of ways in order to further his musical growth and understandings about tone, rhythm, melody, harmony, tone color, dynamics, tempo, and repetition and contrast in the music.

Selected Readings

Almost every book on music for young children will have at least one section or chapter on instruments. In addition, some books deal specifically with how to make simple instruments. Some recommended references include:

Hawkinson, John, and Martha Faulhaber, *Music and Instruments for Children to Make.* Chicago: Whitman Publishers, 1969.

Hood, Marguerite V., *Teaching Rhythm and Using Classroom Instruments.* Englewood Cliffs, N.J.: Prentice–Hall, Inc., 1970.

Kettlekamp, Larry, *Drums, Rattles and Bells.* New York: Morrow Publishers, 1960.

Mandell, Muriel, and Robert E. Wood, *Make Your Own Musical Instruments.* New York: Sterling Publishers, 1957.

Swanson, Bessie R., *Music in the Education of Children* (3rd ed). Belmont, Calif.: Wadsworth Pub. Co., 1969, chapters 4 and 5.

Vernazza, Marcelle, *Making and Playing Classroom Instruments.* Belmont, Calif.: Fearon Publishers, 1959.

Weidemann, Charles C., *Music in Sticks and Stones: How to Construct and Play Simple Instruments.* New York. Exposition Press, 1967.

The young child should be given many opportunities to create tunes.
(Photo courtesy of American Music Conference)

8

Creating
Music

All children have the ability to create music. Listen to the infant as he babbles or pounds rhythmically on his crib. Observe the eighteeen-month-old child as he vocalizes a short tune when he builds a tower with his blocks. Listen to the three-year-old as he chants nonsense syllables when he constructs a "farm" in the sand area. And watch the four-year-old as he makes up a tune on the xylophone or step bells. The universal capacity to create is based on the human being's urge to learn, to grow, to discover, to explore, and to build upon what is familiar. This chapter discusses creativity in music. It shows how creativity is a unifying process that uses understandings in listening, rhythmic movement, singing, and playing instruments to arrive at a musical product, e.g., a rhythm, a song, a piece for rhythm or melody instruments, or a musical accompaniment for a story, poem, or drama. The chapter presents many ideas for fostering musical creativity in the young child. And, most importantly, it describes how all musical experiences originate and find ultimate satisfaction in the **239** creative act.

Creativity and Music

When we think of someone who is creative, whether
that person is Einstein, Beethoven, Madame Curie, your
hairdresser, or your former fifth-grade teacher, we think
of one who is curious, motivated, spontaneous, playful,
observant, and flexible. She has lots of ideas, many of
which are different from traditional thinking. She likes
to elaborate on these ideas to see how far she can go
with them. She likes to redefine her ideas and experiences and look at life in many different ways. She is
open to all possibilities. She accepts other people's ideas
and actions. She lets people try out their ideas to see if
they really do work. She is a person seeking the truth
from a world of alternatives. She is a scientist, a poet, an
artist, a dancer, a composer, a mathematician, a philos-
opher, a historian, and a theologian—all integrated into
one human being.

The creative act is a personal expression that indicates the individual's own initiative and past personal
experience. The act may be a discovery of a new ability,
or a new insight or realized understanding, or a venture
into a new realm of experience. This is true whether the
creator is an artist, an auto designer, a space engineer, or
a young child. The creative experience involves the
person and his creative power, his feelings, imagination,
and intellect, the interaction of his experiences, and the
outward form of expressing the creative act.

The creative process starts with the child and ends
in the form of a new expression for the child. When the
young child creates music, he uses his own intelligence
and imagination in reordering and reconstructing what
he already knows into something that is unique and
rewarding *to him*. The process of creativity involves a
personal expression of what he already understands and
feels. It involves the ability to look freshly at the musical
experience and to see it in a new way. The child takes
materials (in music, this is his voice, instruments, and
musical tone) and becomes intensely preoccupied in
fashioning a product (in music, this is a rhythm, a song,
a tonal pattern, a tune, or an accompaniment) that gives

him inner satisfaction. This process involves continuous discovery, exploration, involvement, and self-evaluation. The musical product—a chant, a tune, a rhythmic pattern—often gives the creator a sense of accomplishment and belongs to him in a very personal way. It provides the creator with a sense of wholeness and integration toward realizing all of his potential.

Musical creativity is a synthesizing, unifying experience and, as such, is *basic* to the muic education of all children. This synthesis involves the use of musical elements that are familiar to the child to create a musical product new and satisfying to him. Many musical understandings and skills are used by the child, at his own level, in the creative process. This implies that the child, and not the adult, should be the final judge of whether the creative work is satisfactory. As adults, we need to say: "You certainly tried hard in making up that song," or "How do you feel about what you you did?" rather than: "That is a wonderful song you composed," or "Try again. That tune doesn't sound very good." The adult's role is to encourage and provide the environment for creativity; it is the child himself who must be the final evaluator of his own creative works.

All children, in varying degrees, are creative. Some are more creative than others. Yet, *every child has creative potential.* Almost all educators agree that the development of each child's creative potential is one of the principal goals of education. Musical experiences for the young child must seek to develop this potential. Music, together with all the arts, is an excellent medium for fostering creativity. Through the use of tone, rhythm, and bodily movement, the child can reshape familiar musical elements to create new expressions he enjoys.

Many creative music experiences occur naturally and spontaneously throughout the child's day. The child may suddenly break out in song as he moves up and down on the seesaw or watches older children jumping rope. He may find a pencil and rhythmically tap it against a table. One cannot really plan ahead for these experiences. All one can do is to encourage the child's experimentation and creativity when they do occur and **241** not interfere with his activity. Nevertheless, the adult can plan for many creative activities by arranging the environment to foster discovery and by encouraging the child to engage in certain creative activities (see pp. 242–250 for specific activities). Sometimes these activities can be only incidental to experiences in singing, playing instruments, listening to music, and rhythmic movement. At other times, the planned creative experience can be the focus of the music experience. In any case, the emphasis should be on creating tonal and rhythmic patterns, using various sound-producing objects in the environment, the voice, and instruments.

The creative musical act is one in which music's tonal and rhythmic elements are reshaped and restructured to provide a satisfying musical work for the creator–composer. Children who create their own babbles, chants, songs, rhythms, and tunes are truly composers. Experiences in *creating music* should be contrasted with *making creative interpretive responses to music,* e.g., moving to and dramatizing music, painting and making up stories to music. Creative interpretive response has an important place in music education and is discussed on pp. 147–150. In this chapter we are concerned primarily with ways the young child can create and compose music from tone and rhythm.

The Adult's Role

Children differ in their creative potential. This is due to a combination of genetic and environmental factors (see pp. 43–47). The role that heredity plays in fostering creative responses is still under investigation by researchers. It does seem clear, however, that the child's potential to create can be shaped and developed by his environment. The adult's role is to provide a creative environment. In this setting, various experiences designed to develop the potential of each child to discover and create musical relationships that become significant in his life can occur. Creative experiences in music also should help the young child develop his overall creative response in dealing with his environment. These experiences will assist the child in becoming increasingly comfortable in his use of the expressive creative act. They will help him recognize and utilize his creative potential in all media of musical expression—i.e., listening, rhythmic movement, singing, and playing instruments—and will aid in his growing appreciation of the creative works of others.

Musical creativity cannot occur in an environment that is not creative. What can you do to stimulate an environment that fosters creative response? You should:

- encourage and guide the child in all his creative efforts
- accept the unique individuality of the child and set standards that are reasonable for him to attain
- teach from any occasion that arises
- invite new solutions to problems rather than one set way of accomplishing a goal
- be flexible, and be aware of the child's point of view as it arises from his own needs and interests
- maintain a stimulating environment, with many playthings, books, musical intruments and records, art materials, and other objects that will foster learning and the creative response
- allow plenty of time for the child to experiment with the materials provided
- be more interested in the process of creating than in the final outcome
- eliminate the forced application of adult standards
- ask many *open-ended* questions requiring the child to think of several alternatives, rather than *close-ended* questions in which only one answer is possible. (Examples: Ask: "What instrument might you use with the music?" rather than "Can you use the tambourine for the music?"; or ask: "Can you show with your body how the music makes you feel?" rather than: "Can you hop like me to this hopping music?")

The capacity of the young child to create music and to respond creatively to music can only be fostered in an

243 atmosphere of encouragement, informality, freedom, and stimulation and only where many varied music experiences are made available.

At times, you may need to provide examples for the child in order to stimulate creative activities. Sometimes a model for the child to follow will help him see some possibilities for creating a tune or rhythm and enable him to be more creative in his responses. Extreme care should be taken not to give the impression that the child must do what you do or that only your response is the correct one. Modeling one possible response in itself is acceptable if it is not done too frequently. Remember that all creative artists have followed many examples before "taking off on their own." It is acceptable to give some adult guidance, when needed. Setting the stage for the creative act and helping the child to discriminate between several choices does not stifle creativity. *Guided creative experiences* are recommended in order to foster the child's maximum potential to create.

Some Suggestions and Activities

There are many activities that you can plan in order to guide the child's creative musical responses. Almost all of these activities have been mentioned previously as part of the discussions on listening and rhythmic movement, singing, and instrumental experiences. They are reviewed here so that you can have at a glance a list of suggestions that can foster creative potential. Some recommendations include:

1. Give the child many opportunities to experiment with a wide variety of sound sources, such as:

- tapping a pot or pan
- clashing pots and metal lids
- hitting together two pieces of silverware
- tearing tissue paper or paper bags
- tapping a soda can or bottle with a stick or spoon

- scraping a stick on a notched water pipe
- crumbling leaves
- knocking on a door or table

Invite a variety of rhythmic responses.

2. Always encourage the child's vocal experimentation as he coos, gurgles, babbles, sings a chant, sings nonsense syllables, and creates unusual vocal sounds. Frequently sing back his "songs" to him, and reinforce him with a smile or verbal encouragement.

3. Give the child a rhythm instrument. Encourage him to experiment with sounds and to make up a rhythmic pattern and sequence on the instrument.

4. Encourage the child to achieve various effects on instruments by playing them in different ways and in different combinations.

Freedom to experiment is the key to musical creativity. (Photo courtesy of M. Hohner, Inc.)

5. Give the child a melody instrument—the step bells, xylophone, melody bells, or resonator bells—and en-

courage him to experiment with playing various tones and creating a tune.

6. Using a variety of instruments, have the child create sound effects for given moods. Ask: "Can you play something to show me how you feel at a birthday party? Can you play something to show how you feel when you're scared, or when you're tired and sleepy?"

7. Use body sounds to create a piece of music. If there are several children available, combine these sounds. Some body sounds to try include:

clapping	snapping the fingers
hitting the knees	making kissing sounds
tapping the feet	clicking the tongue
humming	rubbing the hands together
grunting	growling
panting	shuffling the feet

8. As the child watches other children jump rope or bounce balls, chant to him in time with the children's movements, and invite him to make up a tune for the chant. Use traditional children's rhymes such as:

Bounce high, bounce low,
Bounce the ball to Shiloh.

or

Teddy bear, teddy bear, turn around,
Teddy bear, teddy bear, touch the ground.

Also use chant rhymes prevalent where the child lives.

9. Frequently engage in musical conversations with the child, focusing on the child, his clothes, his body parts, his toys, and activities he likes, such as:

When you sing, vary the pitches, rhythm, tempo, and dynamics.

10. Encourage the child to create nonsense syllables, chant them, and add a tune to them. For example:

Me - me - min - ny - me,   See - see - see.

11. Play a "question-and-answer game." Sing a question to the child, and have the child answer. For example:

How old are you? Three.   What col-or is your dress? Blue and yel-low.

Then reverse roles, with the child singing questions and you answering him. In both cases, use a variety of rhythmic and tonal responses.

12. Repeat the "question-and-answer game," using the syllables "ta-ta" for the question and "la-la" for the answer, such as:

Ta   ta ta ta   ta   La   la   la.

13. Give the child two bell bars from a resonator bell set. Encourage him to create a two-tone melody. Later experiences can be expanded to include melodies with three and then four tones. If resonator bells are unavailable, use any other melody instrument. Place masking tape on the two or three tones you wish the child to use.

14. Ask the child to create an introduction to a familiar song. For example, the ringing of hand bells could precede "Are You Sleeping," or a "tick-tock" on the coconut shells or wood blocks could introduce "Hickory Dickory Dock."

15. Read a story to the child. After several hearings over a few days, give him a rhythm instrument. Invite him to devise a rhythm instrument background for the story. If there is a group of children, distribute several different kinds of instruments to accompany the story. "The Three Bears," "The Three Pigs," "The Billy Goats Gruff," and "Jack and the Beanstalk" are particularly suitable for instrumental accompaniment and dramatization.

16. Provide the young child with rhythm instruments as you encourage creative dramatic activities.

17. After the child is very familiar with a story, invite him to describe the story in sound, without having the story read to him at the time he adds the accompaniment.

18. Sing, or play a recording of a song or instrumental piece. Ask the child to create a rhythm instrument accompaniment that coincides with the rhythm and mood of the music.

19. Have the child complete an unfamiliar tune, singing "la-la." For example:

20. Clap and/or play on rhythm instruments questions and answers, such as:

Encourage the child to answer the rhythmic question with a different rhythm that fits the question. Also reverse roles, with the child asking the question.

21. Let the child act out the story or impersonate the characters in a song and improvise bodily movements for rhythmic patterns, songs, and recorded music (see detailed discussion, pp. 143–150).

22. Use singing games in which new words may or must be added to continue the game, such as "The Mulberry Bush," "The Hokey Pokey," "The Farmer in the Dell," and "Looby Loo."

23. Change the words of a familiar song. Have the child use the tune to sing about his Mommy or friend, his pet, what he likes to do, and where he is going.

24. Make up new stanzas to songs.

25. Have the child suggest a variety of ways to sing a song, such as: The child can sing the first verse, the adult the second verse; or the child and adult can alternate the singing of phrases; or the adult can sing the verse and the child can join in on the chorus.

26. Ask the child to make decisions on how a song could be interpreted. Ask questions such as: "Could we clap at a special place? Where? What rhythm instrument would fit well with the music? Should we sing the music fast or slowly? loudly or softly? Why?"

27. Beat a steady, slow pulse on the drum or another rhythm instrument, or play a steady accompaniment on the piano or harmony instrument. Ask the child to play another rhythm that is faster moving and that fits with the steady beat.

28. Read a poem to the child. After several hearings over a few days, encourage him to chant the poem in a steady rhythm and create a tune for the words.

29. Combine vocal experimentation with rhythm instruments. Have the child make up vocal sound rhythms, alternating with rhythms played on rhythm instruments, such as:

Vocal sounds:

mm mm (click tongue)

Instrumental sounds:

30. With several players, play a rhythm game. One person taps and/or claps some rhythms about ten seconds long. The second person follows immediately and then the third person, etc. The speed should be kept constant, but the rhythm should be varied. Continue practicing until a flowing rhythmic piece is achieved.

31. Give the child an Autoharp. Have him experiment by playing chords and individual strings. Invite him to make up various chord sequences, tunes, and mood effects on the individual strings.

Summary

All children have creative potential to use the elements of music to make up rhythms and tunes that give the "composers" satisfaction. This creative potential manifests itself in infancy as the child creates his own vocalizations and rhythms, and it continues throughout life. The creative act in music is one in which the child uses what he already knows to create a musical product that has meaning for him. The adult can foster the child's creative potential by providing many materials for musical experimentation, by encouraging the child in the creative process, and by being open, flexible, and innovative when working with the child. Many creative expressions occur spontaneously; they can also be planned. Since the process of creating music involves the use of all the elements of musical expression (listening, rhythmic movement, singing, and playing instruments), it provides one of the most important experiences for the musical growth and development of the young child.

Selected Readings

Experiments in Musical Creativity. Washington, D.C.: Contemporary Music Project, Music Educators National Conference, 1966.
Contains several examples of innovative music experiences with young children.
Hickock, Dorothy, and James A. Smith, *Creative Teaching of Music in the Elementary School.* Boston: Allyn and Bacon, Inc., 1974.
Contains many suggestions for creative experiences in music.

Creating Music   Hope—Brown, Margaret, *Music With Everything*. London: Frederick Warne and Co., 1973.
> *An excellent description of the creative process in music. Many practical experiences for grades K–6, but with implications for all children.*

Marsh, Mary Val, *Explore and Discover Music*. New York: The Macmillan Co., 1970.
> *One of the best books on creativity and music; contains many practical examples.*

Maslow, Abraham R., *Toward a Psychology of Being*. New York: Van Nostrand Co., 1971.
> *An important book about the "self-actualized" person, with many implications for fostering creative growth.*

Mayeski,Mary, Donald Neuman, and Raymond J. Wlodkowski, *Creative Activities for Young Children*. Albany, N.Y.: Delmar Publications, 1975.
> *Excellent, practical examples of creativity in all curriculum areas.*

Maynard, Fredelle M., *Guiding Your Child to a More Creative Life*. Garden City, N.Y.: Doubleday and Co., 1973.
> *Easy-to-read, focusing on play, art, music, dance, family activities, and books.*

Paynter, John, and Peter Aston, *Sound and Silence: Classroom Projects in Creative Music*. London: Cambridge University Press, 1970.
> *Vivid description of activities with English schoolchildren.*

Self, George, *New Sounds in Class*. London: Universal Education, 1968.
> *A very useful guide to activities for developing musical creativity; contains many fine suggestions for use with preschool-aged children.*

Torrance, E. Paul, *Creativity in the Classroom*. Dubuque, Iowa: William C. Brown Co., 1970.
> *A clear discussion on creativity and the child.*

Winsor, Charlotte B., ed., *The Creative Process: A Symposium*. New York: Bank Street College of Education, 1976.
> *An excellent reference on the nature of creativity and its significance in early childhood education.*

Musical praticipation fosters the child's development of his own concepts about music. (Photo courtesy of Sally Gale)

9

Promoting Conceptual Growth

One of the important goals of providing musical experiences for the young child is to develop his ability to understand the tonal and rhythmic art of music. Through listening, rhythmic movement, singing, instrumental experiences, and creating music, the child will gradually form concepts or broad understandings about the elements that comprise music, i.e., dynamics, tempo, tone color, rhythm and beat, pitch and melody, harmony, form, and musical style (see pp. 79–87). As a result of the child's growing awareness of these elements, his concepts will become clearer and more defined, resulting in a greater understanding and appreciation of the music he listens to, creates, and performs. This chapter discusses the nature of concept formation in music and offers many specific suggestions on how to develop the child's concepts of music and its basic elements.

Building Concepts of Music

The conceptual growth of the learner is considered to be one of the major goals of education. Yet few people have **255** an understanding of the meaning of conceptual growth.

What is a concept? How is it formed? Why is conceptual growth important? A discussion of the concepts that can be developed through musical experiences is found on pp. 79–87. To review, a *concept* is a person's mental construction of an idea or image that forms after he perceives or experiences an object or event in his environment. It is a generalized understanding that the person builds as a result of his experience and that remains with him after that experience. A concept represents the person's unique attempt to organize what he perceives about the environment into relationships that have meaning for him. It is a person's way of making order out of his experiences. A concept cannot be taught. Rather, it is formed, built, clarified, developed, and extended by the child's own mental and physical activity on objects and events in his environment. The child forms countless concepts about his world as he uses his five senses, as he manipulates objects, as he solves problems, as he creates, and as he questions.

A concept is quite vague and general in its initial stages but becomes more refined through further experience with the particular object or event. During every experience, the child builds upon his previous understandings to form changing concepts about what he perceives and knows. Concepts emerge, grow, change, and become clarified as a result of the child's experiences. For example, as he hears many types of music, a young child begins to build his own concepts of vocal tone qualities. The baby learns to recognize his mother's voice. He then hears his relatives speaking and singing, and his concept of vocal quality expands. He hears children singing and listens to the rock singer on a record or on television. His concept of vocal tone color continues to expand as he hears an opera singer, a church chorus, and a concert choir. In preschool, his teacher may play music sung by American Indians or an Israeli or Danish folk singer. His concepts of vocal tone color will continue to grow and become clarified as a result of his continuing experiences in listening to songs sung by many different people and choral groups.

The first step in concept formation is using the senses to perceive objects and events. In music, this means that the child must have many experiences in

256

hearing music and in seeing and touching objects that produce music. Over a period of time, the child begins to build his own system of structuring and relating his present musical experiences to past experiences. He forms mental images about what he hears today and relates these to what he heard yesterday. He notices differences and similarities in the music and in his experiences. He begins to focus on a particular attribute of the music—perhaps its beat or its tune—and responds by moving or singing. He organizes his thinking about his musical experiences and recognizes that sometimes the music is fast and sometimes it is slow and that sometimes the tune is sung by a woman and sometimes by a man. Every time the child listens to and experiences music, his concepts about music develop.

Musical response and the development of concepts start at birth and continue throughout a person's life. The infant hears sounds in his environment. He perceives differences between his mother's and father's voices. He listens to the soft singing of his mother's lullaby and the loud music on the radio. He experiments with his own vocal sounds. He joyfully kicks the jingle bells that are suspended from a string tied to his crib. He grasps a rattle and makes different sounds on the wooden boards of his crib. Each time he experiences music, he is developing concepts about music and sound. The more experiences the child has with music, the more concepts he will develop.

In order for the child to develop concepts about music, he needs to be given a wide variety of experiences with the materials of music, i.e., tone and rhythm. He needs to be provided with many different kinds of listening experiences—listening to sounds from the environment, to live and recorded music, to musics from many cultures and historical periods, to vocal, instrumental, and electronic music. He needs to experiment with making and performing music—by using sound makers in his environment and by using his own voice and other instruments. He needs many opportunities to develop concepts about music. The more experiences he has and the more he is given the chance to respond to music, the greater is the probability that he will develop musically.

257   Through many experiences with music over a long

period of time, the child develops many concepts about music. He begins to feel and then know that human voices sound different from each other, that some music is faster or louder than others, that music has a beginning and an end, that there is a steady pulse in most music, that some music is smooth and flowing, that some music is jagged and accented, that the pitches of tones in a melody move high and low, and that there is a wide variety of musical styles. Some musical concepts emerge relatively early in life, e.g., concepts about dynamics, tone color, and tempo. Some musical concepts develop much later, e.g., concepts about harmony and form. Nevertheless, all understanding about and enjoyment of music have their roots in the musical experiences of early childhood.

Activities to Promote Concept Development in Music

What can you do to promote the child's conceptual growth in music? In general, provide a wide variety of daily experiences in listening to, performing, and creating music so that the child has ample opportunity to develop his own understanding of music. Offer the child many opportunities to listen to different types of music, to make music with his voice and on sound makers and instruments, and to create music. Provide a balanced repertoire of singing and instrumental selections from many sources. Move frequently with the child to the rhythmic feeling and overall mood of the music, and/or encourage the child's own movements to music. Above all, help the child perceive the music, respond to it with his body and mind, and eventually verbalize what he feels and knows.

The child's understandings also can be developed through specific activities with various aspects of music, including dynamics, tempo, tone color, beat, duration and melodic rhythm, pitch and melody, harmony, phrase, repetition and contrast, and musical style (see next section for detailed discussion). Many of these activities have been mentioned previously in earlier chapters of this book and are summarized on the remaining pages of this chapter. Use these activities on a daily basis, and make them an important part of every young child's musical experience. They should be enjoyable and meaningful to the child and lead to his overall conceptual understanding of musical experiences.

Developing Concepts of Dynamics

There are many beginning experiences that will help the young child develop concepts about dynamics. You can:

1. Play any recording for the child. Turn the volume control high and then low at time intervals of about thirty seconds. Also gradually turn the control louder, softer.

2. Swing or rock the child gently when the music is soft and vigorously when the music is loud.

3. Play a piece that is loud and then a piece that is soft.

4. Sing to the child loudly, softly.

5. Clap, or hit objects for the child—loudly and softly. Say "loud" or "soft" in a loud or soft voice, as appropriate.

6. Play a rhythm instrument loudly when the music is loud and softly when the music is soft.

7. Move to the music, using large movements for loud music and smaller movements when the music becomes softer.

8. Chant rhymes and statements to the child in a loud, soft voice. Vary the dynamics of your voice.

Some later experiences that you can use to help the child develop concepts about dynamics include:

1. Ask the child to play rhythm instruments loudly or softly, as appropriate, to accompany the dynamics of the music. Also clap and use other body rhythms (patting, tapping) to highlight the music's dynamics.

2. Ask the child to use big movements for loud music and small movements for soft music. "Can you get bigger when the music gets louder? Can you get smaller when the music becomes softer?"

3. Discuss whether the music heard is loud or soft.

4. Imitate the movements of a large, heavy elephant or a small, agile bird. Ask the child to add a rhythm instrument accompaniment (loud or soft, as appropriate) to show how the animal moves.

5. Experiment with singing a song loudly, softly. Change the dynamics suddenly, gradually. Evaluate effect.

6. Play excerpts from two recordings. Compare their levels of loudness.

7. Classify pieces according to their dynamics ("This is soft music. This is loud music."). *Do not* use the terms "high" and "low" for dynamics, as these terms should be reserved for pitch (see p. 79).

8. Relate dynamics to energy level by asking: "What do you do to play (or sing) louder, softer?" (You use more or less energy.)

9. Make up a piece of music for a rhythm instrument in which the dynamics change.

10. Show the child the symbols for loud $(\boldsymbol{f})$, , soft $(\boldsymbol{p})$, becoming louder (————————), and becoming softer (————————) as the child sings or listens to music. Use these symbols to reinforce the experience.

Developing Concepts of Tempo

There are many beginning experiences that will help the young child develop concepts about tempo. You can:

1. Play a recording for the child that is fast and then a piece that is slow.

2. Swing or rock the child slowly or fast to correspond with music that is slow or fast moving.

260 3. Sing fast and then slow songs to the child.

4. Vary the tempo of familiar songs. Also sing a song slowly, and gradually get faster, and vice versa.

5. Clap, or hit objects for the child. Do this fast or slow and then gradually faster or slower. Say "fast," "faster," "slow," or "slower," as appropriate.

6. Play a rhythm instrument slowly when the music is slow, and fast when the music is fast. Also change tempo to correspond with the music's tempo.

7. Move to the tempo of the music, using fast movements for fast music and slow movements for slow music. Have the child observe, and/or carry him as you move.

8. Chant rhymes and statements to the child in a fast, slow tempo. Also vary the tempo (begin slowly and become faster, or begin fast and become slower).

Some later experiences you can use to help the young child develop concepts about tempo include:

1. Experiment with and sing a song slowly, fast. Evaluate which tempo seems more appropriate.

2. Play a rhythm instrument at various tempi, and have the child move fast, slowly, as appropriate.

3. Move slowly, fast, and ask the child to add a rhythm instrument accompaniment to your movements.

4. Imitate animals and people and how they move at different speeds. Ask the child to move like a turtle, a lizard, a crocodile, a galloping horse, a train, a bus, an old man, or like anything else that is familiar to the child.

5. Play a fast piece, a slow piece. Ask the child to move as appropriate. Compare the tempo of the two pieces.

6. Play a rhythm instrument, and gradually change its tempo. Have the child move, as appropriate, to the tempo.

7. Give the child a tone block or another rhythm instrument. Ask him to make a steady beat like a fast clock, a slow clock, a fast or slow walk, or a fast or slow dripping faucet.

261 8. Make up a piece for a rhythm instrument that moves slowly or fast or that starts slowly and becomes faster, or vice versa.

9. Relate tempo to feelings and mood; e.g., fast tempo is often happier in feeling than slower tempo. Ask the child to show the movements of a happy and sad tiger, of a happy and sad little child, and so on.

10. Play a recording, or sing a song for the child. Ask him to raise his hands when the tempo changes.

11. Design the beat of the music, showing variations in tempo. Space slower beats further apart than faster beats, as:

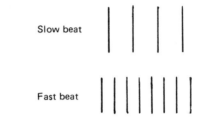

Developing Concepts of Tone Color

There are many beginning experiences that will help the young child develop concepts about tone color. You can.

1. Take the young child around the house and outdoors, and tap various things in the environment with a wooden or metal object as the child observes and participates.

2. Under supervision, provide the child with many sound-making objects as he plays in his crib or playpen. Allow the child to explore his environment, making sounds as he hits a table leg, the wooden floor, or the metal garbage can.

3. Take frequent walks with the child, calling attention to various environmental sounds (see also p. 101–3, 135).

4. Tape-record environmental sounds and replay these for the child.

5. Record the child's own vocalizations and play these back for him.

6. Take the child to watch an older child practice his instrument or a musical group rehearse (see p. 101–103).

7. Encourage different family members to sing to the child.

8. Play a wide variety of recordings that feature different vocal, instrumental, and electronic tone colors. Include church choruses, rock singers, opera singers, folk singers from other cultures, children's voices, and men's and women's voices. Also include such various instrumental combinations as jazz and rock groups, solo instruments, orchestras and bands, ethnic music ensembles (Indonesian gamelan orchestras, Russian balalaika groups, West African drumming and xylophone groups), and other instrumental combinations.

9. Play various rhythm instruments for the child as he watches.

10. Show the child how he can experiment with his voice. Whisper, hum, make "oooo" sounds, make animal sounds, whistle, cough, growl, and grunt. Encourage the child to combine these sounds to make a vocal composition.

Some later experiences you can use to help the young child develop concepts about tone color include:

1. Continue to play a wide variety of instrumental, vocal, and electronic music. Call attention to what voices (or instruments) are performing.

2. Give the child a mallet or stick. Have him experiment in obtaining interesting sounds by striking objects with the mallet or stick.

3. Invite the child to experiment with his voice to change its qualities. Have him try to imitate sounds of birds and animals, the wind, ghosts, dripping water. Have him experiment with grunting, growling, whispering, puffing, whistling, and coughing.

4. Provide a wide variety of rhythm instruments for him to experiment with and play.

5. Play a game. Have the child close his eyes and then identify who is talking—his mother, his sister, or his

father.

6. Play a game. Choose two contrasting rhythm instruments with which the child is familiar. Play them behind the sofa or door. Ask the child to select which instrument he hears. Once aural discrimination is developed, choose three or more instruments for the game.

7. Play a recording that highlights a particular tone color. Show the child a picture of the instrument (or a picture of a man, woman, child, group of people, as appropriate).

8. Play singing games such as "The Muffin Man" (see Appendix) or "Who Is Tapping at My Window?" A child closes his eyes as someone else (a child or adult) sings to him. The child must guess who sang.

9. Take the child to live music rehearsals or performances. If possible, let the child hear each instrument, touch it, listen to how a tone is produced, and try to make a tone by himself.

10. Play a recording that highlights changes in tone colors. Ask: "Can you clap when the woman begins to sing? Can you raise your hands when the piano starts to play? Can you point to the correct picture when the child or man begins to sing? Can you stand when the violin plays and sit when the trumpet plays?"

11. Allow time for frequent sound exploration on instruments such as the Autoharp, piano, or tone bells. "Can you play the Autoharp a different way? Let's see you try another way to make sound on the bells."

Developing Concepts of Beat

There are many beginning experiences that will help the young child develop concepts about beat. Since beat is fundamental to overall musical response, use these activities very frequently, if not on a daily basis. You can:

1. Rock, swing, and bounce the child to the beat of any piece of music.

2. Play recorded music, and tap the beat for the child on a rhythm instrument or by hitting a nearby object.

3. Take the child's hands and clap them in time to the music's beat. Say "beat, beat, beat . . ." to coincide with the beat of the music.

4. Let the child watch and hear the steady beat of a windshield wiper, a faucet dripping, a ball being bounced, and a clock ticking.

5. Play many recorded examples of music with a strong beat (American Indian or African drumming, Hawaiian chants, rock and march music, dance music from Latin America, square dance music, and dance music from many countries of Europe, Africa, and Asia).

6. Clap, stamp, move the entire body to the beat of the music as the child watches and then imitates you.

7. Play a metronome for the child. Then set it to coincide with the beat of a recorded piece. Sing a song and match its tempo to the metronome's beat.

8. Rock the child in a sleeper or rocker, or swing him on a swing, or move him rhythmically on a seesaw. Chant to the beat of the child's movements.

Some later experiences you can use to help the young child develop concepts about beat include:

1. Continue moving with the child to the beat of recorded selections and to songs you sing. Walk, clap, and stamp your foot with him.

2. Have the child move in a variety of ways to the music's beat, e.g., clapping, tapping, hitting his lap or thighs, walking, marching, running, swinging his arms, moving his knees, swaying back and forth.

3. Chant to the beat of the child's movement as he jumps rope, bounces a ball, swings on a swing, moves on the seesaw, walks, and runs.

4. Ask the child to walk or run or skip. Add a rhythm instrument accompaniment to match the child's beat.

5. Move rhythmically in a steady beat without music. Ask the child to watch your movements and match them by adding a steady beat on a rhythm instrument.

6. Use a metronome to accompany the child's singing.

265 Also set a metronome to accompany the beat of a

recorded piece of music. Move rhythmically with the metronome.

7. Have the child click his tongue or make other vocalizations (see p. 263) to accompany the beat. Also have him say "beat, beat, beat . . ." to the music's beat.

8. Visually design the beat, making up-and-down movements in the air and on paper or the chalkboard to

show steady beats

| | | |

and strong and weak beats

| ||| | ||| or | || | ||

9. Show long and short tones through sustained or short movements and symbols. For example:
Say: "**one**-two-three" or "**one**-two-three-four." Clap on the first beat and snap fingers on the weaker beats. Also jump, step, or bend on the stronger beats, and stay still for the weaker beats.

10. Play "paddy cake" games, hitting the child's hands on the beat and strong beat. Also have the child imitate a rocking horse moving back and forth to the beat.

11. Ask the child to imitate various objects and/or things that move as he moves to the beat. "Can you step like a monster, a calf, a mouse, a horse, a soldier? Can you keep in time to the beat of the music?"

12. Play a piece of music. Do not clap in time with the beat. Ask the child to raise his hands when the clapping matches the music's beat.

Developing Concepts of Duration and Melodic Rhythm

There are many beginning experiences that will help the young child develop concepts of duration and melodic rhythm. You can:

266

1. Tap and clap many rhythms for the child.

2. Play a long tone on the triangle or gong. Follow this by playing a short tone on the rhythm sticks. Continue alternating the two sounds.

3. Play drumming music from various cultures, including the American Indians, Polynesia, West and Central Africa, the Caribbean, and the Arabic countries.

4. Sing to the child, using the syllables "mah" or "dah." Alternate tones that are held a long or short time.

5. Take the child on many walks to hear long and short tones and rhythms in the environment. Listen to door bells, the ringing of dinner or church bells, the sounds of sirens, the blaring of horns, and the chirping of birds.

6. Encourage the child to make up interesting sounding rhythmic patterns on rhythm instruments. Allow for frequent experimentation.

7. Using the voice, imitate various tones in the environment, such as a siren, a blaring horn, a clucking hen, a chirping bird, a ringing door bell, and a chugging train.

8. Swing the child in the air for a series of long tones, moving each time the tone is sounded. Bounce him for short tones.

9. Hold the child's hands and move them as you sustain a tone. Sing some short tones and move the child's hands in a jerky, abrupt manner.

10. As the child watches, clap a rhythmic pattern, then stamp it, and then tap it. Encourage the child to repeat your sounds and movements.

11. Frequently clap the rhythmic pattern of the child's name, such as

12. Frequently chant nursery rhymes and words to the child, accenting the rhythmic flow.

Some later experiences you can use to help the young child develop concepts about duration and melodic rhythm include:

1. Ask the child to play long tones, short tones, on the triangle. Move in a sustained way for long tones and in a short, abrupt way for short tones.

2. Frequently clap and tap names, jingles, rhymes, words, and the texts of songs. For example:

Billy Brown

I had a little shadow

Nick nack paddy whack

3. Listen to and imitate on instruments and with the voice various rhythms in the environment, e.g., rain, a faucet dripping, a horse galloping, a train departing from the station, a bird chirping.

4. Echo-clap a wide variety of rhythms. Have the child clap whatever you clap. For example:

Adult

Child

On the last beat, say "Go." Also use rhythm instruments and tapping of the feet to add interest.

5. Play "follow the leader." Say: "Can you do what I do?" Clap and use the body, and vocalize rhythms. Have the child imitate you. For example:

(clap, snap) "boo-boo - boo" (child imitates)

6. Use rhythm instruments, especially the rhythm sticks, tambourine, or wood and tone blocks, to play the

rhythms of words, rhymes, words of song texts, and rhythms of tunes.

7. Use rhythm instruments for imitating rhythms in the environment, e.g., the hoofbeats of a horse, the crowing of a rooster, skipping or running, the beeping of a horn.

8. Move your hand in one direction, and ask the child to sing a sustained tone as long as the hand moves. Also move abruptly and ask the child to sing short tones to correspond with the movements.

9. Show long and short tones through sustained or short movements and symbols. For example:

———————————   ———

long   short

10. Raise hands when a tone in the music is held very long, e.g., the "lu" tone from "hallelujah" in the song "Michael, Row The Boat Ashore" or the "star" tone from "Twinkle, Twinkle Little Star."

11. Isolate a repeated rhythmic pattern from a song or recording. Clap this pattern whenever it occurs, and add a rhythm instrument accompaniment to it. For example:

♩ ♪   shoo fly

♩ ♩ ♫♫ ♩ skip, skip, skip to my Lou

♩ ♩ ♩ ♫ a frequent rhythmic pattern
found in rock music

12. Walk for slow, even rhythms, and run for fast, even rhythms.

13. Send messages using drum talk. Say: "Can you tap 'I like you' on the drum? Can you tap 'My name is Amanda' on the drum?" After much experience, tap a drum message, and ask the child what the message was. Also, use two drums, and tap drum messages to each other.

14. Clap two rhythms. Say: "Are they the same or **269** different?" For example:

Here is rhythm one: ♩   ♩   ♩

Here is rhythm two: ♫ ♩ ♫ ♩   ♩

"Yes, they're different." Use many different rhythmic patterns.

15. Clap a rhythm, and ask the child to add words to fit the pattern.

16. Clap three rhythms, two of which are the same and one that is different. Identify which rhythm is different. For example, say: "Which rhythm is different?"

Here is rhythm one: ♩   ♫ ♩   ♩

Here is rhythm two: ♩   ♫ ♩   ♩

Here is rhythm three: ♫ ♩   ♫ ♩

17. Have the child imitate you as you clap the rhythm of a tune while singing it. For example, clap the rhythm:

♫ ♩   ♫ ♩ for "This old man, he played one. . ."

18. Play a guessing game. Clap the rhythm of a familiar tune, and ask the child what tune it is. Later ask the child to clap a "mystery tune," and call on someone else (you or another child) to guess which tune has that rhythm.

19. Sing a tune with "la." Encourage the child to add words to fit the tune's rhythm.

20. Design the rhythmic pattern of familiar tunes or parts of tunes on a paper or chalkboard, and have the child point to the design as the rhythm is sung or played. For example:

―― ―― ― ――   or   ― ―― ― ―― ― ――
Skip,   skip,   skip to my lou   The   far - mer   in   the   dell

Developing Concepts of Pitch and Melody

For beginning experiences you can:

270   1. Sing many songs to the child as you hold and/or rock him. Often let him touch your face and mouth as you sing.

2. Play many recordings that feature either high or low pitches (examples: soprano or bass solos, flute or cello solos, women's choruses, men's choruses).

3. Take the child on frequent walks to hear sounds in the environment that are low or high in pitch. Listen to birds singing, the wind whistling through the trees, sounds made by boats in the harbor, sounds at the gasoline station.

4. Imitate vocal sounds made by the child, accentuating various high and low pitches.

5. Record the child's vocal sounds, and play these sounds back for him.

6. Chant poems and rhymes, using rising and falling vocal inflection.

7. Make sounds for the child on various pitch levels. Encourage him to imitate these sounds.

8. Play the pitches on various xylophone-type instruments for the child as he watches. Sing "high" when the pitches are high and "low" when the pitches are low.

9. Hold the child. Place him high in the air as you sing high tones and say "high." Place him near the floor as you sing low tones and say "low."

10. Push the child on a swing. Sing "up and down" using high and low pitches as he swings. Also do this as the child moves on a seesaw.

11. As the child walks up stairs or walks up on the steps of a slide, sing ascending tones to match his upward movement. Sing lower tones as he descends.

12. Make up many chants using the child's name or describing what he has or what he is doing.

13. Play many familiar tunes to the child, using a xylophone-type instrument such as the step bells; song, resonator, and melody bells; the xylophone, and the marimba. Make sure the child is in a position to watch. Also play tonal patterns from these tunes.

Later experiences for developing concepts of pitch and melody include:

271

1. Use many of the techniques outlined for developing the child's ability to sing on pitch, as outlined on pp. 178–183.

2. Imitate sounds in the environment, using varying pitch levels.

3. Play familiar tunes and tonal patterns on the step bells or on a vertically held xylophone as the child observes the up-and-down movements.

4. Use the entire body or the hands moving up and down to show pitch levels. First, the child can imitate you as you play the high–low pitches on an instrument. Then the child should be invited to try this on his own.

5. Frequently encourage the child to make up his own songs and tunes.

6. Engage in musical conversations with the child, such as:

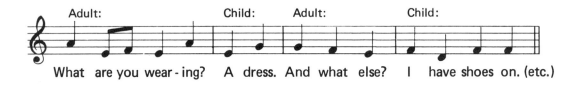

7. Play two different Autoharp or ukulele strings or resonator or tone bells. Discover how the pitches vary according to the size of the string or bell bar.

8. Always provide the children with the starting pitch when singing as a group. Practice singing the starting pitch of a song after hearing it sounded on the pitch pipe, piano, or melody bells.

9. Give the child two resonator bells with contrasting pitches, e.g., C and G, or D and B. Sing or play

$$C \, ^G \, C$$

and have the child repeat this on the bells. Repeat, using other patterns such as

$$C \, ^{G \, G} \, C$$
or
$$^G \, C \, ^{G \, G} \, C$$

Try three contrasting pitches if the child does very well with two. If resonator bells are unavailable, use another melody instrument (see pp. 211–215).

10. Sing or play a tune for the child, making one error in pitch. Encourage the child to recognize the error and indicate this by raising his hand when he hears it.

11. Invite the child to echo tonal patterns sung or played. For example:

12. Sing the tune of a familiar song, using "la," or play the tune on an instrument. Ask the child to name the song.

13. Encourage the child to sing a familiar tune with "la." Have the other children or another adult guess the name of the song.

14. Invite the child to find the high and low pitches on a piano, guitar, melody bells, and other instruments.

15. Ask the child to sing or play tonal patterns for you or for another child to imitate.

16. Sing or play two tonal patterns to the child, the second of which is either the same or different. Encourage the child to say whether the patterns are the same or different. For example:

17. Find objects in the room with high or low pitches when struck.

18. Show the child how to play simple tonal patterns from familiar tunes on the step, melody, or tone bells.

273

19. Show high and low pitches for familiar songs by designing the pitch levels on paper or on the chalkboard. For example:

```
          —
 — —             ———        or    —  —  ———   — —  ———
    —            ———              Jin - gle  bells,   jin - gle  bells
Ring a-round the   ro  -  sy
```

Developing Concepts of Harmony

Many studies completed during the last few years have shown that harmonic concepts in young children are relatively slow to emerge and only begin to be clarified during the elementary school years. Nevertheless, certain activities can be used with the young child to help form the basis of his conceptual structure for understanding harmony. These activities include:

1. Frequently sing to the child using just the voice and then using a harmonic accompaniment.

2. Have the child experiment with making harmony on the step, resonator, or melody bells by giving him two mallets. Also let him make harmony by playing two or more simultaneous tones on the piano.

3. Encourage the child to experiment with harmony by strumming the Autoharp, ukulele, or guitar and by listening to the simultaneous sounds. Use the word *harmony* when you add an accompaniment to the child's singing. Say: "I'm now going to play *harmony* on the ukulele" rather than "I'm now going to play the ukulele."

4. Take the child to hear many choral and instrumental rehearsals and performances.

5. Play an Autoharp accompaniment for the child's singing. Help the child to strum the Autoharp as you finger the correct chords.

6. Play the melody of a familiar tune on the piano. Then add an accompaniment. Compare the sound. Then play the accompaniment alone, and ask the child to listen to it. Compare the melody with the accompaniment.

274

For beginning experiences, you can:

1. Sing to the child, slightly slowing the tempo at the end of each phrase.
2. Sing to the child as you hold him. At the start of each phrase, slightly shift his position.
3. Sing to the child as you hold and walk with him. At the start of each phrase, shift direction.
4. Sing to the child. Accompany the singing with a rhythm instrument. Play the instrument on alternating phrases and then on the first beat of every phrase.
5. Chant many poems and nursery rhymes to the child. Emphasize the spoken phrase. Make your voice rise in the middle of the phrase and fall at the end of the phrase.
6. Play recordings for the child that have distinct phrases. Hold the child on the lap and move with him in different directions as each phrase is heard.
7. Have the child watch as you move your hands and/or body in rainbow-shaped arcs

to the musical phrase.

Later experiences useful for developing the young child's concepts of phrase include:

1. Occasionally use the phrase-by-phrase method of teaching new songs (see p. 188).
2. Show phrases through bodily movement. For example, sit on one phrase and stand on the next, or change the direction of movement for each phrase.
3. Illustrate and emphasize the need to take a quiet breath before and after singing each phrase.
4. Show the child how to move his hands in rainbow-shaped arcs to the phrases. After many experiences in

275

imitating you, have the child move to the phrase by himself.

5. Recite many poems and nursery rhymes with the child. Emphasize the need to take a breath before each phrase.

6. Help the child alternate the singing of phrases. For example, the child can sing phrases 1 and 3, and you can sing phrases 2 and 4. In a group situation, one child can sing phrases 1 and 3, and all the children can sing phrases 2 and 4.

7. Add a different rhythm instrument accompaniment for each phrase of a song.

8. Help the child to count the number of phrases by putting up one, two, three fingers to indicate the number of each phrase.

9. Add an instrument or clap to the first beat of each phrase.

Developing Concepts of Repetition and Contrast

Concepts of form, involving repetition and contrast, usually begin to emerge after the preschool years. Nevertheless, certain activities can be used with the young child to help develop these concepts. You can:

1. Rock or move the child in time with a recorded piece of music. When the music changes its tempo, dynamics, melody, tone color, or mood, change the type of movement.

2. Play a rhythm instrument to accompany a recorded piece of music as the child observes. Change to another rhythm instrument when the music changes.

3. Frequently sing over and over again a short tune or tonal fragment as you rock the child. For example, sing:

Sleep, sleep, go to sleep   OR   Sleep my lit - tle child.

Repeat the pattern many times as you continue the same rocking movements.

4. Play the "same–different game" using rhythmic and tonal patterns (see pp. 269–70, 273).

5. Have the child imitate you as you raise hands or stand (sit) whenever there is a change in the music's tempo, dynamics, melody, rhythm, tone color, or mood. Tell the child that the music has changed.

6. In rhythmic movement, ask the child to move only when the main section starts and not during the introduction.

7. Ask the child to raise his hands or play a rhythm instrument every time he hears a given pattern in the music. For example, whenever he hears the rhythmic pattern

in "Skip to My Lou" or the "e-i-e-i-o" tonal pattern in "Old MacDonald," he should respond.

8. Use many activities listed on pp. 258–264 to help the child develop concepts of repetition and contrast in dynamics, tempo, and tone color.

Developing Concepts of Musical Styles

Young children ages three and four often have surprising insight into musical style. Many children can recognize that music is for a parade, or that it is Chinese or American Indian music, or that it is rock music or dance music. These concepts emerge, of course, because of prior experiences with music of those styles. Beginning concepts of musical style probably start at age two or three, as the child listens to music on television or is taken to various musical and cultural events in the community. Some activities that will help the child to develop concepts of musical style include the following:

1. Sing and play a wide variety of music from many cultures and historical periods.

2. Take the child to many musical events in the community—a rock or jazz festival, a parade, a classical music concert, an ethnic dance celebration.

3. Let the child watch educational programs on television that deal with the life, culture, and music of other countries.

4. If available, provide opportunities for the child to see and hear ethnic instruments being played.

5. When playing a piece of music or singing a song, briefly explain to the child that the music was written a long time ago by a composer or that it comes from a place that is far away. Depending upon the child's maturity, you might show him pictures of the people who live in the country where the music is performed or a picture of the composer who wrote the music.

Special Approaches for Developing Musical Concepts

Over the years, several educators and musicians have developed specific approaches for promoting the young child's ability to respond to music. Each approach aims at fostering conceptual growth and musical response in the very young. Each emphasizes the importance of a musical education beginning in early childhood. And each uses bodily movement as an important means for achieving musical response in the young child. Some of these approaches include:

- the Carabo-Cone method
- Dalcroze eurhythmics
- the Kodály system
- Orff–Schulwerk
- Suzuki's Talent Education Program

If you are interested in details of the techniques used in these approaches you should refer to the Carabo-Cone, Kendall, and Landis and Carder references at the end of this chapter, or write to the following: Carabo-Cone Center, 881 Seventh Avenue, New York, New York 10019; Dalcroze School of Music, 161 East 73rd Street, New York, New York 10021; Kodály Musical Training Institute, 525 Worcester Street, Wellesley, Massachusetts 62181; Orff–Schulwerk Association, Division of Music, Ball State University, Muncie, Indiana 47306.

Summary

As a result of the child's experiences with music, he will form concepts (mental images or ideas) about music and its dynamics, rhythm, melody, harmony, and form. These concepts will emerge, grow, and change as a result of frequent and significant musical experiences. Your role is to provide a stimulating, varied, and creative musical environment so that the child has many opportunities to develop his own concepts. You can provide a wide variety of musical activities for the young child to help foster conceptual growth. You should also become acquainted with various systems and approaches designed to foster musical response in young children, including the Carabo-Cone method, Dalcroze eurhythmics, the Kodály system, Orff–Schulwerk, and Suzuki's Talent Education Program. Each of these approaches has something to offer the young child as he responds to music and grows in his conceptual understanding of what he experiences.

Selected Readings

Carabo-Cone, Madeline, *A Sensory-Motor Approach to Music Learning,* 4 vols. New York: MCA Music,1974.
Presents specific techniques for developing musical responses in young children.

Kendall, John D., *Suzuki Violin Method in American Music Education.* Washington, D.C.: Music Educators National Conference, 1973.
Summarizes the approach of the Japanese music educator Shinichi Suzuki.

Landis, Beth, and Polly Carder, *The Eclectic Curriculum in American Music Education: Contributions of Dalcroze, Kodály, and Orff.* Washington, D.C.: Music Educators National Conference, 1972.
Excellent description of specific approaches to music education of young children. Lists many sources for further study.

Nye, Robert E., and Vernice T. Nye, *Music in the Elementary School* (4th ed.). Englewood Cliffs, N.J.: Prentice–Hall, Inc., 1977.
One of the things the authors describe in this excellent book is music and the learning process and they present a clear analysis of the basic elements of music and the processes of concept formation.

Spitzer, Dean R., *Concept Formation and Learning in Early Childhood.* Columbus, Ohio: Charles E. Merrill Publishing Co., 1977.
A general discussion.

Woodruff, Asahel D., *Basic Concepts of Teaching.* San Francisco: Chandler Publishing Co., 1961.
A very readable explanation on what concepts are and how they are developed.

Zimmerman, Marilyn P., *Musical Characteristics of Children.* Washington, D.C.: Music Educators National Conference, 1971.
A basic reference on music concept formation in children.

Part Three

APPENDIXES

Appendix A

Songs for the Young Child

A Song List

There are many songs appropriate for the young child. Following is a list of some of these songs, all of which are frequently found in song books and music series. In addition, include in the child's song repertoire simple popular songs, holiday songs, folk songs from America and countries around the world, songs from the child's cultural and ethnic background, and songs he creates. Also use children's chants common to the culture, such as "Rain, Rain, Go Away," and clapping and jump-rope chants. Some recommended songs include the following; many are found immediately following this list.

ABC (The Alphabet Song)
All Around the Kitchen
All Night, All Day
All Together Here We Go
Alouette
Angel Band, The
Animal Fair
Are You Sleeping? (Frére Jacques)

A Tisket, A Tasket
Baa Baa Black Sheep
Bear Went Over the Mountain
B–I–N–G–O
Bluebird, Bluebird
Bought Me a Cat
Bow Belinda
Bus, The

Bye, Bye, Baby
Bye, Bye, Baby, Bye
Chiapanecas
Chua-Ay
Clap, Clap, Clap Your Hands
Clap Your Hands
Come Up, Horsey
Cuckoo
Daddy Shot a Bear

Dame, Wake Up
Dance Thumbkin, Dance
Da-ye-nu
Did You Ever See a Lassie?
Did You Feed My Cow?
Do a Pretty Motion
Down in the Valley
Epo I Tai Tama E
Everybody Do This
Everybody Loves Saturday
    Night
Farmer in the Dell, The
Fiddle-Dee-Dee
Fly, Manu, Fly
Frére Jacques
Go In and Out the Window
Go Tell Aunt Rhodie
Good News!
Good Night, Ladies
Happy Birthday
Havah Nagilah
He-Nay Mah Tov
He's Got the Whole World in
    His Hands
Hello Everybody, Yes Indeed
Hey Betty Martin
Hey La La La
Hi-Dee-Roon-O
Hickory Dickory Dock
Hokey Pokey, The
Hole in the Bucket
Hot Cross Buns
Hush, Little Baby
I Put My Hands Up High
I Want to Be a Farmer
If You're Happy
I'm a Little Teapot
I'm Going to Sing
It's Raining, It's Pouring
Jack and Jill
Jacob's Ladder

Jim-Along, Josie
Jingle at the Windows
Jingle Bells
Johnny Works with One
    Hammer
Johnny's on the Woodpile
Jump Down, Turn Around
Kumbayah
Lazy Mary
Les Marionettes
Let Everyone Clap Hands
    With Me
Little David
Little Tom Tinker
London Bridge
Looby Loo
Love Somebody
Mary Had a Little Lamb
Mary Has a Red Dress
Michael Finnegan
Michael Row the Boat
    Ashore
Miss Mary Jane
Miss Polly Had a Dolly
Muffin Man, The
Mulberry Bush, The
My Hat It Has Three Corners
O What a Beautiful Morning
Oh, When the Saints
Old Gray Cat, The
Old Grey Mare, The
Old MacDonald
One Finger Keeps Moving
One Little Elephant
One Man Went to Mow
One Potato, Two Potatoes
Paw Paw Patch
Polly Wolly Doodle
Put Your Finger in the Air
Rabbit in the Wood, The

Rain, Rain, Go Away
Riding in a Buggy
Ring Around a Rosy
Rock-a-bye Baby
Rock-a-my-Soul
Row, Row, Row Your Boat
Sa-Chi-Chi
Santa Claus is Coming to
    Town
Santy Maloney
She'll Be Comin' Round the
    Mountain
Shoo Fly
Shortnin' Bread
Six Little Ducks
Skip to My Lou
Spider and Spout
Sweetly Sings the Donkey
Ten Little Indians
The More We Get Together
There Was a Man
There Was an Old Lady
This Old Man
Three Blind Mice
Three Little Chickadees
Twinkle, Twinkle
Under the Spreading
    Chestnut Tree
We Wish You a Merry
    Christmas
What'll We Do with the
    Baby?
What Shall We Do?
Where is Thumbkin?
Whistle, Mary, Whistle
Who is Tapping at My
    Window?
Yankee Doodle
You Are My Sunshine
Zum-Gali-Gali

The Music and Words of Some Songs

286 The following songs have been found to be used frequently by many parents and teachers of young children. The letter-name of the starting tone of each song is written before the first note. In addition, chord markings for songs are written above the notes. The chords should be repeated on each beat until a new chord is indicated.

The songs are categorized in three groupings: (1) limited vocal range, (2) expanding vocal range, and (3) wide vocal range. The songs in the first category will be the easiest for the young child to sing accurately; the songs in the third category will be more difficult. The songs in each category are presented alphabetically.

Copyright restrictions have prevented us from using a more representative collection of songs suitable for young children (see Chapter 6, Singing), and in addition, these restrictions necessitated the reprinting of several songs which may be in too high a key for most young children to sing. In using these songs with children, place them in keys which the children can sing more comfortably (see page 184).

Limited Vocal Range

A - TISKET, A-TASKET

Cheerfully   D   Traditional Game Song

A - tis - ket, a - tas - ket, a   green and yel - low   bas - ket,

A7   D

I wrote a let - ter to my love and on the way I dropped it.

I dropped it, I dropped it, And on the way I dropped it,

A7   D

A   lit - tle {boy/girl} picked it up and put it in {her/his} pock - et.

Directions:
Form a circle and sing while one child ("it") carries a
letter or handkerchief and walks on outside of circle.
"It" drops the letter/handkerchief behind child of his or
her choice. This child picks it up and runs after "it."
"It" must run to vacant place in circle before being
caught.

BYE, BYE, BABY

Southern

Bye, bye, ba - by, ba - by bye;

My lit - tle ba - by, ba - by, bye.

BYE BYE, BABY BYE

French

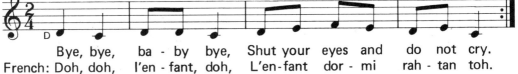

Bye, bye, ba - by bye, Shut your eyes and do not cry.
French: Doh, doh, l'en - fant, doh, L'en-fant dor - mi rah - tan toh.

CHUA-AY

Filipino Folk Song:
Mountain Province

Slowly

Drum beat or clap throughout   Chu - a ay, tal - lum - a - lay

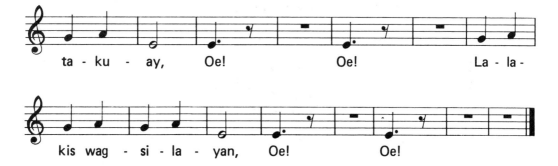

ta - ku - ay, Oe! Oe! La - la -

kis wag - si - la - yan, Oe! Oe!

This is a rice-pounding song to help workers make it easier to pound the rice. The words mean "Pound the rice, hey, hey, Clean it well, hey, hey." Have children dramatize the rice-pounding with their fists.

Courtesy of Ruth Imperial Pfeiffer, "Nine Philippine Folk Songs for Use in Grades 1 to 6." A Terminal Project Presented to the Faculty of the Graduate School of Music, University of Hawaii, May 1973.

CLAP YOUR HANDS

Traditional Chant

1. Clap, clap, clap your hands, clap your hands to - geth - er.
2. Tap, tap, tap your feet, tap your feet to - geth - er.

Other verses:
Touch your head
Rub your nose
Hit your knees
(use other body parts)

CUCKOO

Traditional Chant

Cuck - oo, where are you? Cuck - oo, where are you?

Cuck - oo, I see you, Cuck - oo, I see you.

FLY, MANU, FLY

Hawaiian nose flute melody

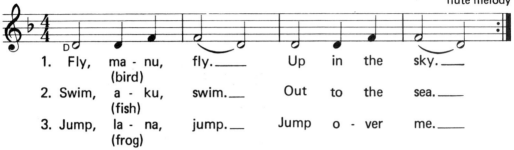

1. Fly, ma - nu, fly.___ Up in the sky.___
   (bird)
2. Swim, a - ku, swim.___ Out to the sea.___
   (fish)
3. Jump, la - na, jump.___ Jump o - ver me.___
   (frog)

Reprinted with permission of Marion A. Todd, State of Hawaii Department of Education. Words by M. Todd, based on Hawaiian nose-flute melody.

GOOD NEWS

Spiritual

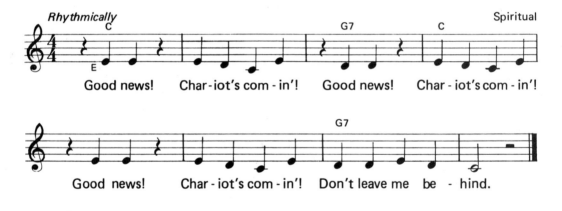

Good news! Char - iot's com - in'! Good news! Char - iot's com - in'!

Good news! Char - iot's com - in'! Don't leave me be - hind.

GO TELL AUNT RHODIE

Traditional

1. Go, tell Aunt Rho - die,___ Go, tell Aunt Rho - die, __
2. The one she's been sav - ing, The one she's been sav - ing, The

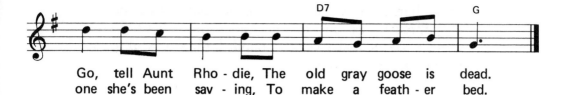

Go, tell Aunt Rho - die, The old gray goose is dead.
one she's been sav - ing, To make a feath - er bed.

3. She died in the mill pond, *(3 times)*
Standing on her head.

4. The goslings are crying, *(3 times)*
The old grey goose is dead.

5. The gander is weeping, *(3 times)*
The old gray goose is dead.

HOKEY POKEY

You put your right foot in, You take your

right foot out, You put your right foot in ___

And shake it all a - bout, And then you

do the hok - ey pok - ey And you turn your-self a - bout,

And that's what it's all a - bout. *Hey!*

Directions:
Form a circle. Do all motions indicated by text. On "do
the hokey pokey" put both hands high above head and

shake hands and wrists. On "that's what it's all about"
clap three times (on "that's," "all," and "about.") Use
other parts of body; eg. left hand, both knees, fingers,
elbows, stomach, head, etc.

HOT CROSS BUNS

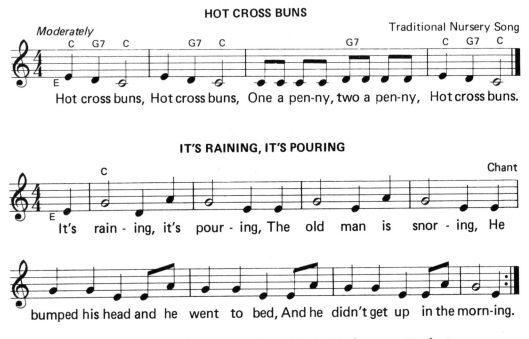

From Boardman and Landis, *Exploring Music: Kindergarten Teacher's
Reference Book* (New York: Holt, Rinehart, and Winston, 1966).
Reprinted with permission of the publisher.

JINGLE BELLS

Jin - gle bells, jin - gle bells, Jin - gle all the way,

Oh, what fun it is to ride in a one horse o - pen sleigh.

LES MARIONETTES

French

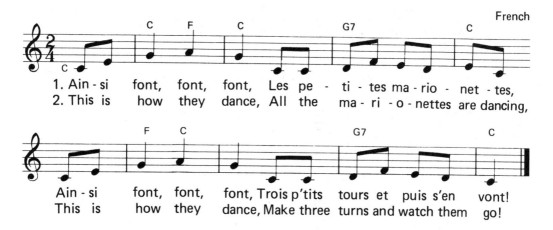

1. Ain - si font, font, font, Les pe - ti - tes ma - rio - net - tes,
2. This is how they dance, All the ma - ri - o - nettes are dancing,

Ain - si font, font, font, Trois p'tits tours et puis s'en vont!
This is how they dance, Make three turns and watch them go!

LOVE SOMEBODY

Moderately

American Folk Song

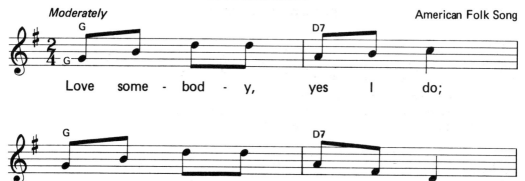

Love some - bod - y, yes I do;

Love some - bod - y, yes I do;

Love some - bod - y, yes I do;

Love some - bod - y, but I won't tell who.

MARY HAD A LITTLE LAMB

Simply

Traditional Nursery Song

1. ⅞ Mar - y had a lit - tle lamb, Lit - tle lamb, lit - tle lamb,
2. And ev - 'ry-where that Mar-y went, Mar-y went, Mar-y went,

Mar - y had a lit - tle lamb, Its fleece was white as snow.
Ev - 'ry-where that Mar - y went, The lamb was sure to go.

3. It followed her to school one day,
   School one day, school one day,
   Followed her to school one day,
   Which was against the rule.

4. It made the children laugh and play,
   Laugh and play, laugh and play,
   Made the children laugh and play,
   To see a lamb at school.

ONE MAN WENT TO MOW

English Folk Song

1. One man went to mow,
2. Two men went to mow,
3. Three men went to mow,
} Went to mow a mead - ow.

Sing this to complete Verse 1

One man and his dog, Went to mow a mead - ow.

Sing this to complete Verse 2

Two men, one man and his dog, Went to mow a mead-ow.

Sing this to complete Verse 3

Three men, two men, one man and his dog,

Went to mow a mead-ow.

RAIN, RAIN, GO AWAY

Traditional Chant

1. Rain, rain, go a - way, Come a - gain an -
2. Sun - shine's here to stay, Now we can go

oth - er day, Lit - tle (John - ny) wants to play.
out to play, Oh —— what a love - ly day.

RIDING IN A BUGGY

Traditional Folk Song

1. Rid - ing in a bug - gy, Miss Mar - y Jane,

Miss Mar - y Jane, Miss Mar - y Jane,

Rid - ing in a bug - gy, Miss Mar - y Jane,

I'm a long way ____ from home.

2. I've got a house in Baltimore,
   In Baltimore, in Baltimre,
   I've got a house in Baltimore,
   And it's full of chicken pie.

3. I've got a girl in Baltimore,
   In Baltimore, in Baltimore.
   I've got a girl in Baltimore,
   And she's three stories high.

WHISTLE, MARY, WHISTLE

American Folk Song

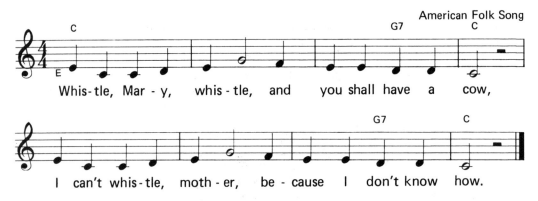

Whis - tle, Mar - y, whis - tle, and you shall have a cow,

I can't whis - tle, moth - er, be - cause I don't know how.

Expanding Vocal Range

A, B, C

Traditional

A, B, C, D, E, F, G, H, I, J, K, L, M, N, O, P,

G7 **C** **G7** **C** **G7** **C** **G7**

Q, R, S, T, U, V, Dou - ble U, X, Y, Z.
(W)

C **F** **C** **G7** **C** **G7** **C**

Now you've heard my A, B, C, Tell me what you think of me.

BAA, BAA, BLACK SHEEP

Moderately

Traditional Nursery Song

D **G** **D**

"Baa, baa, black sheep, have you an - y wool?"

A7 **D** **A7** **D** **G**

"Yes sir, yes sir, three bags full, One for my mas - ter and

D **A7** **D** **G** **D** **A7** **D**

one for my dame, And one for the lit - tle boy who lives in the lane."

CHIAPANECAS

Mexican Folk Song

Brightly

Clap hands × ×

F **C7**

f Sing "Chia - pan - e - cas," Ay ay, Ay ay,

Sing "Chia-pan - e - cas," Ay ay, Ay ay,

Sing "Chia-pan - e - cas," Ay ay, Ay ay,

Sing "Chia-pan - e - cas," Ay ay, Ay ay!

DO A PRETTY MOTION

American Folk Song

1. Do a pret - ty mo - tion, Tra - la - la - la,

Do a pret-ty mo - tion, Tra - la - la - la, Do a pret-ty

mo - tion, Tra - la - la - la, Rise, Su - gar, rise.

2. That's a pretty motion, tra-la-la-la. . .

EPO I TAI TAMA E

Maori (New Zealand)

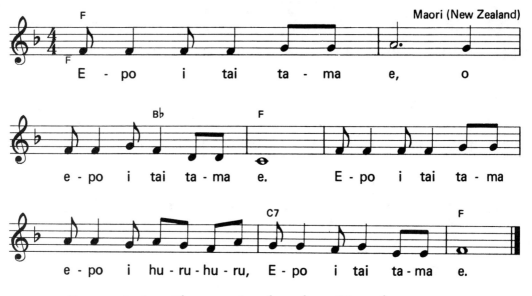

E - po i tai ta - ma e, o

e - po i tai ta - ma e. E - po i tai ta - ma

e - po i hu - ru - hu - ru, E - po i tai ta - ma e.

Pronunciation: Eh-po ee tie tah-mah ay. Hu-ru hu-ru.
Directions:
Measure 1: Hit lap with both hands.
Measure 2: Hands criss-crossed, slap chest.
Measure 3: See measure 1.
Measure 4: Hands up, down, up, down (on the four beats).
Measure 5: See measure 1.
Measure 6: Hands slap chest twice, up in air twice (with fingers wiggling).
Measure 7: Same as measure 6.
Measure 8: Same as measures 1, 3, 5.

Reprinted with permission of Marion A. Todd, State of Hawaii Department of Education. Transcribed and adapted by M. Todd, Honolulu.

FIDDLE-DE-DEE

Liltingly

English Folk Song

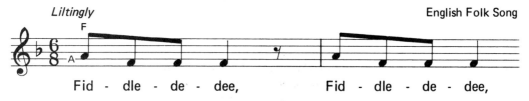

Fid - dle - de - dee, Fid - dle - de - dee,

The fly has mar-ried the bum-ble-bee.

1. Says the fly, says he, "Will you mar-ry me,

And live with me, sweet bum-ble bee?"

HEY, BETTY MARTIN

Brightly

Traditional

1. Hey, Bet-ty Mar-tin, tip-toe, tip-toe,
2. Can't get a boy, a boy to please her,

Hey, Bet-ty Mar-tin, tip-toe fine; Hey, Bet-ty Mar-tin,
Can't get a boy to please her mind; She wants to find a

tip-toe, tip-toe, Hey, Bet-ty Mar-tin, tip-toe fine.
boy to please her, She wants to find a cer-tain kind.

3. I found a boy, a boy to please me,
   I found a boy to please my mind;
   I found a boy, a boy to please me,
   I found a boy, a certain kind.

HICKORY, DICKORY, DOCK

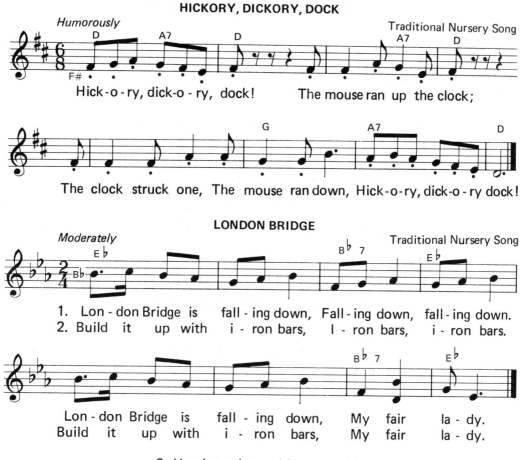

Humorously

Traditional Nursery Song

Hick-o-ry, dick-o-ry, dock! The mouse ran up the clock;

The clock struck one, The mouse ran down, Hick-o-ry, dick-o-ry dock!

LONDON BRIDGE

Moderately

Traditional Nursery Song

1. Lon-don Bridge is fall-ing down, Fall-ing down, fall-ing down.
2. Build it up with i-ron bars, I-ron bars, i-ron bars.

Lon-don Bridge is fall-ing down, My fair la-dy.
Build it up with i-ron bars, My fair la-dy.

3. Here's a prisoner I have caught,
   My fair lady.

4. Then off to prison he must go,
   My fair lady.

Directions:
Verse 1: Stand opposite child. Join hands by making arch above head. Lower hands on "falling down."
Verse 2: Raise hands in arch. Other children march under arch and go around in a circle.
Verse 3: Trap one child in between the lowered hands, and gently sway the "prisoner" in between the four hands. Other children sing and clap.
Verse 4: The two children who formed the bridge hold the "prisoner" in between them, and walk to the "prison."

MICHAEL, ROW THE BOAT ASHORE

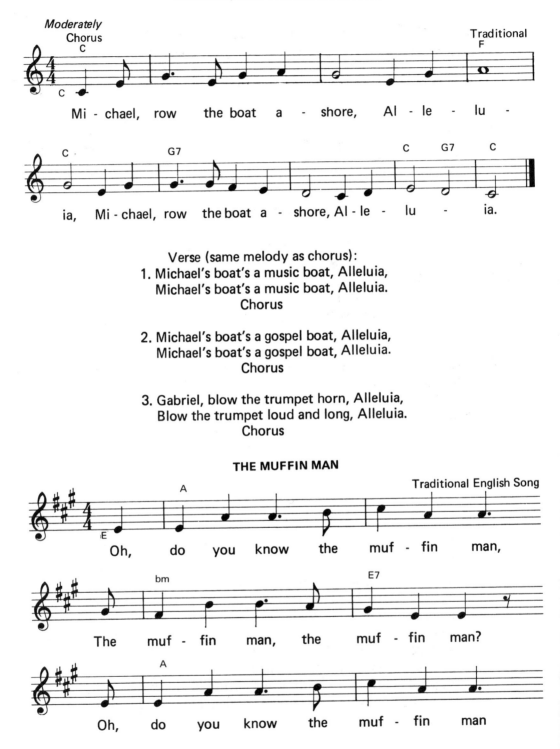

Mi - chael, row the boat a - shore, Al - le - lu -
ia, Mi - chael, row the boat a - shore, Al - le - lu - ia.

Verse (same melody as chorus):
1. Michael's boat's a music boat, Alleluia,
   Michael's boat's a music boat, Alleluia.
   Chorus

2. Michael's boat's a gospel boat, Alleluia,
   Michael's boat's a gospel boat, Alleluia.
   Chorus

3. Gabriel, blow the trumpet horn, Alleluia,
   Blow the trumpet loud and long, Alleluia.
   Chorus

THE MUFFIN MAN

Oh, do you know the muf - fin man,
The muf - fin man, the muf - fin man?
Oh, do you know the muf - fin man

That   lives   in   Dru - ry   Lane?

Directions:

Child sits on chair, facing away from others. Another child is chosen to be "the muffin man." He sings verse 1 as he stands behind the seated child. "The muffin man" returns to his or her place. The seated child turns around and identifies the "muffin man" by singing verse 2 and pointing to that child. Continue the game with other children having turns.

THE OLD GREY MARE

Southern

1. Once I had an old grey mare, Once I had an old grey mare,

Once I had an old grey mare; Sad - dled her and rode her there.

2. When I got there she got tired;
   She laid down in an old court yard.

3. Then they begin to sing and pray;
   She jumped up and run away.

OLD MACDONALD

American Song

1. Old Mac - Don - ald had a farm, Ee - i - ee - i -
2. Old Mac - Don - ald had a farm, Ee - i - ee - i -
3. Old Mac - Don - ald had a farm, Ee - i - ee - i -

o,   And   on   that farm   he   had some chicks,
o,   And   on   that farm   he   had some ducks,
o,   And   on   that farm   he   had some pigs,

Ee - i - ee - i - o.   With a chick-chick here, and a
Ee - i - ee - i - o.   With a quack-quack here, and a
Ee - i - ee - i - o.   With an oink - oink here, and an

chick-chick there, Here a chick, there a chick, ev'ry-where a chick-chick,
quack-quack there, Here a quack, there a quack, ev'ry-where a quack-quack,
oink- oink there, Here an oink, there an oink, ev'ry-where an oink - oink,

Old Mac-Don-ald had a farm, Ee - i - ee - i - o.
Old Mac-Don-ald had a farm, Ee - i - ee - i - o.
Old Mac-Don-ald had a farm, Ee - i - ee - i - o.

SPIDER AND SPOUT

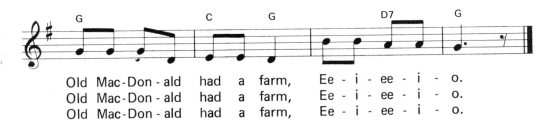

The een-sey ween-sey spi - der climbed up the wa - ter spout;

Down came the rain and washed the spi - der out;

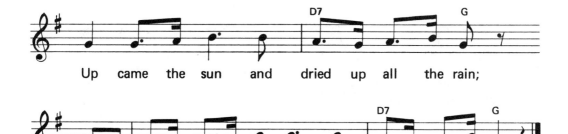

Up came the sun and dried up all the rain;

And the een-sey ween-sey spi - der climbed up the spout a - gain.

Directions:

Phrase 1: Move fingers upward in spider-like climbing motion.

Phrase 2: Move palms downward, with fingers moving. On "washed" move hands sideways in opposite directions.

Phrase 3: Make large circle over head with the arms.

Phrase 4: Repeat motions for first phrase.

SWEETLY SINGS THE DONKEY

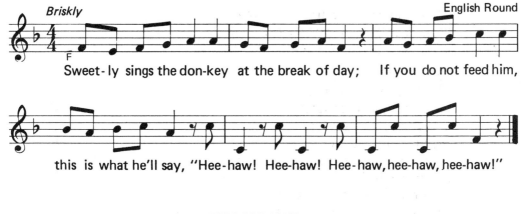

Briskly   English Round

Sweet-ly sings the don-key at the break of day;   If you do not feed him,

this is what he'll say, "Hee-haw! Hee-haw! Hee-haw, hee-haw, hee-haw!"

THIS OLD MAN

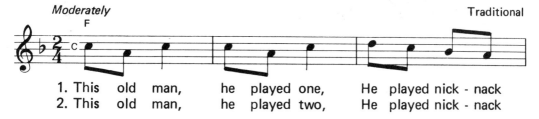

Moderately   Traditional

1. This old man, he played one, He played nick - nack
2. This old man, he played two, He played nick - nack

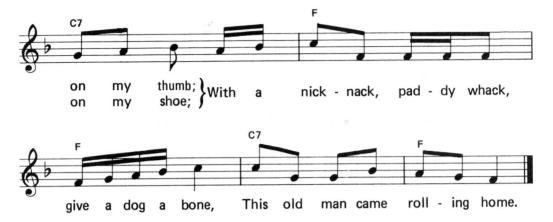

on   my   thumb;   With   a   nick - nack,   pad - dy   whack,
on   my   shoe;

give   a   dog   a   bone,   This   old   man   came   roll - ing   home.

Directions:
"This old man": point with finger.
"He played one": put up one finger of one hand.
"Nick-nack": criss-cross second and third fingers of both hands.
"Thumb": put up thumbs.
"Nick-nack paddy whack": criss-cross second and third fingers (four times on the four beats).
"Give the dog a bone": put out both hands, palms upwards.
"This old man": point with finger.
"Came rolling home": using both hands, make rolling motion in circle in front of body.

Other Verses:
  2. shoe: point to shoe.
  3. knee: point to knee.
  4. door: point to door.
  5. hive: interlock fingers of both hands.
  6. sticks: hit second finger of one hand on second finger of other hand.
  7. up in heaven: point to sky.
  8. gate: make gate by joining fingers of both hands.
  9. time: point to wrist watch.
10. over again: clap twice.

TWINKLE, TWINKLE, LITTLE STAR

Quietly — Traditional Nursery Song

Twin - kle, twin - kle, lit - tle star, How I won - der what you are. Up a - bove the world so high, Like a dia - mond in the sky. Twin - kle, twin - kle, lit - tle star, How I won - der what you are.

WHAT'LL WE DO WITH THE BABY?

Southern

What 'll we do with the ba - by? What 'll we do with the ba - by? What 'll we do with the ba - by? O we'll wrap it up in cal - i - co, Wrap it up in

cal - i - co, And send it to its pap - py, O.

Wide Vocal Range

ARE YOU SLEEPING?

Brightly   French Folk Tune

Ding, ding, dong; Ding, ding dong, Are you sleep - ing, Are you sleep - ing,

Broth - er John, Broth - er John? Morn - ing bells are ring - ing,

Morn - ing bells are ring - ing, Ding, ding, dong; Ding, dong, dong.

French	*Spanish*
Fre - re Jac-ques, Fre - re Jac-ques,	Fray Fe-li-pe, Fray Fe-li-pe,
Dor-mez vous? Dor-mez vous?	Duer-mus tu'? Duer-mus tu'?
Son-nez les ma-tin-nes, *(twice)*	To-ca la cam-pa-na, *(twice)*
Ding, din, don! Ding, din don!	Tan, tan tan! Tan, tan, tan!

DAME, WAKE UP

Traditional English Song

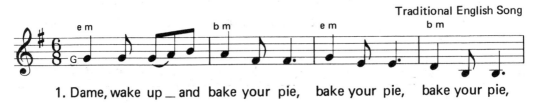

1. Dame, wake up — and bake your pie, bake your pie, bake your pie,

Dame, wake up_and bake your pie on Christ-mas day in the morn-ing.

2. Guess what's in the Christmas pie. . .

3. Meats and apples and spice say I. . .

DA - YE - NU
(pronounced "die - yay - noo")

Passover; Traditional

Da-da-ye-nu __ Da-da-ye-nu __ Da-da-ye-nu, Da-ye-nu, Da-ye-nu __

Da-da-ye-nu __ Da-da-ye-nu __ Da-da-ye-nu, Da-ye-nu, Da-ye-nu.

HEY LA LA LA LA

Chinese Folk Song
Translated by
Margaret Pang

Hey la la la la Hey la la la Hey la la la la Hey la la la

Tien koong chu tsai sha - ya Dee shang kai hoong hwa - ya
Sky shows the rainbow__ on the ground blossoms red flowers. __

Hey la la la la   Hey la la la la   Hey la la la la la   Hey la la la la.

Note: Children can clap, play drums or tambourines on beat, move hands to imitate rainbow and flowers falling to ground.

HUSH, LITTLE BABY

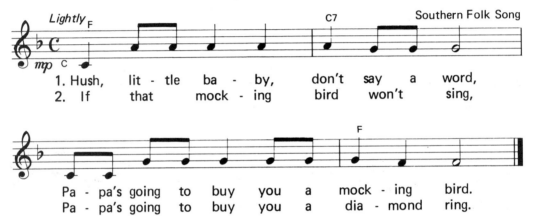

Southern Folk Song

1. Hush, lit - tle ba - by, don't say a word,
2. If that mock - ing bird won't sing,

Pa - pa's going to buy you a mock - ing bird.
Pa - pa's going to buy you a dia - mond ring.

3. If that diamond ring turns brass,
   Papa's going to buy you a looking glass.

4. If that looking glass gets broke,
   Papa's going to buy you a billy goat.

5. If that billy goat won't pull,
   Papa's going to buy you a cart and bull.

6. If that cart and bull turn over,
   Papa's going to buy you a dog named Rover.

7. If that dog named Rover won't bark,
   Papa's going to buy you a horse and cart.

8. If that horse and cart break down,
   We'll take a walk all around the town.

IF YOU'RE HAPPY

Traditional

Joyfully

If you're hap - py and you know it, clap your hands, *Clap Clap*

If you're hap - py and you know it, clap your hands, *Clap Clap*

If you're hap-py and you know it, then your face will sure - ly show it,

If you're hap - py and you know it, clap your hands. *Clap Clap*

LITTLE DAVID

Spiritual

Lit-tle Da - vid, play on your harp, Hal - le - lu, Hal - le -

lu, Lit - tle Da - vid, play on your harp, Hal - le - lu. _____

LOOBY LOO

Lively

American Singing Game

Here we go loo-by loo __ Here we go loo-by light __

Here we go loo-by loo __ all on a Sat-ur-day night __ I

put my right hand in ___ I put my right hand out __ I

give my right hand a shake shake shake and turn my-self a - bout. __

2. left hand   3. right foot   4. left foot   5. whole self

Directions:
Form circle. On the "looby loo" part, participants clap or stamp or create other movements. On the "I put my right hand in . . ." section, all participants act out directions in the song.

MULBERRY BUSH

Brightly

Traditional Singing Game

1. Here   we   go   round   the   mul - ber - ry   bush,   the
2. This   is   the   way   we   wash   our   clothes,   we

mul-ber-ry bush, the mul-ber-ry bush, Here we go round the
wash our clothes, we wash our clothes, This is the way we

mul - ber - ry bush,
wash our clothes, } So ear - ly in ___ the morn - ing.

3. This is the way we hang our clothes. . .

4. This is the way we iron our clothes. . .

5. This is the way we fold our clothes. . .

6. This is the way we paint the fence. . .

7. This is the way we rake the leaves. . .

Directions:
Form circle. Move around the circle, walking to the left.
On other verses, dramatize the words of the song.

ROW, ROW, ROW YOUR BOAT

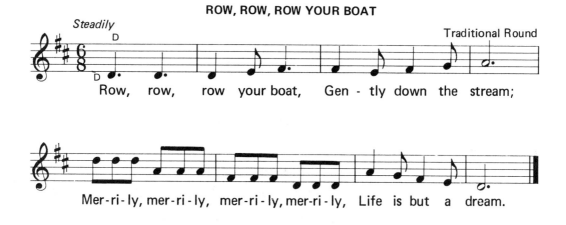

Row, row, row your boat, Gen - tly down the stream;

Mer-ri-ly, mer-ri-ly, mer-ri-ly, mer-ri-ly, Life is but a dream.

SHOO, FLY, DON'T BOTHER ME

American Folk Song

Briskly

Shoo fly, don't both - er me, Shoo fly, don't both - er me,

Shoo fly, don't both - er me, For I be - long to some - bod - y.

I feel, I feel, I feel, I feel like a morn - ing star;

I feel, I feel, I feel, I feel, I feel like a morn - ing star. So

Directions:
"Shoo fly": move hands away from body, as if chasing
fly away.
"Don't bother me": point to oneself.
"I feel": point to oneself.
"Morning star": make diamond shape with thumb and
forefingers of both hands.

TEN LITTLE INDIANS

Traditional

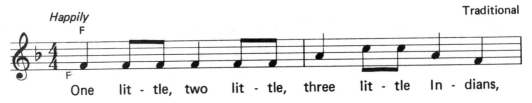

Happily

One lit - tle, two lit - tle, three lit - tle In - dians,

Four lit - tle, five lit - tle, six lit - tle In - dians, Seven lit - tle, eight lit - tle,

nine lit - tle In - dians, Ten lit - tle In - dian boys.

THE MORE WE GET TOGETHER

Gaily

German Folk Song

The more we get to - geth - er, to - geth - er, to - geth - er,

The more we get to - geth - er, the hap - pier are we!

For your friends are my friends and my friends are your friends,

The more we get to - geth - er, the hap - pier are we!

WE WISH YOU A MERRY CHRISTMAS

Vigorously

Traditional English Song

We wish you a Mer - ry Christ - mas, We wish you a Mer - ry Christ - mas,

We wish you a Mer-ry Christ-mas, And a Hap-py New Year!

Good ti-dings to you wher-ev-er you are;

Good ti-dings for Christ-mas and a Hap-py New Year!

WHERE IS THUMBKIN?

Traditional Game Song

Cheerfully

Where is thumb-kin? Where is thumb-kin?
Where is point-er? Where is point-er?

Here am I. Here am I. How are you this morn-ing?

Ver-y well I thank you. Run a-way. Run a-way.

3. Where is middle man?   4. Where is ringman?

5. Where is pinky?

Directions:
"Where is thumbkin?": hands behind back.
"Here I am": thumbs up, out front.

"How are you this morning?": wiggle right thumb.
"Very well, I thank you": wiggle left thumb.
"Run away": place right thumb behind back.
"Run away": place left thumb behind back.

Other Verses:
Use correct finger. Repeat actions as in verse 1.

Appendix B

Resources

Music Series

A number of publishers during the last few years have published music series for school children in grades K– 6. These series usually contain at least one book and accompanying recordings for use in kindergartens and preschools. The books offer suggestions on teaching music to children, and present many songs and listening-movement activities. These books provide excellent sources of music for the very young. The songbooks and recordings can be ordered either from the publisher or from a local music outlet. These series include:

Birchard Music Series: Kindergarten. Evanston, Ill.: Summy-Birchard Co., 1959.

Comprehensive Musicianship Through Classroom Music: Zone I. Reading, Mass.: Addison-Wesley Pub. Co., 1972.

Discovering Music Together: Early Childhood. Chicago: Follett Pub. Co., 1968.

Exploring Music: Kindergarten. New York: Holt, Rinehart and Winston, 1975.

Growing With Music: Kindergarten. Englewood Cliffs, N. J.: Prentice-Hall Inc., 1966.

The Magic of Music: Kindergarten. Boston: Ginn Co., 1965.

Making Music Your Own: Kindergarten Book. Morristown, N. J.: Silver Burdett Co., 1971.

Music for Young Americans: Sharing Music, Kindergarten, 2d. ed. New York: American Book Co., 1966.

New Dimensions in Music: Music for Early Childhood. New York: American Book Co., 1970.

Spectrum of Music: Teacher's Resource Book for Kindergarten. Riverside, N. J.: The Macmillan Co., 1974.

This is Music: Kindergarten and Nursery School. Boston: Allyn and Bacon Inc., 1965.

Recordings and Record Series

There are literally thousands of recordings which can be used in the musical education of the young child. Using the criteria that the music played for the child should serve to introduce him to the rich and diverse heritage of musics of the world, here is a list of some record series and recordings which are particularly suitable. You can order them from the record company or your local dealer. Continue to search for other records for the young child. Remember to provide a balanced diet of listening experiences.

Bailey, Charity, *Music Time with Charity Bailey* and *Sing a Song with Charity Bailey.* Folkways/Scholastic Records.

Barlin, Ann, *Dance a Story.* RCA Victor Records.
Four albums with eight records and story books.

Bowmar Orchestral Library. Bowmar Records.
Excellent for listening and movement activities. For starters try albums 51–54, 62, and 68.

Children's Record Guild Series. Franson Corporation.
Many excellent rhythm records.

Courlander, Harold, *Ring Games.* Folkways/Scholastic Records.
Circle games of Alabama black children.

Early Early Childhood Songs (Ella Jenkins). Folkways/Scholastic Records.

Electronic Music. Folkways.
A fine collection of comtemporary music.

Guthrie, Woody, *Songs to Grow on.* Folkways/Scholastic Records.

Headstart With Music. Creative Playthings Inc.

Hughes, Langston. *Rhythms of the World.* Folkways/Scholastic Records.

Instruments of the Orchestra.
> *Try the albums produced by Capitol, Columbia, Decca, Golden, Vanguard, or Victor Records.*

James, Phoebe, *Creative Rhythms for Children.* Children's Music Center, Los Angeles, distributor.

Jenkins, Ella, *Call and Response, Counting Games and Rhythms for the Little Ones,* and *Rhythm and Game Songs for the Little Ones.* Scholastic/Folkways Records.

Listen, Move, and Dance, Vols. 1 and 2. Capitol Records Distributing Corp.

Meet the Instruments. Bowmar Records.
> *With two filmstrips.*

Mother Goose Songs and Children's Songs. Bowmar Records.

Music for Children. Angel Records, Capitol Records Distribution Corp.
> *Simple songs inspired by Carl Orff. Encourages creative movement.*

Music for Creative Movement, Vols. 1 and 2. Lyons Music Co., distributor.

Musical Mother Goose. Golden Records.
> *Nursery songs.*

Purdy, Helen G., *The Downtown Story.* Folkways/Scholastic Records.
> *A story with song of sounds of doors, elevators, buses, and other sounds of the city.*

Purdy, Helen G., *The New House—How Honey Helped.* Folkways/Scholastic Records.
> *Recorded sounds of sweeping, water running, dishwashing, and other sounds in the home.*

RCA Victor Basic Record Library for Elementary Schools: The Listening Program, The Rhythmic Program, The Singing Program.
> *While all the recordings from these three series are useful with young children, albums one and two from each series are particularly appropriate.*

Rusty in Orchestraville. Capitol Records.
> *The sounds of the instruments.*

Ruth Evans Childhood Rhythms. Ruth Evans, 326 Forest Park Ave., Springfield, Mass.

Schwartz, Tony, *1, 2, 3, and a Zing, Zing, Zing.* Folkways/Scholastic Records.
> *Street games of New York City children.*

Schwartz, Tony, *Sounds of My City.* Folkways/Scholastic Records.
> *Sounds and songs of New York City.*

Seeger, Pete, *American Game and Activity Songs for Children.* Folkways/Scholastic Records.

Singing Games for Little People. Kimbo Educational.
> *With teacher's guide.*

Small Dancer, The, The Small Listener, The Small Player, and *The Small Singer.* Bowmar Records.
> *Music for rhythm instruments, creative movement, and singing.*

323

Songs from Many Cultures, Vols. 1 and 2. Kimbo Educational.

Sounds I Can Hear. Scott Foresman and Co.
Introduction to various sounds.

Sounds of New Music. Folkways Records.
Contemporary music.

Tipton, Gladys, ed., *Adventures in Music.* RCA Records.
A basic series for listening and movement activities. Each album has an excellent teaching guide. Begin with the first four albums of the series.

World Library of Folk and Primitive Music. Columbia Records Educational Dept.
Excellent collection of music from around the world.

Young People's Records, Franson Corporation.
Many excellent records for the young child, including some songs and music for creative movement and dramatic play.

In addition to the previous list of records and record series, the recordings which accompany the music series listed previously are highly recommended for use with young children.

Glossary

Some Musical Terms

Accent.   A louder stress on one tone than on the others.

Beat.   The steady recurring and progressive pulse of the music; the rhythmic feeling in music which makes you want to tap your foot or clap evenly.

Chant.   A semi-spoken song; a song using only two or three tones in a repeated manner.

Chord.   The simultaneous sounding of three or more tones.

Duration.   The relative length of a tone.

Dynamics.   The degree of loudness or intensity of sound.

Harmony.   The simultaneous sounding of two or more tones.

Intensity.   The relative loudness of a tone.

Introduction.   An opening section of a musical work which sets the tempo, mood, and key of the piece.

Melodic Rhythm.   The rhythmic pattern of the melody; the rhythmic pattern of the words in a song.

Melody.   A succession of tones of different pitches organized in a rhythmically meaningful way.

Meter.   The grouping of beats into strong and weaker pulses, such as *1–2*, *1–2–3*, or *1–2–3–4*.

Phrase.   A musical "thought" or idea, comparable to a sentence in speech.

Pitch.   The relative highness or lowness of a musical sound.

Rhythmic Pattern.   Tones of different duration organized as a recognizable unit.

Tempo.   The speed of a piece of music.

Theme.   An important melody of a piece of music.

Timbre.   See *Tone color.*

Tonal Pattern.   A succession of rhythmically organized pitches having unity and interest.

Tone.   A sound having pitch, duration, loudness, and tone color.

Tone Color.   The distinctive timbre or quality of a sound which distinguishes it from other sounds.

Tune.   See *Melody.*

330

331